THE FIRST —
Introdu
Karate • Ke

and the mystic drills of Zur Khane Dervishes
• Ninjas • Meditators • Mountain Ascetics • Firewalkers •

ZEN COMBAT was greeted as "a new kind of book about the Japanese arts of attack and defense. Not just another karate manual, ZEN COMBAT is the complete guide to the bare hand techniques of *karate* and *aikido; kendo* sword technique of the samurai warrior; *kongo* and *jitte* stick fighting techniques; *kyudo* fantastic 8-foot archery bow; and many other styles of fighting never previously described in books outside Japan."

Forty years ago in *TRUE* magazine the author introduced the "empty hand" martial art of karate to the USA, first wrote of the "mysterious power" of the oriental warrior. Now, after a lifetime of study, this revised edition for the first time explores "*ki*-power"—that very same "secret teaching" the Chinese elders castigated young Bruce Lee for revealing to the foreign devils.

over 400,000 copies sold of the original edition
and now a new and largely rewritten expanded edition with an
exciting new chapter on the secret power of martial arts
KI ENERGY (alias Ch'i or Qi)
which is also seen to be the root of Oriental healing arts of
acupuncture, shiatsu, even Christian "laying on of hands"

Appendix–Datebook of Sports Events
from Sumo Tournaments to Firewalk Rites

Profusely illustrated with 150 drawings by the author
after photos or ancient Oriental books

Cover calligraphy "KI" is by ANDO Misaki, "Chuggy"
Calligraphy this page "Zen-Sword-Brush"—see page 8 or 122

ZEN

This is an original publication—revised—not a reprint.

COMBAT

JAY GLUCK

PERSONALLY ORIENTED

ASHIYA, JAPAN

DEDICATION

IN MEMORIAM

NAGAO-SENSEI

at the bar of law,
as at the archery butts,
a damned straight shot—

Printed in the United States of America

Originally published in
BALLANTINE ORIGINAL PAPERBACK
Copyright © 1962 by Jay Gluck
U.S. printings 1962, 1974
Canadian printing 1963
Mexican Spanish editions 1964, 1977
Persian language magazine edition [partial] 1965

Revised and enlarged edition by
PERSONALLY ORIENTED BOOKS
13-5 Yama Ashiya-cho, Ashiya 659 JaPAN
Fax country code 81-797-22-9224
Internet: gluck@knet.gol.com
Copyright © 1996 by Jay Gluck

Distributed in the Western Hemisphere by
WEATHERHILL New York
Tel 1-800-437-7840; Fax 212-966-4860

ISBN   4-89360-038-9
Library of Congress Catalog Card Number 93-92623

The paper used in this publication meets the minimum requirements of
The American National Standard for Information Sciences
Permanence of Paper for Printed Library Materials, ANSI Z39.48-1984

CONTENTS

空手
empty hand
karate

I. A BULL STORY

THE BULL WAS RELUCTANT. He trotted back and forth at a respectable distance, sizing up with his bulging excited eyes the lone man tormenting him with stones. As the bull wheeled toward him, the man who was unarmed and clad only in shorts, feigned retreat. The bull lowered his head, snorted and charged.

The man suddenly turned to face the bull and set his feet firmly in the sand. At the last instant, he pivoted back on his left foot; as the shoulder of the thousand-pound beast brushed his naked abdomen, he yelled and brought his right hand out in a swordlike slash at the back of the bovine head. The bull bellowed in pain as its right horn broke off at the root. It was some ten inches long and three inches across the base.

The man went into a boxer crouch and attacked with his bare fists before the bull could ready itself for another charge. Short trip-hammer blows drove into the animal's ribs, and it went down, lowing, onto its knees. He grabbed it by the remaining horn, threw his left arm around its head and levered it over onto its side. One last blow to the heart finished it.

The bull had been provided by a slaughterhouse in Tateyama, near Tokyo, Japan. Less than three minutes after it answered the challenge it was pronounced unfit for beef due to excessive damage. The unorthodox slaughtering by Oyama Masatatsu, 'Mass,' karate champion of the world, had been too rough.

Witnessing 'rushes' from a documentary-in-progress on this event started me on a strange pilgrimage among mystic oriental strongmen. The death of the bull, I must admit, bothered me —even though he had been on the way to the butcher's block. Thankfully in my pilgrimages I was not to participate, however passively, in any further blood sacrifice. Looking back at my path from the heights, each step seems a step up in developing a sort of psychic arms control system.

My quest had been set in motion when I started lessons in Japanese *sumi,* or India ink, painting in order to develop my cartooning style. The connection should be quite obvious, as all seemingly ridiculous associations soon seem obvious when you've been Out East too long; or as long as I have.

It all began because I just couldn't get the flimsy little bamboo brush to draw me a clean line. I was beginning to see that my whole occidental heritage had caused me to form a block against the technique of strength through delicacy the brush seemed to demand.

"Zen ken shu!" my white-bearded painting teacher had said to me one day. "Zen meditation is the sword is the brush! Understand one and you understand all. But you cannot come to understand one without the other two."

So I took to crossing bamboo swords with my aged painting teacher who, true to ancient tradition, was one of the highest ranking masters of Japanese *kendo* fencing. To remedy my Madison Avenue slouch over the drawing board, he also had me learn to twang the great eight-foot bamboo Japanese long-bow with its yard-long bamboo arrows.

After months of strenuous effort wielding bamboo sword, bamboo brush and bamboo longbow with its bamboo arrows I still wasn't going anywhere. I had the same fault in all, old master said: too much concentration on the tool. "Think too much about sword, you lose sight of the end. Perhaps you understand easier if you saw swordplay without sword."

So old master took me to the bull butchery movie. After seeing it I still wasn't sure of what he meant, but decided this "swordless swordplay" worth a look. He arranged for me to meet Oyama, writing the formal letter customary to all oriental introductions. Interspersed with the Chinese ideographs basic to written Japanese, he drew in minute tick-tack-toe diagrams I had never seen in Chinese or Japanese. I questioned these.

OYAMA
MASATATSU
'MASS'

"Oyama's real name is Choi Yong-I. He's Korean," old master explained. He folded the letter and handed it to me. I was reminded of my *sensei*'s considerable prewar travels in Korea.

What I took in my hands was to turn out to be a ticket to a seven-year-long pilgrimage among mystic strongmen down Tokyo and Kyoto alleys, to lonely Japanese villages, up mountains in Japan, across high passes in Afghanistan, to gyms in Thailand, dervish drill halls in Iran, yogi ashrams in India and Nepal; to temples, gyms, shrines, hermitages; to meditate like a Buddha, be thrown about like a rag doll, dance with dervishes, and walk on red hot coals with sweet old ladies.

Master of the Barehand Kill

I looked up Mass (pronounced halfway between green moss and high mass) Oyama at his house in the outskirts of Tokyo. I got myself lost in the warren of unnumbered streets and houses. The local policeman took me straight to his door, for all karate adepts are registered as carrying a lethal weapon —their hands. Once there, I was led down the hall through myriad sliding-paneled rooms, out to the backyard where I saw a number of odd-looking posts padded with leather and straw. They resembled parking meters. Oyama, dressed in a comfortable polo shirt, had evidently been exercising here. There was no other equipment but these posts.

He came over, greeting me with a gusty "hello." He read the letter of introduction. As it was in Korean, he spoke to me in a lilting, breathy speech that acquainted me with the garlic-and-pepper *kimchi* pickles he'd had for lunch. Getting no reaction, he switched over to the staccato but more familiar Japanese, occasionally trying a sentence in English, he, as it seemed everybody, was studying.

I told him of my interest, asked him about karate, could he demonstrate for me. I knew only the bull story I had seen in the movie, had heard equally implausible tales of people breaking boards, bricks and stones. As he set up an anvil of barbell disk weights on a brick base, he told me of an assembly of Buddhist monks held near Canton, China, about A.D. 525. He said the meeting had been called by the Indian priest Daruma, and I was on home ground for I recognized Daruma as the patriarch Bodhi-darma—"he who understands the law of life" —from my study of Zen Buddhism. Daruma had originated the meditative sect of Zen, which dominated the thinking of China for centuries and was an important factor in the shaping of Japanese civilization. His philosophical and scientific theories still direct Japanese fencing, painting, tea ceremony, etiquette and athletics. When Daruma emigrated to China, the country was split into many warring kingdoms and bandit baronies. The Canton warlord disarmed the civilian population.

As Mass recounted this ancient tradition, he placed two bricks side by side before him.

"So, when this Chinese warlord disarmed everyone, yet failed to protect them from bandits and feuding barons ..."

On the bricks he carefully lay, one flat atop the other, two barbell disk weights, adjusting the whole for solidness.

"... the Buddhist monk Daruma called his disciples to his cave. He said to them, 'War and killing are wrong.'"

Mass placed his open left hand, knuckles down, upon the anvil thus formed, cushioning it on a folded towel.

"'But so is it wrong not to be prepared to defend one's self. Thus shall it be ...'"

In his left open palm he placed a 22-pound (10 kg.) stone, shaped like a flat football, thick as a brick, with the black color and smooth sheen of a barbell iron.

"'… We may not have knives, so make every finger unto a dagger,'" he quoted. He grasped the rock with his fingers and thumb and pressed his knuckles into the cushioning terry cloth for firmness.

"'Our maces are confiscated, so make every fist a mace.'"

He forced air from his lungs, drawing his shoulders back and down. The rising tension in his muscles and his concentration forced his face into a smile.

"'Without spears, every arm must be unto a spear …'"

As he inhaled to the pit of his stomach, he drew his right arm up horizontal, elbow pointed straight out, open hand cocked, thumb up, two inches in front of his shoulder. His voice rasped as he spoke against his final, filling inhale.

"'… and make every open hand unto …'"

His forearm shot down like a spring released. The edge of his open hand hit the stone with a crack! "'… a sword!'" he exhaled explosively.

He sat back and the Mona Lisa-like smile settled out into a broad grin of satisfaction. "Then he taught them his new fighting system, the *go-shin-jutsu-karate*, the self defense arts of the open hand. This took place some 14 centuries ago in China, and I, Oyama Masatatsu of Korea and Japan, continue the tradition of the 'open hand.'"

I picked up the two halves of the neatly sheared stone. I knocked them together. They were solid. I examined the 'cutting edge' of his hand. Except for a callous slightly off center which contrasted sharply with his smooth palm, they were normal and unbruised. "Aren't you afraid you'll break your hand?" I asked.

"Never hurts if I do it right and I do it right only when I am not afraid. You can do anything, if you're not afraid."

"'The only thing we have to fear is fear itself,'" I quoted.

"Hah!" he boomed. "You've been reading our Zen sages!"

"Well …" An aide brought two cups of the bitter green tea oriental convention demands. Mass joined me.

I returned my gaze to the fragments in my hands and said I thought that fear or no fear, it takes a tremendous amount of strength to crack bricks and rocks bare-handed, that such a fighting technique itself was quite fearsome. Mass disagreed, confided it was a "trick"—the trick being to know yourself and your opponent.

"Karate is for self-defense only," Mass assured. He hated fighting or people who fight, adding sadly as though to himself, "but I've had to fight all my life." Koreans have always been known as a hot-headed people. "Domination by others for four thousand years ... too small or too disunited to kick back ... So, we fight amongst ourselves."

Mass's father was a Yangban, a noble, eligible to wear the black horsehair high hat of honor. He was a real Korean, if hot-headedness is the criterion. His favorite sparring partner was Mass's mother. Once he struck her too hard and Mass reacted, knocking him through the door. This most serious crime against the ancient Confucian code brought the whole village of Wa-Ryong-Ri Yong Chi Myo'n Chul Na Do—near Gunsan—to the village square to hear his case. He was the village problem child, a Korean rebel without a cause (if not without cause).

"They even blamed the bad crops on me."

They cleared him on the technicality that there was no precedent for judging him. But since Korea was obviously too small for both father and son, Mass headed for Japan. Here he was just another Korean immigrant with a stretch in the coal mines waiting for him if he should become a problem. It was 1938, he was 16 years old.

He worked his way through a small college as a milkman and ricksha boy, somehow holding his temper despite the vicious prejudice he suffered as a Korean in the Land of the Gods. He blew off steam at boxing and Greco-Roman wrestling. These sports didn't satisfy him, "... too inefficient, too slow, too undisciplined." He tried judo, but here too, he found too much restraint—"You have to hold back or you'll put your partner through the wall."

Then he met Funakoshi, the grand old Okinawan karate master who was trying to introduce the sport into Japan. Watching Funakoshi in action, Mass knew immediately that this was what he had been looking for. There was no holding back in karate. In a match punches were pulled a split second, a fraction of an inch, before contact. In actual use, instead it is at the instant of impact, like cracking a bull whip. The pull-back takes as much strength, or more, than the punch. The hothead had found his safety valve.

"Funakoshi kept me out of trouble, straightened me out." That, he explained, is what is meant by the strong ethics and morals behind this 'art.' Only the pure of heart can really succeed and Funakoshi purified him with the white-hot iron of work and responsibility.

After World War II, Mass, a fiercely patriotic Korean—there was not yet 'North' or 'South'—discovered that he was being used by phony compatriots and that he had earned himself an unsavory reputation. A karate elder, also a Korean patriot, advised him to take the ancient 'cure,' to seclude himself on a mountaintop doing ascetic exercises and Zen meditation. In effect, become a twentieth-century Daruma. He did. He came back to civilization a year and a half later with long hair and a wild beard, shouting his "hello" with a smack at a telephone pole that rattled the wires. Then he devoted himself to karate and left politics alone.

In the democratic atmosphere of the sport he rose as fast as ability allowed. In 1947, a few months after coming out of the mountains, he won the All-Japan Championship in a grueling series of elimination bouts in which not a few contestants eliminated themselves. They didn't show the proper mental and physical control and landed blows with full impact instead of snapping back at the next to the last instant and just tipping the "target" to let him know he'd been hit. Mass fended off every such overeager blow thrown at him, himself threw nothing but perfectly controlled snap-taps. He was promoted to the fourth grade of black belt.

When first I interviewed him for *True* magazine way back in 1957 he admitted to holding a black belt of "sixth rank, the highest."

Some of Oyama's friends even then claimed he was eighth or ninth grade. Anything above sixth rank is a mark of the athlete's standing as a gentleman and valuable citizen in the eyes of his peers, not only a degree of karate ability. No man will admit higher than sixth. The highest honor is the red belt (my kendo sensei wore one), the rank beyond ranking reserved for one or two, usually masters of a school. In 1961, Oyama became eligible to wear red, but preferred not to. He was still a superb athlete, beyond rank, when he died in 1995.

Oyama toured the States in 1952, alias Mass Togo, junior partner in a "brother" pro-wrestling team with fourth rank judo champ Endo, the Great Togo, a California nisei— American of Japanese descent. In judo, he had noticed that many holds were identical to Greco-Roman wrestling. Karate was even more evidently like boxing, Greco-Roman and Pier Six brawling combined—the same tricks, but more scientifically applied.

Karate recognizes 37 vital points on the human body. Some are the knockout spots of boxing or the pain hold points of wrestling. Some are needle healing points in acupuncture. Nine are below the belt, 14 in back and 14 clean with Queensbury.

The tour was uneventful till the Togo brothers got to Minneapolis, where Togo Senior had bottom billing and Mass was not even listed on the program. Main feature was Dick Real, 6 feet 7 inches, pro-grappling champ, who offered $1,000 to anyone who could down him, freestyle. Mass, 5 feet 8 inches and then 170 pounds, fourth grade black belt in karate, jumped at the chance and got into his 'working' trunks.

The champ came in slow and low at a crouch, looking for a chance to get his special stranglehold on Oyama. Mass saw that Real's defense was perfect, leaving no opening—any karate chop or hand-sword attempted would only result in Mass's being pinned. So he threw a feint, a nose-crushing eye gouge, with his left. Real moved to block the terrifying and illegal (if real and connecting) thrust and threw up his hands. Mass switched his objective, grabbed Real's hands, jerked him close and ground a twisting jab to his breast plate. Real staggered. Mass threw another pair of left and right fist hammers to the same point. Real went down glassy-eyed after three minutes of ring time.

That night, the newly rich Togo brothers moved into a better hotel. Their surprise visitor found them anyway; a soft-spoken giant with a child in tow. After a short chat, Mass started to show the boy a few karate tricks. The father watched, then interrupted, took Mass's hands in his own and said, "Gentle as a baby, and yet these did what they did a few hours ago. These hands aren't those of a human, or my name is not Jack Dempsey."

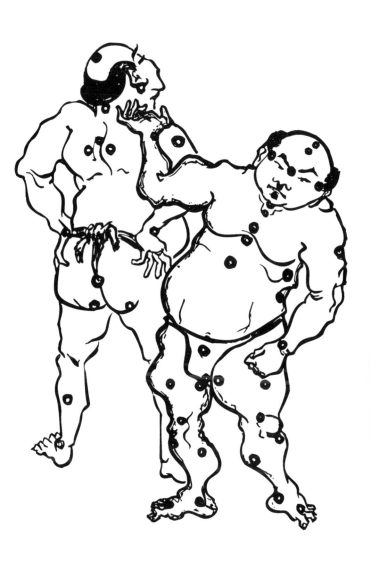

KARATE TARGET POINTS ON THE BODY

After Minneapolis, Mass was a main attraction. In Des Moines the audience hooted down his karate demonstration with cries of 'fake.' Recalling the $1,000 gimmick that had given him his break, he made the same offer to anyone who could match his brick busting. A local policeman who boasted loudly of his third rank judo black belt took up the challenge. He grasped the brick, sneered a couple of wisecracks at Mass, strained to build up the strength needed for the smash. Mass noticed that his hands had started to sweat and was about to warn him when the egotist made a nasty ethnic crack. Mass shut up.

"Sweat is the worst thing possible," he says. "I always keep a towel handy to wipe any off." The American's fist snapped down against the brick, with more than enough force to crumble it easily, said Mass, "… if he'd done it right." The cop's sweaty hand slipped and was mashed and bloodied. The brick wasn't even chipped. Furious, he ranted. He said there was some trick afoot, but that, instead, he'd take on Mass—"the sneaky yeller crook"—for the purse. Mass was angry, too, so he accepted.

The American changed clothes. When he came out, Mass bowed, as much for karate etiquette as to calm himself down. The Yank wondered aloud if the money even existed. Mass assured him it did and the bout began. Mass faced him, fists at hips in the basic ready position, seemingly leaving himself wide open. The Yank threw a brutal roundhouse, which Mass adeptly sidestepped. As he did, he looked into his opponent's wild eyes and realized he had a madman on his hands. He stayed on the defensive, evading everything, till an opening presented itself and he launched a trio of twisting heart and breast plate blows, "which I don't think I held back much. I heard a sickening sound I'd never heard before," Mass said. Down went the hothead with seven ribs broken. A minute and a half had gone by on the clock. The crowd was unlike any he'd seen before, or since. It took a police riot squad with motorcycle escort to get him to his hotel safely.

After that, the challenger from the audience was a regular feature, with a limit set at two minutes. Mass says that in six months of demonstrations in 32 states, he found Americans fine sportsmen and good losers. "I guess the one exception proved the rule."

His fastest fight, and the one he first feared would be his toughest, was in Chicago against Dan Calendar, 250-pound ex-wrestler, boxing and judo instructor in the police training school. The man was coolheaded and moved smoothly, alternating a boxing with a judo approach, erect at 6'4". He knew how to take full advantage of his tremendous height. Mass doesn't remember too well what happened next; he says his actions were by then mostly automatic reflexes. Dan threw a right hook, keeping his left cocked to follow through with either a haymaker or a judo grab. Mass fended with a left sword-hand, an openhanded stab into the air over his head, coupled with a vertical leap to overcome Dan's height, and a lightning pair of openhanded chops with the same left hand, one to Dan's now unprotected neck and the other to his temple. Dan went down, his left hand still cocked to protect him from the right that never came. He was out cold for two hours after only ten seconds in the ring.

The bigger they are, the harder they fall—and vice versa. His toughest go was against a small boxer barely his own height. This man, Becker, had marvelous footwork. When Mass threw a blow, Becker was usually someplace else. Mass even went out of the ring once, "I missed a blow and slipped—I had let him put me on the offensive with an art that is meant for defense." But Becker's sparring was ineffective and even if he could have gotten a haymaker past Mass, it probably wouldn't have been enough to jolt the karate man. Time was all on Becker's side. Mass dusted away Becker's jabs like pesky flies. The crowd was tearing the house down. Mass, never much of a karate leaper, used several to close in, but Becker just danced away. Suddenly Mass leaped backward. Then, before Becker was fully cognizant of the significance of this odd maneuver, Mass made a leaping lunge forward to land a sometimes lethal *chudan tsuki*, fingers extended in a fencing jab to the solar plexus. Becker collapsed bare seconds before the bell.

"Becker would never lose a street fight," said Mass. "Too smart, too cool. What a fight that was! What a karate-ka he'd have made."

A year later, another group of karate experts toured the United States. At a demonstration before 50 United States judo men, they did things like splitting a stack of five one-inch boards. United States judo expert Charles Yerkow couldn't crack one over his knee. Yerkow told reporters he didn't think a hard-hitting boxer could match this, even with knuckles protected. Oyama agreed, "It isn't the force of the blow so much as control." One hundred years ago Sasagawa Shigezo, legendary giant son of a famous jujutsu master, established a legend by knocking out a charging bull with his bare fists.

Sasagawa may have wanted to try his fists because a *kempo*, or Chinese karate, expert had just previously been brought to Japan and matched against the shogun's jujutsu (also jujitsu) champion. The fight was close, was called a draw, but the jujutsu champ sank into oblivion and the kempo man was lionized. To this day Japanese acknowledge that, all else being equal, a karate man will best a judo man.

Mass confessed he toyed with the idea of going to America to become a "one-man tag team" in *puro-resu*, pro wrestling. But, since most homicide departments would frown on this, he also considered going to Mexico and becoming a swordless bullfighter. "But I have aversion to blade—and killing."

But first he wanted to take some ancient-style training. This involved hiding away on a mountaintop with a box of books— ancient classics—living simply on wild herbs and fruits as he did for a year and a half before winning his first championship. He would rise with the sun, pick out a nice, healthy-looking full-grown pine tree and give it 200 or more fist-hammer blows before every meal. "When the tree was dead, I would be ready to come down."

Mass took this mountain training at least once every winter. One year he took along with him a sparring partner, a French savate expert and holder of a high-ranking black belt in judo, who had been sent to Japan by the French national judo organization to study karate, aikido and Chinese kempo. (I was to meet him some years later in the main aikido dojo, become good friends and look him up again in France.) André Nocquet said Mass had them out barefoot in the snow. Before dawn every morning they did an hour of exercise and freestyle karate-savate-judo and anything-goes grappling. "Then," says André, "we'd eat a breakfast for a medieval monk and spend the rest of the morning yelling poetry at each other, me in French, Mass in Korean or Japanese, before our midday work-out and hermit's lunch."

After a 19th-century woodblock printed book

SASAGAWA KILLS HIS BULL

Mass dismissed Greco-Roman wrestling and savate. "We do everything they do and more." As for use against just plain brawn, the tales of single karate or judo aces routing whole mobs are commonplace, and since that first *True* article martial arts movies have made them almost trite.

In perhaps the first, *Bad Day at Black Rock*, Spencer Tracy set an example in 1964 never since surpassed. A one-armed, aging, seemingly cowardly war veteran, he avoided and evaded the taunts of a giant bully, refusing to fight him till he finally had no alternative as the bully attacked him. He moved out of the way like lightning, and what followed will go down as a classic in Hollywood fight scenes. Two or three blows and the country doctor bends over the bloody, broken hulk of the bully and pronounces, "Somehow, he'll live."

Karate dojos throughout Tokyo reported several new students who were amputees or cripples—and Spencer Tracy fans. Since then the therapeutic value of martial arts has been proven.

While we sipped our tea an assistant had set up a stack of 31 heavy Japanese ceramic roof tiles. When he finished talking, Mass went over, squatted before them like a Buddha in meditation and, after the proper centering preliminaries, gave them a short downward jab with his fist. Twenty-seven split. (Mass can break 30.) He showed me his unbruised knuckle. "Direct blows don't hurt."

I said that my hand would have broken like an eggshell if I did that.

"Not if I taught you how," he countered.

I barely tip the scales at 130 after a Sunday dinner and my five-foot-seven frame bends in the blast of my Mazda RX7's exhaust like a bamboo in a typhoon. Mass is only about an inch taller but a good 60 or 70 pounds heavier. His arms are so large his shirts must be tailor-made, and friends claim he can split his monster-size shirt collars by flexing his neck.

I was to see students smaller than I break a dozen tiles.

Fundamentals: Emptying the Hand

Mass asked if I would like to see some karate group work. He dressed and I joined him and we left, picking up enroute three neighborhood junior karate-ka black belts and an American of Korean descent, Richard Kim. Dick was then Mass's personal *deshi*, "disciple," a black belt holder in karate as well as a judo and boxing enthusiast and who had even more recently become one of the first Americans admitted to the exclusive school of aikido, which I discuss later.

We took a bus across Tokyo to the East End where black market stalls of the old "Yen PX," the theaters, burlesque houses and neon-gilded plywood honky-tonks of Tokyo's Coney Island-Broadway, the red-light district and ancient geisha section of Yoshiwara, renowned from ancient woodblock prints, ring the wharf-side gashouse slum of Tokyo.

We left the bus and entered the maze of narrow, crowded but, surprisingly, not dirty streets.

Mass stopped in front of an old and run-down temple gate. In front of most Japanese and all Korean Buddhist temples stands a large roofed gate with three portals, the center one for passage and the other pair housing two nightmarish wooden sculptures of temple guardians, the Oriental Gog and Magog. They are usually armed, but the pair Mass pointed out were unarmed. "Karate guards the sacred grounds," he said.

Now I understood something that had puzzled me, when, visiting Nara, ancient 7th-century capital of Japan, to research our travel guide *Japan Inside Out*, I had stopped by to see some 1,200-year-old statues of the twelve guardians of Buddha. Each was armored, but differently armed—bow, sword, lance —except the fiercest one whose postured hands were empty. I had since seen many such ancient empty-hand sentinels, posing puzzle number two—Why didn't Japan learn karate a millennium ago? Was it a period of such peace and simple living that they didn't need it? The ancient novel, *Tale of Genji* (available in paperback translated by either Arthur Waley or Edward Seidensticker), indicates it was probably so. They did adapt graceful karate postures into their dance, however.

These *nio* statues (below), gripping the ground with their toes like cats, are still a good basic lesson in karate Mass pointed out, striking an identical pose and daring the five of us to budge him. We totaled over three time his weight, but he might as well have been rooted there. When we exerted our maximum against him, he seemed for an instant to give and I found myself seated some distance away, a fifth part of a semicircle of sprawling bodies around a laughing karate master. "Give and snap back," he roared.

The four students brushed themselves off and, at an order from Mass, assumed four basic ready stances, all of which I had seen before in those ancient "nio" statues in Nara, and which my old fencing master had recently taught me for kendo. They differ from boxing or fencing stances in that no effort is made to offer as small a target as possible by leading with one foot and hand. Instead a stance is taken that will

21

enable the fighter to change stance instantly, to retreat to either side or rearward or attack with either or both hands or feet or all. This stance is more like that of the bowie knife fighters or medieval Italian two-rapier fencers. (The Japanese sword is light, yet with a two-handed grip, and may be used two-handed, switched from hand to hand or in pairs.)

Breath Control

When the feet are properly positioned, they force other parts of the body into springlike tension. The abdomen is particularly affected. Orientals consider the abdomen the seat of the soul. A villain to us is black hearted; in the Far East he is black stomached. It is the center of balance, of action.

"All my attention, all my training, all my thinking is centered on my abdomen," Oyama said.

The wooden temple guardians show an exaggerated abdominal muscular development. Not great ripples of muscle, but rows of knots. One group runs in two arcs parallel to the lower ribs, looking like an extra pair of ribs, and the other in rows running perpendicular over the lower ribs. These are not muscles for hefting weights, they are for speed and power; more akin to the leg development of a track man than the brawn of a weight lifter. Most modern karate men are smaller, less exaggerated versions of these statues. Oyama himself was rather an exception, relatively heavy and beefy.

The wasp waist of the weight lifter is also undesirable. The Oriental athlete is characterized by a barrel belly that, with his less accentuated chest cage and small posterior, forms an almost perfect cylinder the length of his trunk. Breathing does it—the soul in the stomach idea. Daruma had taken the yoga breathing drills and the Chinese Taoist "magician" breathing techniques, studied them and formalized them. Our modern scientific techniques of breathing had been carried to scientific perfection fourteen centuries earlier in the Orient.

The maintenance of balance in motion depends on breathing. The Zenist and Taoist say there are four types of breathing: that with the shoulders, the chest, the lower abdomen and with the toes. The warrior is concerned with the first three.

Breathing with the toes, I leave to the philosophers.

Breathing with the shoulders is considered in China and Japan, the breathing of a sick man. Run up some flights of

SEVENTH-CENTURY TEMPLE GUARDIAN STATUES

stairs—four to six, depending on your capabilities—and you'll find yourself panting; almost no chest motion, but a pumping action from the shoulders. The relatives of a sick bedridden Japanese who gets to the point of breathing with the shoulders notify the lawyers and priest.

The way most people breathe normally is with the chest, as stressed in American athletics: "Breathe with the chest; develop the chest expansion; build up a chest expansion of, say, three inches." I've a chest expansion of $5\frac{1}{2}$ inches and couldn't run up two flights of stairs. Evidently there's something wrong with the theory that if you breathe with the chest you will develop a big chest expansion. (Now in my late sixties, after years of light meditation but no exercise, I can do 3-4 flights.)

Breathe with the lower abdomen, which accounts for the Japanese man's style of wearing the obi sash low on his kimono, the black belt low on his karate blouse, and the present-day older white collar workers wearing their trousers as if they were growing out of them.

The pressure low and freedom above is an aid to control. But again beware, for the improper following of these instructions brings about the exact opposite results. The Japanese military for seventy years prior to the defeat in 1945 stressed this misconception of *hara-no-chikara*, "belly strength," not knowing what they were doing. They foolishly wedded the low obi and high belly band, as seen in some of the ancient guardian statues, with the "belly warmer," or *hara-maki*, to conform to modern uniform styles. This created in effect an abdominal support. According to returned prisoners taken to Siberia, the Russians saw swathes of good material going to waste in these *hara-maki* and confiscated them with the reputed result that 30 percent of the Japanese prisoners soon died of fatigue or easily fell prey to diseases when deprived of their abdominal support.

The cowboy's low-slung belt, alone, amply illustrates that we of the West know most of these things which comprise the Japanese martial arts, but were not aware of them. To us the heart is the esthetic "center." We have expressions like "I have no stomach for something" if scared—conversely, a brave man "has guts." As for our stomach being anything more than just the seat of emotion of the weak person, we're not aware.

"Breathing is with the pit of the stomach," Oyama demonstrated. Repeated deep breaths with the chest cause giddiness, due to an imbalance of oxygen in the blood system that's worse than being short of breath as it takes all the strength away and dulls the senses, leaving you off balance and defenseless. Take a deep breath into your chest, through your nose, mouth tightly shut. Breathe deep, show off your expansion, throw back your shoulders. Now, as you exhale slowly, force your shoulders down, stretch your neck—up, not forward. Exhale naturally until the chest feels comfortable … about halfway between full expansion and contraction.

I followed Mass's instructions, inhaled deep but slowly, holding the chest cage rigid, forcing the air into the stomach.

"No," he said, "not the upper stomach, the soft belly … force it to the groin." He took his belt off, then tied it tightly around my stomach just below the lower ribs. "Force the air down, down … force your feet, if you're standing, or your seat, if you're sitting, right through the ground."

24

BREATHING

My dad was a top trumpet player, lead cornet with Original New Orleans Five in the twenties, first trumpet with Paul Whiteman just before I was born, jammed with chums Louie and Bix at Jazz and in sweet was a match for Bunny, for years first horn with the Russ Morgan Orchestra, then Ray Bloch's house band on Ed Sullivan's show. He was a trumpet player's trumpet player. He read the early version of this chapter in *True* magazine. He thought about it, followed the instructions. "If someone had taught me this when I was seventeen, I'd have become the greatest trumpet player in history."

Do that a few hundred times a day till breathing with the pit of your stomach comes natural, and see how it improves your agility. It will also condition your abdominal muscles, improve your posture, digestion, and constitution. You can use this for therapeutic exercise, for nervous stomach, insomnia or general tenseness; with no possible harm even if you don't do it right. The complicated hatha yoga techniques can do no more, and they can be dangerous, too easily done incorrectly without a teacher present.

Mass claimed he never heard of a karate man who had ulcers or any constitutional irregularities and many of them eat good hot Korean foods smothered in red chili peppers. I checked, and what he said also holds for fencing and judo and aikido men and any of the old style Japanese painters, actors, and dancers who use this same conditioning before undertaking their arts. Yet Japan has the world's highest ulcer rate—1,000,000 judo, karate and kendo men don't make much of a dent in a population of 125,000,000. This breathing technique was priest Daruma's great discovery, the heart of karate and indeed the heart of all the Chinese, Korean and Japanese martial arts and an important factor in the fine arts and scholarly study-discipline.

"Fail to master breath control," Mass warned, "and you can do nothing in karate except possibly a few cute tricks, and certainly none of the good ones."

One of the guardian sculptures had his mouth open, the other's was closed. They personify *in* and *yo*, or yin and yang, passive and active, the two main aspects of breathing, inhale-exhale. This dualism permeates all Oriental culture. "The karate man attacks on exhale, active. Man is vulnerable to attack when inhaling, passive," said Mass, repeating what my fencing master had taught me. "Inhale always through the nose, mouth closed, it clears the mind. American slang for a dull-witted person, I have heard, is 'mouth breather,' so it shouldn't be news to you. When you attack, attack instantaneously with bounce and recoil, like the cracking of a whip, exhaling explosively through the mouth. Karate-ka usually yell when attacking, and, coming from the pit of the stomach like an opera singer's high C, they really sound off. Wild animals roar and primitive savages and scared infantrymen give battle cries when they attack. We have just made a science of doing what comes naturally."

Mass advised watching your opponent and timing his breathing so you can attack when he inhales. Try, he said, to do something active suddenly while inhaling. "See? You're off balance." Oyama went through one of his shadow boxing drills, sounding off his breathing and snapping every offensive motion on an exhale. There are a score or so of such drills—they can be done in any room and are excellent "constitutionals." A few basic ones are detailed below.

Turning to defense, if your opponent is aware of balance of breathing—and many a fighter is, instinctively—simply "freeze." The static man is dangerous. You can not tell what he's going to do next and when he does attack, he has no inertia to overcome as a moving man does when he wants to shift direction. The best defense is to avoid a fight, but if fight you must, let your opponent attack. You are then morally and legally right in defending yourself, and have the tactical advantage. The best defense is not the offensive, it is the counteroffensive. The man who is ready, not the man who attacks first, wins.

A man can defend himself by parrying while inhaling but an attack launched is like an arrrow—once it leaves the bow, it is shot and cannot be redirected. Be ready always. Parry and counterattack instantly while your opponent is most vulnerable and you can use his forward momentum in addition to your own power against him. To the karate-ka—as to any budo-ka—the battle is won or lost the instant the first punch is started on its way.

"It isn't in boxing," I contradicted.

"For one or both of two reasons," answered Mass. The first, he said, being that a boxing match is usually between two equals. How often is this true in life? Almost never. The second is that boxers spar, looking for openings, while karate-ists (more correctly, karate-ka) spar mentally, intuitively—you might say, by telepathy—as they do in all Oriental sports. That's why to the uninitiated, sumo wrestling looks like the waltz of two hippopotami. There is no light jabbing, every attack is meant to be a haymaker and a bout between experts will usually be a few seconds or days of staring each other down, followed by one lightning counterstroke. "At least," said Mass, "that's the ideal."

The temple guardians stare cross-eyed through you. Odd Oriental art! But if you're an ex-aerial gunner, you can see it's not so odd.

The eyes have a double focus. The individual eyeball focuses like a camera lens and the two eyes in unison zero in like a stereopticon. Sitting in the middle of a 270-degree movie screen in a mock-up turret waiting for a lantern slide Zero to buzz from somewhere or other, several of us Grumman TBM gunners-to-be found that we could effectively sight a greater area if we did not concentrate our vision as we would naturally do, cutting down on side vision. By "crossing" the eyes for near viewing, yet forcing the individual eye focus for distance, dead-ahead vision was reduced slightly, while the view out of the corners of the eyes was clarified and overall vision was equalized. This is similar to recommended night sighting to bring the rods of the eyes into play, but what relationship there is between the two I leave to the opticians. Oyama prescribed this same system of "cross-eyed" vision for guarding against an unseen opponent who might attack from any direction or for when you are surrounded by several attackers.

For a single opponent, he sticks to the western idea of manliness. "Look him straight in the eye. A coward can't take it and any man gives his actions away in advance through his eyes."

I thought that pretty occidental. It doesn't sound like the stock idea of the indirect Oriental who never looks straight at anyone. Mass answered that it's just universal. Equals look eye-to-eye. To the ancient sages, all men were equal who strove for the ultimate equality which is the reason for living. This averting eyes downward started as a mark of respect to a senior and got out of hand when seniority became universally associated as meaning "I am bigger, better than you are—bow, peasant." You will never see a karate man or a judo man bow and scrape. "But we will gladly bow our heads to someone we respect—though never while talking to him."

I told Mass of our old gun-sighting trick. He shrugged. "There's nothing new in karate or judo or anything. We just put them all together a special way. Anyone can do it."

The steadily gathering crowd awakened Mass to reality and he ushered us off.

I canot tell a lie, Hon. Father. I did it with my
bare hand-axe, karate-style.

28

道場
dojo – way place

II. IN THE DOJO

WE CAME to a large building I at first took to be a stable and passed through a carriage gate into a barren schoolyard where small groups of teenagers were doing snappy calisthenics, and continued on into a clapboard barn. We removed our shoes at the door and stepped up onto the two-inch-thick padded rush mats. These are the 3 by 6 feet *tatami* used in traditional Japanese houses and are softer to the fall, as well as far cheaper then than our canvas pads—though many dojo have since switched to canvas as handmade traditional mats got too expensive, and some use imitation plastic.

The one room was about 50 by 70 feet, completely floored with tatami. The walls were bare wood with a border, about seven feet up, of small name tablets, each bearing Chinese ideographs—four usually—and grouped under larger boards with a single Japanese number. These numbers stood for karate ranks, and the higher the number, the fewer the accompanying names of the members of this dojo, or gym. Only a handful stood under the 六 – "6" group.

Yamaguchi Gogen, master of the dojo and dean of some 200,000 karate-ka looked every bit the "Cat." He was 5 feet 5 inches tall, perhaps weighing 135 pounds including sweat suit and red belt. Past the half-century mark then, his hair covered his shoulders and his eyes were as wild as a temple statue's. When he walked, I'd swear his feet didn't touch the ground. Most of the students present were teenagers and most of these averaged 110 pounds with few as heavy as 130. In tough neighborhoods such as this, police are wary of karate groups but both Oyama and the "Cat" refuted the popular notion that they breed gangs, pointing out that no student in good standing has gotten into serious trouble. If they hear of one going astray, they straighten him out, give him something to do, to take pride in, some place to let off steam. There's a natural tendency for a young sport to want to blood himself, but the dojo channels that tendency by contests for the coveted black belt and the first grade. He knows if he fights outside, expulsion from the group is immediate.

Four youths formed a square facing diagonally six feet apart. Each held in front of him two three-quarter-inch pine boards a foot square, back to back, grains matched. Behind each stood four more youths, bracing him like a rugby scrum. The "Cat" ordered a student into the center of the square and gave him a nod. He took his stance, inhaled and the twenty holders were visibly jolted as the 130-pounder slashed out to either side simultaneously, kicked forward with the ball of his bare foot and punched rearward. All eight boards clattered to the ground, halved. The "Cat" criticized him for slashing left and right, saying he should have stabbed one "for variety."

Another two-board sandwich was held up and the "Cat" lunged like a swordsman, bare fingertips extended, and the halves clattered to the floor.

"Cat" called a match. Several of his teachers squared off. All higher ranking men present teach those lower while themselves learning from the highest rank holders and the "Cat." One fourth ranker performed a graceful ballet against five opponents of third and second ranks. Oyama indicated with a sweeping motion, "None of your pawing boxing extensions or bolos. Everything is for in-fighting or stand off out of range and leap in like a tiger. A tiger paws at play, only."

The fourth-ranker had taken four of them out on "point" in one fell swoop, executing a graceful tour jeté in which he raised effortlessly straight off the ground and then zoomed forward at eye level height. He "flew" with his left leg tucked up beneath him and with right leg extended. In midair, his left leg shot out to one side, the ball of his foot scoring between the eyes of his first opponent. Simultaneously, his right hand slashed down catching a second man at the point

"The Cat"

MASTER YAMAGUCHI GOGEN — THE CAT

on the crown of the head (fatal if full power), an inch to the rear of the highest point on the skull. An instant later, his right leg, which had come in when the left one shot out, went out again catching the third man in the center of the breast plate, the favorite target of French savate and Berber *rabah* kickers. This spun the kicker around, and, as he touched the ground, his left arm swung out, the heel of his palm catching number four on the chin—not "on the button" as in a boxing knockout, but just above the cleft about a half inch below the low point of the gums. Number five jabbed viciously at the ballet fighter, who caught his fist at the belly like a shortstop taking a line drive, spun him with his own momentum and then took him out with a karate chop to the neck just above the right shoulder blade.

The leap had taken the fighter about twelve feet, much of it at shoulder height. He had struck four men out from midair. He landed facing the direction from which he had come, in fighting balance.

"And some people," laughed Mass, "seem to think karate can be made easy, can be mastered by wishful thinking." He stressed that the only easy road lay through sustained hard work, lots of it. It would be almost impossible to learn any real karate without a teacher, for there were certain principles which set it, as all the oriental martial arts, apart from any western counterparts. The first, of course, was the breathing. The second was tension, both extension and contraction, which gives the karate hand such hardness, the whipping karate blows such power. Without mastering these two basics, one's antics might look like karate to the ignorant, but in a fight it would be a dance of suicide.

"Actually, dancers make the best karate-ka," Mass said. "But almost anyone can learn. I have only one prerequisite to studying here; you must like music. If you haven't got rhythm, you can't learn karate. You cannot become a black belt karate-ka without a teacher, but there are a few karate tricks you can learn easily, for defense or for calisthenics," he said. And practicing these can help you get the knack of the breathing and the extension. Let's take a look at a few.

After this demonstration, the victor went back to his corner of the dojo where he was supervising several students skipping rope with barbells on their ankles. Oyama said this is a major contribution to karate by Koreans, who like to fight with their feet. Country folk in Korea say you can tell which houses karate men live in as these don't have front doors. They supposedly leap over the roof into the back garden and come in through the rear porch door.

"The wife of one of the foreign embassy officials to whom I teach karate tried that trick of wearing weights on her feet all day before going to a ball. She said she danced on a cloud all night, has done it before every dance since," said Mass. "You should see her legs now."

The Uniform

Mass and I changed and he showed me how to put on the karate uniform of "pedal pushers" and tough waffle weave blouse, fastened with the eight-foot-long cotton belt. The belt, whether the novice's white, the beginner's brown, the adept's black or the grand masters' red, is tied the same. Take the belt at its center, which place against your abdomen just at or below the navel. Bring the two ends flat around the hips, taking care not to twist the belt—not the small of the waist as with your trouser belt but just encompassing the top of your hipbone. Pull tight in front (you'll have two loops around you), tight enough that you feel the support it gives you in

32

BASIC MUSCLE CONDITIONING

the small of the back. Now tie a square knot—left end over right, right over left—which should lie flat just on or below your navel. Let loose ends flap free, or if too long tuck in, as you prefer. One size of belt fits all.

Karate-ka use many of the calisthenic tone-ups that western-ers do. Twenty or more sit-ups daily are minimal for developing the abdominal muscles. When two practice together they can anchor each other's legs, sitting facing each other, legs partially enmeshed so that each man's feet are under the knees of the other. Each can then do sit-ups alternately with the other.

Push-ups are also basic. But a variant is to do them on the parallel bars. Dumbbells and barbells are also used in conventional ways. However, weight lifter muscles should be avoided by not using overly heavy barbells. You want speed of action, not spectacular weight. Mass called such excess beef, "sukiyaki meat. . . and it didn't do the cow any more good than it will you." Barbells should run maximum about two-thirds your own weight.

33

Other drills to be done in pairs round out the muscular toning developed by push-ups and sit-ups. For neck muscles, lie face down, as if doing push-ups, but rest on your elbows. Have your partner stand astride you, hands on your head and pushing down. Raise your head slowly against his pressure, hold it there, then lower it slowly. He should balance his pressure to allow you to barely make headway against him.

For the loins, stand with feet apart, set solidly. Have your partner mount you, face to face, his legs around your waist and arms around your head. Now bow your trunk forward slowly, until as near to horizontal as possible. Then raise your trunk slowly. When adept at this, try doing knee bends with the added weight of a passenger.

Leg muscles can be strengthened by having your partner mount you from behind, standing with his feet on the back of your thighs just below the hips. You must have your legs set well apart, both to give him footing and maintain yourself as well. Now walk forward, slowly. A lumbering King Kongish gait should be possible once you get accustomed to the new balance.

For the back muscles, kendo drills (mentioned in a later chapter) are done, but using a heavy cudgel in place of the light sword—make good baseball batter warm-ups, too.

That Not So Empty Hand

Conventional karate uses about 15 hand forms for attack. There are many others in specialized schools—ripping hooks, gouges, the finger-fists as lethal as a tap hammer or a woman's high heel. These require much special training, but they follow the same principles as the few basic ones mentioned here.

The basic hand form is that used in the notorious karate chop and finger lunges. It looks like a simple, flat open hand. It's anything but simple. This is the hand-sword, called *shuto* when used to chop like a saber; *nukite* used for lunging like a rapier. Merely flattening your palm and stiffening it is not a shuto or nukite, any more than an untempered iron sword is a fine steel blade. The successful tensing of this hand is basic to all karate hand forms. Master it, or master none. Broken arrows in the following diagram show direction of tension, extension or contraction. Solid arrows indicate direction of strike.

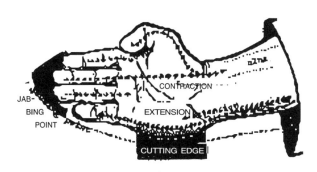

CONTRACTION

EXTENSION

JAB-
BING
POINT

CUTTING EDGE

THE HAND-SWORD

Hold the palm flat, as a straight-line extension of the forearm. Press your fingers together to get the feeling of tension. Now relax again, this is not the direction of tension we want, but the feeling must be understood. Now pull on the thumb, or more correctly, have the thumb pull on itself from within, so that it tries to ride back to the wrist and cocks itself as shown. Do not just bend the thumb, that is not a karate hand and is ineffective. You will find this easier to do if you have practiced a few times the deep breathing outlined earlier. You should exhale, straining from the pit of your stomach (like an imitation of a movie wolfman, in a highly sibilant near growl), so that the imagined cord or line of force, on which you are pulling to retract the thumb, seems anchored in your abdomen. Pulling in the thumb, you will notice a reaction, naturally, in an outward force, an extension, stiffening your other fingers. Now pull in on the three fingers except for the pinkie, which all the reacting extension should be allowed to work out through.

Your fingers will bend inward a trifle, the longer midfinger will shorten slightly in relation to the others (which is fine, a safety factor). You may find it hard to keep the fingers from separating, but keep at it. When done correctly, your forearm will feel like an iron rod, not because you are muscular, but because of pure tension.

Faults to avoid: don't allow the wrist to bend, as it may tend to bend backward, or to the side, the thumb side. The fingers may also tend to bend to the pinkie side. The whole hand-sword should form a perfect plumb straight line, the spine of the "sword" running down the middle finger, across its raised, almost distended, knuckle and straight up the ulna, the inner and larger of the two bones of the forearm. Stand erect, breathe deeply, or you will feel pain in your shoulder blade, scapula.

Your upper arm muscles will also be tensed. Your whole arm will feel as if spring-mounted. The inner softness of your palm should now feel as solid as a leather punching bag. As long as the tension is maintained (which can be indefinitely, as it is not physically tiring, but rather stimulating), the cutting edge of the sword, the side of your palm, will also feel like hard-packed leather glued to the bone, rather than the loose sinews it normally is. Hit a flat, hard surface with your normal, untensed, palm edge. Tense muscles as above and hit it again. The consciousness of contact, which in its extreme is pain, is far less when hand is tensed. Practice making this hand position fifty or more times per session until it can be done instantaneously, unconsciously.

Drilling the Hand-Sword

Oyama led me over to where an initiate was being started on the hand-sword stab or lunge. The equipment used is very simple to duplicate. Take a box about a foot square and a foot deep. Actually, a large bucket will do. Fill it with flour or sand—flour is easier. Place it on the floor. Stand as if up at bat, left foot alongside the sand box, right off behind it, looking down directly from above the box. Make the hand-sword. Cock your arm back, hand alongside your ribs. Breathe deep, through the nose. Tense your lungs. Jab your arm down, bending left knee but keeping right straight. Explode your breath out through the mouth simultaneously with your sudden action.

Repeat this at least two hundred times, daily for two weeks, until your hand jabs into the flour or sand up to the knuckles. Then replace contents with uncooked rice or other grain. Repeat exercise until hand jabs in up to the knuckles with ease. Replace with small beans or dried green peas and eventually with smooth pebbles such as you'll find in goldfish suppliers. Finished with pebbles, your hands are conditioned and ready to start cracking pine planks.

CONDITIONING THE HAND DAGGER

This was originally a scholar's exercise and many modern karate-ka still like to practice calligraphy, fancy brush writing. So progress is purposely kept slow to ensure against disfiguring the fingers. Don't rush things; six months is good time. The human solar plexus, even the rib cage, against which this attack is used, is a lot softer than beans.

Hand daggers, or finger jabs, are conditioned this way. Jab with forefinger alone or fore- and middle fingers combined. Make sure you contract them so end joint bends just slightly.

Many condition their toes in this same way.

The chop, using the blade or side of the palm, is conditioned in the same way as the mace, illustrated below.

Other fists and semi-fists begin with a hand-sword extension. As you contracted thumb, so now contract last two joints of the four fingers, also on breath exhale. Let hand bend back slightly at the wrist so that the heel of the hand shoves forward as the direct extension of the forearm. This is *shotei*, hand piston (following page), and is used for striking the chin in a jab or uppercut. Work it straight forward like a piston. You can deliver more force to target, with less training, than with your closed fist. This is especially handy for the amateur, and most effectively used by women as it takes no conditioning.

HIRAKEN   SHOTEI

Hiraken (above left), broad-hand, is made like *shotei*, except follow through a bit more contracting the two finger end joints so that they are tight as the thumb and the wrist again straightens. Result is a solid paddle, main contact area evenly distributed over the heel of the hand, inside mound of the palm, side of thumb, and end knuckles of four fingers. This is used in a simple slap, but just as a slap from the flat of a sword is more effective than a slap from a Ping-Pong paddle so is this slap much more effective than a simple slap. Women use it without further conditioning or training as a normal slap. It is more effective if the slap is not a bolo, but a short whip, delivered with forearm, upper arm held in close, allowing elbow to jolt outward as a counterforce.

Tetsui, in English variously fist hammer, mace or skull cracker. It also is a follow-through for the heel hand and fist hammer. Continue contracting the four fingers until they are completely rolled into a fist. Then complete the contraction of the thumb until it pulls down over the second joint of the fingers.

Don't just make a fist and think you have a mace or karate fist. The karate closed fist must be literally rolled inward, contracting from the fingertips as outlined above. One effect of this is that your hand is inured to pain or damage without hardening or further conditioning. After drilling for a while you should note a slight broadening of the palm, similar to the broadening of chest and shoulders that any healthy exercise brings about, and that deep breathing drill will also cause, regardless of whether or not physical exercise accompanies.

Karate Fists

The fist hammer mentioned above is the basic closed fist. Looking at it from above you will note that the knuckle of the middle finger is in a direct line with the ulna. Contact point is not the breadth of the fist, but the middle knuckle and forefinger knuckle.

Some karate-ka purposely smash the cartilage of these two knuckles, then knead it so that it heals as one immense super knuckle. Oyama had this karate knuckle. He conditioned it by pounding it with a hammer. He invited me to and I smashed it with all my might, to no avail. I drove thumb tacks into the cartilaginous lump. Oyama had no feeling in it.

The Cat has no such knuckle, being more of a leaper and slasher. Oyama himself believed it is wrong to develop this knuckle, wrong to disfigure the body "as presented by heaven" in any way. Long-term conditioning will naturally build up the knuckle, but you should not try imitating Oyama's karate super knuckle, it is a mistake.

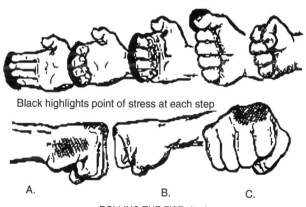

Black highlights point of stress at each step

A. B. C.

ROLLING THE FIST (top)
Crosshatch shows contact area on—
A) FIST HAMMER, MACE B) URA-KEN, BACKHAND C) BASIC FIST

KNUCKLE JAB

The properly contracted karate fist is used in combat like the ancient Roman gladiator used his short sword: jab conventionally with *seiken*, standard knuckle jab; smash downward on the crown of the head like a mace or ax; whipping inverted with *uraken* backhand; whip a slash at the temple, or driving the thumb knuckle into your opponent's vulnerable temple.

Ninth fist form is the *ippon-ken*, single-knuckle fist. Make by contracting the fist with the middle finger lagging behind the others so that its knuckle stands out as in the picture. Use this for thrusts and jabs to the upper lip, right at the point where the central flange of nose cartilage joins the upper lip.

Equipment

Parking meterlike posts had customers when we got to the dojo. One was being newly set up and Oyama explained its design to me (sketch facing). The standard Japanese height of these posts is 140 to 150 cm, 55–60 inches. This may be too low for tall Americans, so feel free to modify this to shoulder height of tallest gym member, or your own if for private use.

The standard padding is rice straw with the outer flaky sheath removed. Oyama believed this is too hard. And as karate is for use against living beings, the hard-packed post does not duplicate the human target in hardness or resiliency. It also leads to deformation of the fist and joints, again unnecessarily. Oyama experimented with new punching posts covered with heavy sponge—this is also more easily handled and more easily available outside of Japan. Standard western style heavy punching bags, especially those rope-anchored at top and bottom, can be used.

Mass rediscovered some ancient Chinese tricks for fist training which require no dummy or post—more on that later.

"PARKING METER" TRAINING POST

Stance

There are an unlimited number of postures in karate and
these are often mistaken by occidental writers for ready stances.
These other postures are striking and parrying and other
moving positions. There are several ready stances but a few of
the basic ones of general value are:

Straight stance, or *musubi-dachi*, at attention but shoulders
relaxed, feet together from toe to heel. Hands may be set in
hand-sword, in which case let them hang naturally. If you are
extending properly, this natural position will not be at your
sides, but the palms will be against the front of the thighs.
This is the formal Japanese stance from which the standing
bow is made. Japanese do this in place of the handshake. It is
customary to open all karate and judo sparring or training
with a bow.

Alternatively, contract into your mace, fist hammer, allowing
the forearms to contract so that they bend at the elbows and
bring your fists naturally up to hip level, hammer head down.

Both of these positions can also be taken in the *hachiji-dachi*
variant, a duck foot stance heels together and toes apart, feet
set at about 60 degrees. Do whichever is more comfortable.

The immovable stance, *fudo-dachi*: start from the duck foot,
above, and spread feet apart one big step. Common fault is
insufficient spread. Distance between toes should be about
that between shoulder and wrist.

From this, move on to—

Sanchin-dachi, three-attack stance, by moving either leg back the length of your foot, bringing forearms up, fists to shoulder level a foot out from body, hammers facing in. Rock slightly on feet, shift weight back and forth to get the feel of stance.

From this, move on to—

Shiko-dachi, 'waiting' or 'beckoning,' an extension of above, rear foot, either one, is moved back as far as you can comfortably do so—about the distance from your Adam's apple to fingertip plus a few inches. Rear foot is turned 90 degrees to forward one, knees are slightly bent for stability so you can bounce your torso up and down and dodge. Various hand positions can be worked in this stance, most common being to hold the forward hand open at shoulder level in *shotei*, hand piston, with rear hand horizontal across the stomach, palm up, in a hand-sword, or *nukite*, for jabbing.

Pivot on either foot to reverse this stance, changing your lead. There is no conventional left or right lead in karate. Ambidexterity—all-around balance—is striven for. Rock back slightly to put all weight on rear foot, freeing the front foot for kicking. Rise on your toe, bring front foot back, still free. Get the feel of the endless variations in posture possible. Try on either leg. Return to *shiko-dachi*. Then move on to—

Horseman stance, *kiba-dachi*, by turning your feet again parallel and sitting lower in your imaginary saddle. The hands will return to fists, hammer down, set before your hips as in *fudo-dachi*, the immovable stance, rather as if you are holding the horse's reins.

Stork leg, *tsuru-ashi-dachi*, is moved into by shifting weight to either foot, sliding free foot close, then raising leg as in diagram. Don't rock upper trunk, try to keep it vertical or you lose balance. From this position you practice your kicks.

Move through these stances in succession. Make all outward moves on the exhale, all withdrawal and closing moves on the inhale. Move slowly. Move in time, try a 3-4 time waltz record accompaniment. Move gracefully and don't be afraid of having graceful mistaken for effeminacy. There is no power without gracefulness.

A powerful man is graceful. A graceful woman, a power.

FUDO	KIBA	SANCHIN	SHIKO	TSURU
Immobile	Horseman	Three-attack	Waiting	Stork

KARATE READY STANCES

Tempering the Iron Fists

The plain fist is simply pounded against the parking meter, or semirigid stuffed bag. It is used in an arrow-straight jab. Start thumb out and up (palm up, that is) and pivot the fist on the axis of the forearm 180 degrees as it pistons forward so that on contact your palm is down, your thumb down and inside. Contact point is the middle- or middle and forefinger knuckles. Deliver blow with explosive expulsion of air.

Now from *fudo*, or immovable stance, try series of one-two-one-two alternate hand jabs. Try snapping them so that they bounce back into ready position as fast, or seemingly faster than, jabbed outward.

The hand ax or karate chop is practiced standing in front and slightly to one side of the parking meter, snapping the *shuto*, hand-sword, edge of the palm against the pad. Again note that the forearm twists on its own axis 180 degrees, starting from palm up position and reaching a palm down just before contact. Again try snapping this.

This snap is essential to karate bouts, as all blows must be pulled before contact to avoid maiming your sparring partner. In combat they are more effective if snap-pulled in the same way just at the instant of contact. A whip snap is far more destructive than a whiplash.

43

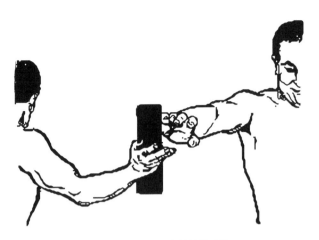

CONDITIONING HAND AX

Alternate this with hammer pound to top of padded meter, or palm up outside chop, which involves no pivot or twist of forearm.

Take immovable stance, *fudo*, or three-attack stance, *sanchin*. Raise forearms vertical so that fists are near your cheeks. Fist form is middle finger knuckle extended slightly. Snap fist down in backhand, counteraction of elbow snapping inward slightly. This is a knockout blow if delivered at base of nose or on cleft of chin (illustrated on page 40). Easily blocked, true, but usually unexpected.

Fist hammer, or mace or skull crusher, is practiced seated at a table, or traditionally squatting on your heels and knees at a low pedestal such as Mass built to break the bricks. As a pounding surface use a thick board. Pad it with thick sponge rubber or a few layers of inner tube. Raise fist hammer to eye level and chop down. Raise over head and chop down. Now develop the snap-back in this also.

Special Punching Drills

Take a large beanbag, sandbag or tough cushion 18 inches square, 6 deep. Take push-up position, on fists. As illustrated, shift weight to one arm, draw other fist as far back and high as possible. Strike downward into beanbag in cavity left by

SPECIAL PUNCHING

your first position, as illustrated above. Try this with either hand, for development of fist and muscles of back and wrist.

The "secret" of the karate punch is the snap-back. This is identical in execution to the billiard player's snapshot used to make the cue ball stop dead after hitting the target ball. The soccer player will also recognize the basic technique in the illegal leaping double kick. Oyama rediscovered an ancient Chinese drill for developing this. This is a scholar's drill, especially indulged in by willowy lightweights. It takes no special equipment other than a candle or a sheet of typewriter paper and thread. It must be done in a quiet room in which there is no breeze, not even that of a stray breath. This atmosphere is also especially conducive to meditation.

Stand a candle in normal position. Light it. Flame should be just below shoulder level, so adjust height of your candlestick on table with books, etc. Stand so that with arm fully extended flame is about two inches beyond the flat of your fist. Now strike a forward jab at flame with regular fist, snapping back. The efficiency of your snap-back will be recorded in the reaction of the flame. Develop a good snap and flame will flicker and bend toward you. Start with small birthday candle, and work up. When you can draw the flame out on a three-quarter-inch-thick candle, extinguishing it, you are ready to tackle a bull.

Try a hand-ax slash, whipping your hand just above the flame. Watch its reaction. You should form a partial vacuum in the wake of your stroke which will draw the flame after.

Success in this will be due to developing true power, not to brute strength—meditative breathing as opposed to grunting. Velocity, not force, is effective. Remember, a high velocity .22-caliber bullet properly aimed is more deadly than a lower velocity slug of higher caliber.

Hang a sheet of paper by a thread so that sheet center is at shoulder height. Stand off as above, snap a standard fist blow at the paper, stopping an inch or two short, snap it back. With absolute technique, great power, perfect control, you may make the paper swing. A good karate-ka can accomplish these feats in seven years. Then you can take on your bull.

Pardon My Elbow

Assume *kiba-dachi,* or horseman stance, legs well apart like a tennis player. Fists in any form, but raised to cheeks, forearms vertical. If working at parking meter, stand at 30-40 degree angle off to one side. If at punching bag, stand facing it. Crook elbow so that forearm is horizontal at shoulder level.

Stand facing parking meter or punching bag, at about arm's length, hands at your sides, feet slightly apart. Bring right fist up and place into left hand before your navel. Pivot on left foot 90 degrees, while simultaneously with right foot stepping forward to parking meter at 90 degrees to it, dropping into slight knee-bend crouch, lunging forward with force surging up from left leg, and jabbing right elbow into target at solar plexus level, increasing force of blow by shoving the right elbow with the left hand. This is a simple maneuver easier done than described. It is easily learned for use by women defending themselves against molestation from the front.

Try first elbow attack listed above, following through with:

Squat at anvil table as for exercising fist hammer. You can also use a sandbag on a low stand. Have fist in any position, held at shoulder, with elbow extended out horizontal. Slam elbow down, making contact with target just behind the point of our elbow. Elbow must move down a vertical line perfectly dissecting your torso, from nose to navel.Stand with back to target, parking meter preferred, in close. Practice elbow jabs to rear at various ranges of 6 to 18 inches. Combine with stamping same side foot back. In defense this would plant your heel on attacker's instep while driving elbow into his solar plexus. Follow-through for most people should then be to run like blazes.

Especially for women: stand facing shoulder height target, raise either fist above ear, then slam elbow down. For crowdedsubway mashers, raise arm overhead as if holding strap, bring elbow slamming down forward or to side.

LIMP WRIST

The Not So Limp Wrist

Raise your forearm, hand to eye level. Now bend your wrist all the way forward, fingers pulling in.

This is the most effective parry and counterblow "fist" ("small fist" is what it's called in Japanese). Its uses are endless. It has been poorly renamed "chicken neck" by some American karate-ka in what is no doubt a well-meaning attempt to emulate an oriental nomenclature of such as stork stance, cat stance, horse-man stance. But the Eastern names communicate a sense of strength, of a specialized vector of lines of force. There is nothing strong about a chicken neck (except for Churchill's 1940 quip, "Some chicken, some neck!"), nothing inviting about having a limp wrist as easily wrung.

There is a chicken-beak fist similar to the "small fist" wrist except that the wrist is straight—the fingers are clamped as illustrated to enable you to concentrate all your power on as small a contact area as possible. You can literally peck a man to pieces with this fist, but it is not one of the basics of karate and is really beyond the realm of this introduction. Suffice it to say, the chicken-beak and the "small fist" wrist are used together. The "small fist" should be used in parrying, as illustrated. It should also be used in a backhand slap where one would otherwise use the back of the hand. Oddly, though it enjoys less leverage, it packs more effective punch than even regular fist used backhand. Use against head or face, especially side of jaw, or from waist against solar plexus. Use also as a short jab uppercut when in close.

THE THREE FOOT-CONTACT AREAS
Any may be employed depending on target range, effectiveness

As it comes from an unorthodox position, it does not telegraph its presence and will tak e an opponent by surprise. Very effective against someone behind you. Otherwise use to outside or upward. Held in this way, the hand seems almost impervious to pain or bruising.

My Foot!

The foot is a wicked weapon, but used improperly can be of far greater danger to the kicker than to the target.

The foot is used in several ways. Three parts of either foot can be used as contact points: the outer edge, the balls of the sole, and the knuckles, as illustrated.

The knuckle, as well as the knee, is used only for a kick to the genitals.

I stress the danger of the kick to the kicker because I sat watching Mass while he read through a best-selling American book on what its author called karate. Its author, reputedly, taught movie stars and 'choreographed' martial arts episodes in Hollywood movies. Mass clucked his tongue. "Use this footwork against any real attacker and you are a dead man. This not karate. I don't know what it is except maybe suicide!"

Similar errors in other positions result in loss of most of your expended effort. In illustration #1, below, pounding the fist against a cinder block for "toughening" is not karate and is denounced by oriental karate masters. Besides this, the karate-ka is hunched over. In this position, more force is lost upward from the shoulder than is delivered downward by the fist.

In figure #2, below, body curvature also effects power loss. Elbow blows must always dissect the body center or work at a true perpendicular to it, at shoulder height. This position shown is effective only for holding a cocktail glass at a bar.

In figure #3, this weave leaves karate-ka wide open as he cannot retreat further if attacker throws a follow-up blow. The rear foot is not firmly planted, so can't bear weight if forefoot must be pulled back in retreat. The oddly curved body can't deliver counterblow, especially as rear foot is not planted to act as a base for a blow.

In #4, body curvature again weakens the defender, who cannot move easily to avoid all possible attacks as his body curvature acts as a counterforce to his moving against it. Blows at the main curve points here would be especially effective.

2.   3.   4.

What Not to . . .

Most kickers are off balance once the kicking foot leaves the ground. Some karate books even compound this innate weakness in a kick attack by instructing you to rise up on the toes of your other foot. Nothing could be worse. The standing foot must remain firmly planted, flat and immovable. Actually, an effort must be exerted not only with the kick, but in recoil back against the standing foot. *(Continued on page 52)*

WRONG KICKS

(1) This kick is taught, using the bottom of the foot which diffuses the force of the kick over a large flat surface, in effect canceling out its effectiveness. The form is horrible as the kicker is all hunched over, a position from which he cannot exert maximal effort, and in which his balance is so unnatural that the slightest countereffort on the part of his target will send him sprawling. The flat kick from such a position is thus ineffective.

(2) Any football player can spot the errors in this one—base foot raised off ground, body bent back from center of balance depriving kicking foot of inertia. The target need only slap the kicker's ankle, or kick his base foot ankle, to send him sprawling.

(3) Again, hunched over, using the ineffective flat foot kick, base foot bent at knee to cause loss of kicking force.

(4) Is supposedly to use the "outside edge of foot," which from this position is totally ineffective. The outside edge should only be used in a sideward kick at target below hip level. In this illustration the kicker has had to contort his body to attain this unnatural kick position, losing all force and leaving oneself wide open for counterattack. This kick couldn't crack a raw egg, never mind a tough yeg.

(5) Using "inside edge of foot" in this manner is as dangerous and ineffective as kick number 4, with the added bonus that the kicker has left his family treasure wide open through the whole maneuver. To counter either of kicks 4 or 5, just grab the kick foot as it makes its feathery contact, raise your arm on contact side trapping kick foot, and pin it to your shoulder. Do as you wish, for your kicker foe is now helpless.

Four centuries ago master swordsman-philosopher Miyamoto Musashi, "laments the commercialization of martial arts, resulting in fragmentation of the science, with impractical elaborations and movements based on showmanship rather than efficiency.

WRONG KICKS

With apologies to various 'experts' and 'masters'

The large figure on the left demonstrates correct form
for kick number 2, as posed by Oyama.

OYAMA SIDE-KICKS CORRECTLY

(Continued from page 49)

The edge of the foot is used in side kicks. These are the easiest to learn and by far the least dangerous and most effective for defensive use by novices. Let's take this one first.

I am eight inches taller than my Japanese-American wife, and we Caucasians have proportionately longer arms and legs. Yet her reach, using this side kick, is a good three inches greater than my punching reach. Best use of this kick, almost indefensible, is against shins or kneecap. Use also against abdomen and chest.

This is a fairly conventional kick. The difficulty of it is that it was developed for use by barefoot people—the Japanese and Okinawans wore sandals which they kick off when fighting. Drill this kick only as a balance exercise. When drilling barefoot, make sure to pull the toes back to clear the contact face of the balls of the foot. For defense, drill with shoes on, kicking with just underside of point of shoe. If shoe is a very soft-soled style, you must kick as if barefoot. A moderately rigid shoe, such as most lightweight, rubber-soled or plastic-soled loafers, is bad because neither can you kick with the ball of the foot, nor will the shoe protect your toes in a kick with the tip of the foot. Make sure also, that your shoes fit snugly. Floppy shoes destroy your stance and deprive you of traction. You are better off barefoot than with poor shoes.

The butt of the heel is also used, but only in stomping. For a more effective stomp, bend the foot, toes up slightly—not too much, or you will move the contact point back too far and hurt yourself.

Jumping

Jumping is an essential part of karate. The jump is dangerous to the jumper, for once off the ground you are easily spilled. But it is less important in battle than as a calisthenic. Rope skips with weighted feet should be done regularly. Practice the simple standing high jump, and from a straight standing position, no bending or windup. A first-rank black belter should be able to leap over a four-foot barrier from a straight standing start. Try it first from a crouch over a barrier between knee and crotch height. You should be able to get over hip height after several days of practice. In leaping, the knees fold and snap in to be ready to kick out while in the air or upon touching down with one leg. Practice leaping straight up and kicking out to side at a target about chest height.

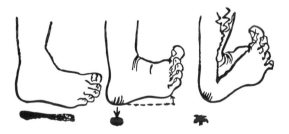

STOMP KICK

Flat foot *(at left)* dissipates force of kick. Correct form *(center)*. Excessive back bend *(right)* causes tension in toes and shins, detracts from strength; contact point too far back on vulnerable Achilles heel.

Use Your Head ...

The head butt is a legitimate part of the karate repertoire, just as in North England's Northumberland it is both the favored way to fight as well as greet a friend. A karate-ka can break boards with his head. A top karate-ka should be able to break bricks. One of the best can crack two bricks or split a pile of twenty roofing tiles. Around the dojo they joke that he earns extra money doing testimonials for headache medicines.

The main things to remember about using your head are:

a) keep it; and b) don't be afraid to use it.

As with all attacks, the head lunge starts from the pit of the stomach and is done on an explosive exhale. You add recoil power to it by snapping the knees back and jabbing back with the elbows and fists. Lunge with the head, do not try a snapback jab, you may injure yourself or at least lose balance.

Woman's Defense Against Attacker

In illustration above, your weight at start when attacked is on your right foot (rear foot). Thrust forward from right foot, giving way with puller to relax his grip on your hair. Direction of thrust of your fists is as closing a circle comprised of your arms. In this way the power behind either fist is greater than if used separately. An effective defense against both arms is almost impossible, especially as the attacker has expended his offensive power. Even should one thrust miss, the other alone has KO force.

WOMEN'S DEFENSE AGAINST ATTACKER

Figures 3, 4 and 5, above, suggest some follow-throughs.

Always follow through, even if it seems unnecessary. Any golfer or baseball batter realizes this: it assures completion of circular motion through extension.

Here, in figure 4, fingers are held semirigid so that they will give slightly upon contact and follow the contour of target's face. Collapse digits so that the ball of the palm will crush attacker's nose, while first and third fingers gouge his eyes.

In figure 5, jerking him down opens another vulnerable point and hitting him while he is in motion falling forward adds much of his own weight to the force of the blow.

Let's Dance: *Pinan* II

Havelock Ellis called love the "dance of life"—karate is the "dance of death." Mass had one entry requirement to his dojo. You must have rhythm, must have a feel for music. First time visitors to a good Japanese dojo may think it's a dance school.

Actually, the war dance is an ancient human institution. Even today in China, the most popular theater is the classical Peking Opera and the most popular acts are those fabulous, brightly costumed sword- and battle-dances.

The most popular movies in Japan are the "easterns"—the oriental two-sword version of our two-gun western, with samurai sword battles in which the participants literally dance out the battle for more dramatic effect. Korea and China have their versions, all available in the U.S. today on ethnic television stations in major cities.

The karate-ka must put the following stances and attack and defense techniques into practice, in quick succession, with rhythmical connections. This is done with a series of drills called 'Forms,' *kata*, as in all martial arts. There are over 50 in the various Japanese schools of karate; Oyama used about 36. Basic are the *taikyoku* and the 5 *pinans*. Perfection in at least four is required for the first rank black belt, *sho-dan*.

One representative drill form, *pinan II*, is shown here in simplified drawings. This dance routine is similar to the so-called Chinese shadow boxing, performed in China both as a dance on stage, as a scholar's calisthenic (*tai ch'i*) and fighter's drill. In China they are practiced in slow motion, then steadily speed up till whirlwind fast.

It begins from the simple Chinese "eight" ﾉﾍ stance, as do most, legs spread and ankles turned 'duck-foot.' It is the ideal ready stance for most efforts, a good tennis stance. Russ Morgan, one of the great trombonists of American music, was asked by a child how to begin to play the slide horn. He replied "First you stand like you're going to serve a tennis ball ..."

Every move is executed with a snap, putting one's total power behind it. All muscles and nerves from toes to scalp must be under tension at all times. All offensive—that is, outgoing—moves are made with an explosive exhaling of breath from open mouth; all recoils on tight-lipped nasal inhale.

Rhythm and tempo are all-important.

Match this to your taste, but a waltz tempo in three-quarter time is about the easiest. If you are in a gym or macho atmosphere and concerned that visitors may think you nuts, or effeminate, try one of the Sousa marches that have been orchestrated for military waltzes. Conversely, just remember, some of the best marches for a dress parade are Strauss waltzes and there's nothing effeminate about the United States Marines drill team.

Go through this drill very slowly at first. (Mass used to say to play an old 78-rpm waltz record at 33 or 45.) Then speed up as you get the hang of the movements. Nowadays some tape players have speed controls for dictation playback and can be slowed down.

BASIC DRILL: PINAN II

57

BASIC DRILL: PINAN II *(Continued)*

58

The same extensions (with breathing and visualizing) and contractions you have learned in making a hand-sword or a fist hammer also here apply to the whole body.

Center these extensions and contractions in your navel as the root of all lines of action.

A full proper karate workout consists of two minutes of meditation, 50 minutes of workout at the parking meters, sandpits and bags, another 50 minutes in *kata* forms and paired off matches.

I still remember my first workout. When I finished, the large after-work group came in for the evening lesson. It was at the Cat's dojo, before Mass had built his own. Mass had stressed my choosing and specializing in forms best suited to my own natural abilities and physical requirements and limitations (for me, size). Then as he moved to get the evening group started, he admonished, "Brain beats brawn in karate."

Mass and the Cat kneeled down on the mats facing the squatting ranks of students. They led them through the deep breathing drill and then all sat, eyes closed, for two minutes of silent meditation, centering themselves. They stood, bowed and paired off.

Oyama rejoined me. "We make them meditate before every workout and encourage meditation at home or at work."

Early in his teaching career Mass chose two new students who were as evenly endowed with natural talents as possible. One he trained purely on calisthenics and workouts, taught him all the tricks. To the other he gave less physical training, but made him do *zazen* meditation every day for half an hour when he awoke and again before his evening workout, squatting like a Buddha, forcing all his internal organs into proper alignment, breathing "right down to his toes" and clearing his mind. After six months, both men came up for their black belt test and he matched them in *shiai*. The first fellow had beefed up and put on ten pounds; the other had grown wiry. The wiry thinker made mincemeat of the muscle boy.

Mass had another ace student he liked to show off at press demonstrations. He shattered bricks and great blocks of ice with his forehead. Mass smiled, "That's all he can use his head for. I think he's brain-dead. It's a great PR show, the press love it. But empty head is not empty hand."

"The immediate goal of karate is to build a healthy mind, the only true self-defense," Mass said. A healthy mind in a sound body, the Latin *mens sana in corpore sano,* breeds confidence and strength. The man or woman possessing these will never be attacked, so need never worry about having to use this terrible fistic A-bomb."

Karate Standards

United States karate will have to police itself as carefully as Japanese groups do. The United States Air Force in Japan did not find it necessary to enact special laws regulating karate. As Major Seth Lurie, director of Public Information, USAF Far East stated:

> The Japanese government in 1950 outlawed the indiscriminate use of karate, thus serving notice on the small criminal element of Japan that the use of this lethal art for foul purposes would be grounds for criminal action against the user.
>
> There is no Far East Air Forces policy against the study of karate…but parallel regulatory policy might be the use of the pistol by military personnel, including air police on duty. An Air Policeman is honor bound to use his pistol only in self-defense and then only when all other forms of self-defense have been exhausted and his life is at stake.

Mass noted that this is identical to the traditional unwritten code of the karate schools. Karate must be recognized as a weapon, just as a trained boxer's fists are. Indiscriminate use of karate should be recognized by the law courts for what it then is, indiscriminate use of a potentially lethal weapon, and punishable under existing laws. Mass was willing to testify in any court in any nation that karate is a weapon and ask that an indiscriminate user should be properly punished.

In Japan such a wise guy might not get off so lightly. He might instead be allowed the great honor of facing his master in a bout. One in which blows are not pulled quite so early.

Empty Hands and Empty Heads

Karate is a dangerous weapon. When Americans in the Far East first became interested in it, several United States Army commandants forbade their troops studying it without prior permission. This was wise. Intelligent self-policing and publi city on strict etiquette by the various karate schools and governing associations quickly overcame this ban.

The United States Far East Air Forces Air Police in Tokyo were put through a special 30-day course at the Kodokan, mecca of world judo in 1956, stressing karate techniques and especially defenses against common karate attacks. This quickie course led to no belt of any color. Several hundred took the course. Several developed sincere interest in the sport and continued it. In 1957 my article "Masters of the Bare-Hand Kill" (first draft of Chapter I) appeared in *True* magazine, then the largest circulation men's mag, and at least seventeen new dojos soon opened. Karate has come a long way since, but too often with excess theatrics, perhaps.

Where to Study

There are now innumerable karate schools in the United States, Europe, worldwide. This martial art has become so popular that most martial art dojos (aikido, tai-ch'i, etc.) are commonly listed in the yellow pages under "Karate –."

There is no dearth of "how-to" books and videotapes—but you can't learn a martial art from a book any more than you can learn to play a piano.

Cocktail Karate

The Japanese, of course, have their own forms of party sports like Indian arm wrestling and other "jam session jujutsu." They differ from ours mainly in being less sports of brawn, more tests of delicate balance.

In this they have a wider base of appeal; the little fellow used to dodging rush-hour traffic and treading on thin ice at the office may find himself with an advantage over the life-of-the-party football center. These wrestling forms are called in Japan various varieties of "sumo." They are excellent light-hearted drills in judo, karate or aiki balance. The illustrations —following on page 63—are from the more than hundred-year-old art masterpiece the *Hokusai Sketchbooks,* or called in Japanese the *Hokusai Manga.*

Crane sumo is played standing on one leg like a crane—which as national bird of Japan, is used as emblem by Japan Airlines, and by what is perhaps Japan's best *sake*, rice wine. There are two forms. In one, you may hop around within a fixed area. In the other and more difficult style you must not move from the fixed spot and the two contestants stand about three feet apart. Slapping, pulling, pushing, anything goes. Loss of balance loses. Releasing the raised leg to use the arm for balance is a self-inflicted TKO. In one version the opponents "peck" at each other, using only one finger, an extreme version of the chicken fist.

Squat sumo sees the contestants squatting on tiptoe, set about three feet apart. Again two styles: in one you lose if you are put off your stance, i.e., if you are set down on your seat or if your heels, or one hand, touch ground; but you may hop about to keep balance. In the tougher type, being set down or moved in any way at all from your assigned spot is a KO.

Shiri-sumo or oriental bumpsa-daisy, is not as picturesque now that most Japanese wear trousers. You may move about, of course, but KO is being knocked off your feet. TKO is releasing your hand grip on your legs. A geisha house version is to stand back to back on a foot square cushion and bowingly bump the opponent off the cushion. I have found Japanese have an unfair advantage in this in being built lower to the ground. Or maybe it's just that the geisha I have contested with are more experienced wrestlers.

Foot sumo is just a leggy version of Indian wrestling. In tougher versions you may not plant your free hand on the floor and it is a combination of squat sumo and foot sumo.

There are other variations, explore your own ideas. Another version of crane sumo is played with arms folded or akimbo and the fighting done with the raised foot. This one can get rough. Experts start from a squatting position and stand up on one leg, coming up fighting. I have found that very few Occidentals can do this one-leg rise, and few enough Japanese. This stand-up is described in the Archery chapter, where the straight rise (two-legged, heels and toes together) is a part of archery ritual and a form of stand-up not expected today out of archers under third rank. Most anyone who can do a formal archery rise (page 170) will find a one-legged rise easy.

Crane sumo

Squat
sumo

One
leg
sumo

Shiri
sumo

Geisha house
bumpsa-daisy

COCKTAIL KARATE

63

Lanny vs 'kaho budo'

Referring back to the meet when Mass won his championship —at that time he pulled punches and snap-tapped, while less traditional contenders were disqualified for hitting full force. He always spoke of gentleness, power of musical rhythm, of strength through circular motion, how meditator beat muscle-builder in controlled test (page 59). Then he originated Full Contact Karate. And other schools followed. Some even developed armored 'space suits' with bubble helmets, more like gear for an extravehicular walk from a space satellite. It is macho. It is exciting. It is Show Biz. It is a gimmick to draw students and crowds and make money. It is gamesmanship— what early 19th-century critics of the unreality of then kendo dojo practice called *kaho kenpo* "flowery swordplay."

It just ain't what the ancients promoted that set Zen Combat apart from barroom brawling. But after all, martial arts teachers don't usually make much of a living without rich patrons, or movie contracts. Gimmicks are a sales pitch alternate.

It isn't a new problem, either. It's precisely what Musashi warned of even four centuries before Hollywood and TV:

> … people make the arts into commercial products…. In martial arts particularly there is a lot of showmanship and commercialization. The result of this must be, as someone said, 'Amateuristic martial arts are a source of serious injury.'

Schools like Shito-ryu (another of the four original contemporaries of Funakoshi) still adhere to old style circular motion. One of the most beautiful martial arts performances I have ever seen was the gentle yankee giant Lannie Dwyer sensei. He is owner-bartender of Bojangles, Kobe karate-ka hangout.

What Is a Black Belt ?

Just what is involved in earning the right to wear a band of black cloth around your midriff? The requirements vary with the schools. Those of Oyama were perhaps the toughest.

The *kyu* ratings, those brown and green belts below the *dan* or black belt, are not strictly regulated in Japan, as they really respect only the black belt. Browns and greens are usually recognized only within individual dojos. In America, after too many easy dans were issued, it was realized how awful it would be to have an international meet between a giant Yank or Dutchman and a peanut Japanese of lower rank and have the giant come off a poor second. The foreign black belts would fade to tattletale gray on the world sports market.

French black belt requirements were early on, if anything, tougher than Japanese. Rank standards in the USA have, as I foresaw in the original edition, stabilized themselves once karate got more of a college campus following, as it was sure to do. Regular competitions have kept international standards of campus and commercial dojo rankings fairly level. And elevation of taekwando, Korean karate, to an Olympic sport, completed the evolution.

The Japanese Ministry of Education early recognized Mass's school, Kyoku-Shin-Kan, on a level equivalent to karate as the Kodokan is to judo. Not all karate organizations in Japan have this Education Ministry certification. Those which do, maintain equally strict standards.

The curriculum for the black belt ranks which Mass registered with the Ministry are:

For first rank: mastery of the two *taikyoku* drills and the five *pinans*.

Second rank: add *saifa*, *kanku*, *tensho* and *sanchin*. This completes the karate-ka's repertoire of *kata* "dance drills." Pinan #2 is illustrated (pages 57–58) as typical. Most seconds should be able to break a brick with the bare hand, but proficiency in *kata* dance drills is far more important.

(All schools of oriental martial arts have similar curricula, similar "dance sets" under different names, different details. This is basic to all, armed or unarmed: kendo fenciing, bo-stave, zen-longbow achery as well as the arts of the empty hand, with their dances ranging fromthe dreamlike sweeps of tai-chi chuan, the radial extensions of aikido, the rounded sparring of Shito-ryu or the joint-jarring full-contact karate).

For third rank, the karate-ka no longer has an empty hand. He must master the basic use of the four-foot and six-foot-long *bo*-staves (illustrated page 142-3), *kusarigama* or scythe-ball-and-chain (page 148). He must show his knife technique both defensive and aggressive, use of the chair, of fighting from a seated, reclining or even sleeping position; use of ashtray, pen and pencil. Then there are *kakudori* "corner capturing" dance routines whereby he demonstrates his ability to cover all conceivable angles of attack and defense.

Fourth rank requires more of these applications of empty-hand techniques to objects. One is now a guerrilla of the first order, capable of projecting a common fountain pen with the lethal effect of a dagger or even ancient samurai's armor-piercer (a ballpen in the handkerchief- or shirt pocket is now a lethal weapon concealed), of using any common household object which might come to hand as a lethal missile or fist supplement.

Fifth rank and higher requires increased proficiency in all the above techniques. But mainly, it is demonstration of being what Japanese call *jinkakusha*, a gentleman of high character and accepted as such by his community. Thus is the 'Way.'

Not commonly known is that martial art rank is not permanent. It is always subject to review. It may be recalled for any infraction of the rules of conduct, for the commission of any crime or misdemeanor, or for misuse of one's award.

In lieu of formal testing, ranks are sometimes assigned on a rough estimation or appraisal, subject to later examination and reassessment. In the early years most US black belts were held on this basis, as few of the Yankee-*dans* had been under close observation by a master long enough to be appraised as carefully as is a Japanese or Korean karate-ka. This, thankfully, changed and international standards are quite even.

Details of all of the basic routines necessary to the initial colored belts and the first rank black belt, plus those for the second and on, can be found in the literature available at your dojo. Always consult your sensei.

Once a black belter retires from active participation and training, he retains the honor of the rank held at that time. Many rise to second or third rank in college, and then taper off in activity. Some suffer minor (or major) injuries which make retirement from active competition advisable.

My favorite Japanese sport cartoon shows a judo white belt novice being flipped about by a suave black belter. In the second frame he bows and asks the black belter to swap belts for a few minutes. Then the white belter in the borrowed black belt flips the real black belter around.

Alas, such is not real life. When the gauntlet is dropped, your opponent won't take notice how you hold up your pants. Performance counts. And those most proficient in the various karate 'empty hand' martial arts are not always the guys in white hats.

zen

III. WHY THE 'ZEN' OF ZEN COMBAT

WHAT REAL DIFFERENCE is there between Japanese and western martial arts? I have found nothing in any of the Japanese or other oriental forms which is completely strange to the West. Basic principles may be shared by the Japanese two-sword samurai ('one who serves') and an American two-gun cowboy, by karate-ka and foil-fencer. Yet, while they may share some common principles, even boast more identical elements than dissimilar, the martial arts of the Orient and the West in the overall are most certainly different.

Basically the difference is a matter of awareness and of approach. Granted, we share knowledge of all the miscellaneous elements with the Japanese, yet we are not aware of any whole these elements might comprise. Japanese masters are aware. Being unaware of the whole, Occidentals have also been unaware of the possibility of a scientific approach, a unified field, thus have made no attempt at an organization or even scientific cataloging of this known miscellany.

Accumulated knowledge and skills of the individual western champion have usually gone to the grave with him. In Asia, particularly in Japan, the champion has been able to pass on the benefits of his experience and discoveries, his "guiding principles," to successors.

The heart, then, of the difference between Japanese and western martial arts is the ability of one to perpetuate itself, thus grow with accumulated experience of passing centuries. This ability to perpetuate itself is due to "Zen."

The western champion masters his skill by intuition: he feels that a certain way is the right way to dive, the right way to swing a bat, the right way to draw a gun. Those who lack this intuition fall by the wayside—in modern sports figuratively, in our more violent past, (and alas, more so today) literally. The Japanese champion was taught the proper way to dive, the proper way to swing his halberd or draw his sword.

Yet Zen is supposed to be intuition—"unlearned intuition," the misleading expression often used by learned Zenists quite unintuitively. Then this same prisoner of words will spend years learning by rote some intricate ceremony of etiquette. What has been overlooked is that intuition cannot be learned, but it can be conditioned; the techniques for conditioning it can be learned.

The many ceremonial arts and skills associated with Zen are technical formulae for sharpening and developing intuition. All through Zen arts learning and intuition go together as inseparably as yin and yang, female and male. Alternatives to this are intuition without learning which degenerates into black magic at its worst or at its best the cockeyed genius champion with the perpetual run of unexplainable "luck"; or the unintuitive learning of the bookish bore who "knows" how to do everything but in fact can do nothing.

Undisciplined, intuition discourages learning. Once undertaken, learning kills intuition. Zen, as it has applied itself in the martial arts, attempts to maintain both in balance.

Takuan, a Zen monk, lived from 1573 to 1645. He invented the pickled radish which bears his name, and greatly advanced kendo, the way of the sword. He was noted as a tea-man, calligrapher, poet and painter, living example of *zen-ken-shu*. Exiled by the shogun, he later won his way back into favor as his Zen teacher. Takuan instructed his students to "arouse the mind without fixing it anywhere."

Daisetsu Suzuki, noted writer on Zen, more recently restated the Zen approach to education for mastery of an art: "Technical knowledge is not enough. One must transcend technique so that the art becomes an artless art, growing out of the unconscious." That is, the techniques themselves must be learned to the point where they may be performed intuitively. Learning the techniques arouses the mind—transcending technique allows "not fixing it anywhere." In short, learn by heart and then forget about it and do what then "comes naturally."

Learning by rote has been the basis of western education since the first Greek student sat in a garden at the feet of the first Greek teacher. It is the basis of western military and athletic drills. But unfortunately the balance of learning technique without dulling the intuition has been upset. The Zenist has at least attempted to maintain the balance—though he has been as much alone in this in his home country as he would be anywhere else.

Zen has been, to the martial arts, an attempt to apply the accumulated knowledge of Confucius, Mencius, Laotze, Buddha, and all the other culture heroes and intellectual giants it has come in contact with, to the sharpening of the intuition. In the martial arts, it has been the unifying and driving factor.

Martial Arts Before Zen

Earliest literary reference to martial arts is in man's oldest extant written story—*The Gilgamesh Epic.* It is inscribed in Sumerian, the first written language, in cuneiform script on clay tablets before 2,500 B.C. Many parts survive in separate fragments from different archaeological excavations in the Tigris-Euphrates valley of what is now Iraq. Our hero Gilgamesh in the city of Uruk is challenged by Enkidu. "So they grappled, holding each other like bulls,...locked together.... Gilgamesh *bent his knee with his foot planted on the ground and with a turn Enkidu was thrown.*" Enkidu admires Gilgamesh's skill and they "embraced and their friendship was sealed." They go on to share adventures like a typical buddy-pair in a modern movie scenario.

Other early literary references to martial arts are Persian and Chinese. By the fifth-century B.C. Achaemenid dynasty there were in Persia fully developed martial arts. Instructional texts on them existed but, except for indirect reference to them, are lost. Persia probably developed the first concept of scientific warfare, including both scientific use of individual weapons and tactical deployment of bodies of disciplined troops rather than symbolic display of massed formations as practiced elsewhere in Asia. Alexander the Great of Macedon studied these. The principal weapons of the Persians or Iranians were the bow and the sword. There was also a jujutsu-like art called (at least in later times) *zur khaneh* or "deception-strength" still practiced today to some degree (pp. 89–94).

The Greeks learned tactics and weapon use from them, but evidently preferred the more easily understandable 'mechanical' sport of Greco-Roman wrestling. Basic tactic of the Persians, as of all Central Asians, was the retreat and counterpunch with the "Parthian shot"—firing to the rear during feigned retreat. This concept, fundamental to all Asian martial arts, has been notably neglected in the West, even though the Parthian Persians regularly beat the pants off Rome's legions: sending Marc Antony back to the waiting arms of Cleopatra, defeating Emperor Phillip the Arab, and capturing Emperor Valerian and all his legion—none of which gets much mention in European history books. In the Far East it is referred to frequently as the bamboo or willow principle —give and snap back.

While Persian tactics and martial arts were dynamic, they were purely mechanical, physical, as their contemporary graphic art indicates.

In China, a record published in 681 B.C. describes "a fist art using hands and feet and all gestures of limb and body." This sport was called *pag* (is this a phonetic coincidence or is it the ancient Latin "pug" of pugilism?) It is interesting only in that it is called a formalized "art."

The Chinese Han Dynasty history of the third century states that the Emperor and his court "preferred *byon*, archery and other martial games to music and beautiful women." This *byon* was demonstrated at drinking bouts as an entertainment. Unlike similar "entertainment" at our western shindigs, it included much "formalized grasping with the fingers" and was limited by a fixed set of rigid rules. It evolves into Korean *suse-ryong*, hand-power order and later *hwal-gwon* or open fist, a complicated and formal martial art. It is also referred to in this period as *gwon*, or fist, and *gwon-yong*, or brave fist— names which indicate it was still mechanical, what we would

From an 18th-Century
Wood-block Book

CHINESE KEMPO

today call a *jutsu*, or technique, rather than a *do*, or way of discipline. There are oblique Hindu references to secret arts and of course a treasure trove of Tibetan tales of superman-lamas. There are Formosan and Indonesian fast-footed combat sports with highly developed kicking, as in Thai boxing.

The *Kojiki*, Record of Ancient Matters, was compiled in Japan in the seventh century A.D. It mentions that the mortal gods Kajima and Kadori used a secret "hand art" to chastise the barbarians of what is now Tokyo. But this was most likely an early form of the recently introduced sumo, a ritualized version of Mongolian wrestling. Sumo has ritual similarities to Persian *zur khaneh* in the closing Bow Dance as well as in the posturing. The ritual aspect of sumo was stressed more and more. Complex rules limited it until it has become a highly specialized and exotic spectator sport with seemingly no practical outside use.

In Korea contemporary to the Period of the Gods in Japan, there were the "eighteen arts of defense." Seventeen used weapons. The eighteenth, written in various homonymous/ homophone ideographs, all meaning "hand-strike," "-blow," "-shove" or "-push," had been borrowed from China.

"Even an egg is strong, if it could adapt its inherent strength and sublimate its weakness."

None of my teachers could understand our story of Humpty Dumpty. "Why, when he hit the ground, didn't he roll?" Stepping over to the table where I sat, my old painting and fencing teacher once had pointed to a legless, red-caped Humpty Dumptylike doll whose fierce face peered out under beetle-brows. "... Like Daruma rolls," he said.

He struck the foot-high doll from the table and sent it bouncing and rolling across the lawn. It came to a halt fifteen feet away, wobbling, but upright and unmarred. I had seen papier-mâché dolls like this from an inch to a yard high at village toy stalls, shrines and fairs all over Japan.

"Maybe if the inventor of the Humpty Dumpty tale knew he could have started a toy industry, he'd have put a rock in Humpty's seat and made him roll, too," I said.

Laughing at this, he said he thought westerners too stubborn, preferring the oak, which the typhoon uproots, while the Oriental prefers the bamboo which not only bends with the gale but is adaptable to life. Flexible, it makes a fine bow; straight and sturdy, it makes the best arrows. It is light and easy to wield, yet strong enough to batter down oak doors. It can be sharpened with a pocket knife, or even peeled with the fingernail, into lances or swords as keen as a razor. Yet its hardness and resiliency repels all but the most direct blows of a steel blade.

To all these athletes with whom I studied, that doll was not just an entertaining toy, it was an ancient and timeless educational tool. It symbolizes a way of life—roll with the punch, keep your balance and you will win. And it keeps alive the memory of a great saint, father—or, at least, godfather —of the many fantastic fist arts in the far Orient.

In the sixth century a highly developed martial art appeared which was not just a matter of simple mechanics applied to grappling, as all earlier forms seemingly were. Nor was it an intuitive "mystery." Significantly, this was near modern Canton at Loyang, cultural melting pot of Buddhism and Taoism and a host of other Asian philosophies. Here Indian swamis and

DARUMA   EVER UPRIGHT

Christians and Persian Zoroastrians are known from oral tradition and portraits on temple wall paintings, to have mingled. Invention of this, the *go-shin-jutsu karate* or "self defense art of the empty hand," is attributed to the culture hero of Zen, Bodhi-dharma, "bouncing" Daruma, "he who knows the Law of Life." He was a saint from India, and noted Yogi. He had lived for several years in Persian Khorasan, northeast Iran, which not long after was to become the home of the Zenlike philosophy-cum-cult of Sufism which "adopted" *zur khaneh* as a training. The Zenist warrior read the ancient classics and poetry while training. The *zur khaneh* leader recites rhythmical poems, such as the *Rubaiyat* of Omar Khayyam and Firdosi's moral epic *Book of Kings*, to condition the gymnasts.

According to the legend, still a modern oral tradition in China, Korea and Japan, it was a period of civil war and banditry. The local warlord near Canton prohibited civilians from possessing arms yet failed to give them adequate protection. Around A.D. 528, Daruma emerged from seven years of meditation in a cave and, as I have reconstructed from a multitude of written and oral accounts and traditions, pronounced that "war and killing are wrong, but so also is it wrong not to be prepared to defend oneself. We may not have knives, so make every finger like unto a dagger; our maces are confiscated, so make every fist like unto a mace. Without spears every arm must be like unto a spear and every open hand a sword."

73

This system required first of all that the fighter divorce himself completely from any association with his weapon—in this case his empty hand, but applicable to any actual weapon. He must divorce himself from any emotion toward his opponent—either the person or the weapon. The system was to be used only for self-defense. It was, in essence, an application of the mental concentration of Zen meditation and yoga to a scientific study of fisticuffs.

Daruma as founder of Zen, harkened back to the Indian meditative Dhyana tradition of Buddha. The basic principle of his martial art seems to stem from an incident in the life of the Buddha who lived about 2,500 years ago. (There have been several Buddhas, one has appeared on earth in each of several *kalpa* or great time cycles, and this one was he of the fourth kalpa, the historic Gautama or Sakyamuni, who on his physical death became the Buddha of our earthly epoch). The young prince was chided by his officers for ignoring his archery and military drill and wasting his time over books and "sitting." Then sitting, Buddha's answer was to take his bow to the drill ground and give a perfect archery performance. The moral evidently is that the healthy awake mind has perfect control over the body.

Daruma seems to have had in mind to teach those with near-Buddha-like minds the essential mechanics of self-defense. For those other followers with lesser mental capabilities perhaps the same mechanics would lead them back toward developing the "Buddhalike" mind.

"Spirit and body shall be inseparably united. Now you are all so overcome with the demands of your bodies that you seem unable to comprehend the benevolence of mind-body unity. I am, therefore, going to give you a doctrine. Train your body, and your mind with it. Then you shall attain higher perception."

He would arm the man of peace; pacify the man of arms.

Both approaches are valid. A pure mind controls the body. The story of Bodhidharma's emerging from years of meditation plays much upon his legs having atrophied—thus the origin of the round-bottom bob-back folk doll. The punchline of the story is usually passed over: he concentrated on his legs and fully restored them. Mastery of the body can lead to a pure mind as well.

74

Yoga Influences

The time Daruma left India was one of a great resurgence of yoga. Daruma was undoubtedly a yoga adept. His approach to the martial arts was new in that it was not a system of mechanics, but rather of intellect. "Mind controls hand" is the yoga principle. The three main parts of the body in yoga are hand, mouth and mind. The second principle that evolves out of this is that mouth enables both control and execution—mind controls, mouth enables. This second principle is what Oyama, and all my other teachers, had in mind when they warned, "Fail to master breathing and you will never advance beyond doing a few tricks."

Yoga was contemplative. The Chinese mysteries of Taoism were intuitive. Their "magical formula" is stated (in Japanese) as *shi-ki-chikara*; or, as expressed in the modern terms of a chemical reaction, idea + spirit (or will) = power. Buddhism was idealistic, and contributed the idea of *ahimsa*, nonviolence, turning the other cheek; and *metta* or goodwill, loving one's enemy. But the Confucianists who controlled the environment, who composed the reality Daruma had to cope with, were practical, Yankee-style pragmatists, realists. They were from some oriental Missouri and demanded "show me."

In India, yoga was usually ecstatic. The ecstasy might sometimes be induced by drug or alcohol, or even by hypnotic technique. It raised the votary above the plane of space and time. This ecstasy plus the hot climate results in, as Albert Schweitzer puts it, "World and Life Negation." Daruma's method of coping with reality was obviously no negation of life. Perhaps it was the more lugubrious climate of China, and later Japan, which drove this attitude of fatalism out of Zen. As a humorist of sorts, a published cartoonist, I have found little more humorless than Indian thought; nothing more humorous than Zen.

In the cosmos of yoga, the *atman* or greater self is differentiated into smaller egos which must strive to be one with the atman. The breath control of the yoga adept, adapted into the martial arts as *ki-ai* (spirit breath), enables the body to draw on the sum power of what the Japanese call the "universal breath" (a yogic concept) and join as one with it.

But the Taoist divides his cosmos into at once opposing and interacting yin and yang (called by the Japanese variously *in-yo, in-ga, in-an*). Hsun-tsu, fourth century B.C., admonished his disciples to "domesticate and regulate nature instead of praising her and meditating upon her." So with this Confucian penchant for rational analysis, obviously workable yoga breathing exercises are analyzed in the Taoist yin-yang reference. Breathing is inhale-exhale, respectively, passive-active, –/+.

Sculpture and Movement

We can see and follow these abstract developments of ideas for they are reflected in the arts. Buddhism introduced statuary into China, in the Greek style of static poses. The Indian animated it with his own ideal, carved the rhythm of a dream world. The later statuary of one and two centuries after Daruma, as preserved in Korea and Japan, shows certain new elements.

In the center of the Korean flag is a circle, bisected by an S-shape which divides the sphere itself into something like the numerals 6 and 9, or tadpoles, one black and one white chasing each other's tail. This ageless Taoist mystic symbol of *yin - yang*, or universal dual female - male, night - day, minus-plus, or in-out and about which ancient sages wrote libr-aries of interpret-ation.is also ex-pressed in pairs of *nio* temple guardian images.

These opposing pairs always represent yin and yang; always one is depicted mouth closed and nostrils flaring in the act of inhaling or at the moment when he has just filled his lungs, while his mate is openmouthed in the process of exhaling explosively. The inhaler will be cocking his fist or drawing a weapon, the exhaler in the process of striking or having just struck.

Paired sculptures are common all over Asia from earliest times, but never before this do these mismatched, contrasting mates appear. Where there was before the balance of static symmetry, there is now the balance of dynamic action. The shrine "lion dogs" of Japan—Koma-inu (Korean dogs) and

Kara-shishi (or Tang China lions)—are Near Eastern in origin, the legendary *shirishi* of ancient Sumer and Babylon, embodiment of the power of divine rule. They appear in pairs all over Asia, but always in matched pairs. Even in Achaemenid Persia, 5th–3rd centuries B.C., which lived under a religious philosophy of dualism. So, too, in modern Thailand (Siam) they are exactly matched.

But from the Tang period (A.D. 618–906) on in China, as well as in the 'cultural colonies' of Korea and Japan, they personify yin and yang and stand one with mouth closed (female principle), the other with mouth agape (male). The earliest of these yin-yang sculptures are approximately contemporary with Daruma. They are from the cave temples of Tunghuan in West China on the old Silk Road, from where Daruma reputedly came. Thus art seems to further support the oral legends of Daruma as preserved in the dojo.

SHISHI LION DOGS

All through Tang Period China and the sculpture it inspired, this and other elements of the martial arts make their debuts. Wall paintings of about 5th–8th centuries in cave-temples of Tunghuan show 'boxers,' probably doing an early form of kung-fu. North Korea was the site of the 4th–7th century nomad kingdom of Kokuryo which sent many skilled migrants to early Japan. Their tombs have murals which show pairs of bare-hand fighters.

New fighting forms appear as the era progresses and, by tradition, the international Tang era was marked by great advances in the martial arts. Under the next dynasty, the more China-centered Sung, an era of peace and high art, they reached their zenith.

The Sung 宋 Dynasty

Perhaps an added insight into the romance of history can be gleaned by taking an event and reinterpreting it in the light of the development of the martial arts. The Nestorian Christians or the 'lost' Christians of Prester John were favored by the early Tang dynasty rulers. But later in the dynasty all monasteries except for one or two were abolished by an edict issued in the seventh month of Hui-Ch'ung, A.D. 890: "The right of the pen (administration), and the sword (war) belongs to the state and they are the two weapons wherewith to govern…. Abolish monasteries, return tax-free inmates to productive ranks of taxpayers … melt down images for coin…." The state needed its tax base back, no more tax loopholes.

An oral tradition in karate and jujutsu relates that monasteries were again disarmed. While this probably had little effect on the Ch'an, or Zen, Buddhists, tradition says that many of them assembled at the Shao-lin Monastery, revived the existing fist arts, reinterpreted Daruma's teachings and formulated *kara-te*, the "empty hand" or "Tang Fist." (In 1985 we went to this monastery in China, took a taxi for a day ride into the country and arrived to find a giant parking lot with 73 tourist busses full of Hong Kong kung fu movie fans, and no kung fu monks.) Not long after this the Tang dynasty was overthrown by the Sung, under whom Zenists were favored. In this period Zen and the Zen arts also reached their zenith, and among other things the tea ceremony was formulated.

The bare-hand basic version of Daruma's self-defense arts of the empty hand now took the popular name of the fist art of *sang-e*, named after a Korean champion. It would seem that Oyama was not the first Korean to make a name for himself overseas as a karate man. The North Korean tribes have long had a reputed fondness for fighting. Early records mention a sport called *char-yok* or borrowed power, which involved "mysteries." By the time of the Koryu dynasty (918-1259) *su-bag* was popular. The winners of frequent contests were awarded military honors and commissions.

In January 1410, in the reign of the Korean king Tae Jong of the Yi dynasty, it is recorded that "military officers in charge of recruiting tested new recruits in *su-bag* and appointed any man who won three matches to the crack National Defense

Troop." And again, "... at Jagji between Yosan and Unzin on the fifteenth day of July every year the people living around gathered there and held games of *su-bag*."

- During this period the fist art makes an important division into *nega* and *wega*—internal and external schools, or spiritual and physical. The inner, spiritual style, becomes more of a scholar's exercise and evolves along the lines of meditative Taoism. The outer, more of a purely martial drill for training of knights or troops, eventually degenerates into unintuitive calisthenics. The exercises of the inner style, which maintain a balance in their development, include such arts as *kempo*, still an exercise of many Chinese scholars and known in America as Chinese shadow boxing. Another of these exercises is *tai-chi-chuan* which evolves more as a practical application of Taoist concepts and is closest to, though more eclectic than, Japanese aikido, though somewhat resembling karate.

The *New York Times Magazine,* way back in the summer of 1956, published photographs of old men doing solo exercises in a Peking public park. Captions explained them as part of the "new calisthenic discipline performed daily by millions of brow-beaten Orientals to bring health to the nation." The *Times* readership included an old China-hand and a few weeks later in the letters to the editor, the error was partially corrected: the contortionists in the photographs were doing *tai-chi* drill-*kata*, now a standard early morning tourist sight, regularly reported by print and TV tourist-journalists.

The *nega* at its most extreme degenerated into the mystic hocus-pocus for which Taoism is unfairly too well known in the Occident. It's easy to understand the popular belief in feats of magic if you have had any experience with any Chinese or Japanese *nega* martial art. There is at least one active modern near-*nega* school, that of aiki-do, which we discuss later. Individual masters, such as Mifune of judo, Oyama and Shitoryu's Mabuni of karate, retain a fair balance.

In aikido, after only a short period of *nega* training in energy-generating drills, a pupil can perform tricks so foreign to one's normal everyday orientation that one can almost believe in levitation, teleportation, thought projection, individual invulnerability or any other waking dreams of wish fulfillment. Oyama, holding off several pushers in front of the temple, was only the first of innumerable examples of some "mysterious power" many adepts develop—as I was to see and learn, as almost anyone can.

It is understandable that practitioners with perhaps insufficient ethical discipline let these fabulous *nega* powers go to their heads when displaying them in *wega* ways in the dojo or before Hollywood cameras.

Zen to Japan

At the close of the Sung dynasty period in China early in the thirteenth century, Zen enters Japan in force. Jujutsu is popularly supposed to have been introduced into Japan around A.D. 1400 by the Ming Chinese scholar Chuen Yuan Pin (Chin Gen Pin in Japanese pronunciation). But this probably refers only to an incorporated school, for almost two centuries earlier other aspects of the martial arts were known in Japan. In the near century of relative peace between the wars of the Genji and the Heike in 1192 and the long-lingering threat of the Mongol Invasion in 1274, the military ability of the individual Japanese samurai degenerated alarmingly. And what little concept the Japanese may have had of military tactics completely disappeared.

Some dozen years before the Mongol threat, when Prince Hojo Tokimune was 10 years old, his father held an archery meet. A century earlier the easy requirements of this meet would have bored the rank and file of archers. But now our Japanese records tell us that none of the archers could even reach the target, much less hit it. Tokimune was (in obvious adaptation of the Gautama Buddha tale) called from his Zen meditation. He mounted his horse, galloped out to the firing range. At full gallop and well before reaching the 200-yard firing line, he released an arrow that split the target. This is the first reference to Zen in the martial arts in Japan. This sport of archery on horseback is called *yabusame* and can still be seen in Japan, played in ancient costume. (See illustration on page 183 and Appendix Calendar.)

When Tokimune became de facto ruler, he formalized the study of archery along strict Zen lines. Not so much because the bow, as modern Japanese archers so smugly insist, is the ideal embodiment of Zen, but rather because the low level of Japanese marksmanship was desperately in need of an intelli-

SAMURAI USING JUJUTSU AGAINST PEASANT
After Woodblock-printed Storybook by Hokusai, circa 1800

gent and productive discipline. Zen technique, which can be applied to anything—even motorcycle maintenance—was applied to archery. Modern Japanese archery of both the Heki (rapid fire, military) and Ogasawara (meditative, ceremonial) schools are both descended from Tokimune.

Japanese military tactics of the time are exemplified by incidents in the two Mongol invasions. In 1274 the Japanese built a defensive wall of excellent tactical design, then lined their men along the top like spectators at a baseball game while an individual champion would stride forth toward the Mongol horde, announcing his pedigree and calling for a challenge. Few got as far as grandfather's name before going down under a volley of armor-piercing arrows and the world's first gunpowder artillery. After the lucky escape of 1274 (the Mongols just went home after a teenage sniper put an arrow through their leader's eye), Hojo Tokimune forced on his warriors acceptance of a minimum of tactical deployment. By 1281, when the Mongols invaded Japan on a follow-up, the Japanese tactical units could hold the enemy at bay long enough for miraculous intervention of the "kamikaze" storm.

This "magical" intervention of the kamikaze stopped the further development of military tactics in Japan for centuries. But in military diplomacy Tokimune's Zen monk advisor, Bukko, set precedents long followed in diplomacy, military tactics and inscrutable business deals. The Mongols sent an embassy to Kamakura, the capital. Zen monks advised "*yu-shin*," and Hojo sat in an "attitude of contemptuous silence" for seven months while the ambassador first fumed, then wondered and finally went home. Then the monks advised "*gen-shin*" (anticipate attack)—a revolutionary concept among a people to whom battle was a symbolic show of masses and extemporaneous dueling of extrovert "heroes."

After 1274, when the invaders turned back, many of the samurai took this as a show of weakness and tended to despise the Mongols and their Chinese and Korean satellites. The Zen priest's admonition, "Fear not the strong nor despise the weak," was put to hard test by Tokimune's internal diplomacy. There is little doubt that without Tokimune's Zen advisors the Japanese would not have come off nearly so well (if at all) in the second, larger invasion of 1281.

One of the last flowerings of sculpture in Japan in this, the Kamakura period, are the seminude *nio,* known definitely to have been carved by Japanese artists. These portray a thorough understanding of the basic concepts of the martial arts, particularly the "empty hand."

The Bushi 武士: The Samurai

During the period of the Civil Wars of the fifteenth century there was an obvious need for development of the martial arts. The direct participation of warrior monks in the fighting provided a ready source of theory: "The man who seeks to obtain enlightenment should not resist intellectual difficulties but rather let them destroy themselves by their own weight."

Monk Takuan developed the idea of Fudo, "nonmovement" —the man in motion has inertia to overcome to change direction. One solidly braced must also overcome inertia. But he whose mind and intuition are ever awake but focused nowhere, whose physical attitudes are passively ready has no inertia.

This becomes the basis of jujutsu and newly developing Japanese way of the sword, *kendo,* gives the spectator sport of sumo the unjust reputation for being static: let your antagonist attack. Then, with no static inertia of your own to overcome, evade, letting the attacker destroy himself by his own forward inertia, adding to it what you may with a swift counterattack.

Fudo may also discourage attack by confusing the attacker. Most people openly "telegraph" the direction—or static state—of their inertia, in so doing revealing the other directions from which they are open to attack. Thus the lack of any such obvious opening, called *suki*, confuses. Paralleling the evolution of kendo and jujutsu is the rise of the *bushi* or samurai. But its greatest advances are made in the long era of peace under the Tokugawa Shoguns, 1604–1867.

All of the various empty hand, jujutsu, forms fall generally, with some overlap, into the two groupings of karate and judo, often grafted onto existing local fistics and adapted to the conditions and needs of a particular time and country.

Karate itself is a term used by several "schools" or formal styles of pugilism claiming some half million adherents in Japan. Largest school is the Go-ju—"hard-gentle"—Ryu, led by Gogen Yamaguchi, the "Cat," with a purported 200,000 adherents and which Mass more or less followed until he himself became master of his own independent school. Funakoshi, Mass's first teacher, introduced *te,* or fist, as it was called in Okinawa, to Japan in 1924. Japan's large Korean populace, such as Mass, has flavored it with *su-bag*, a savate extraordinary.

Judo, now an international sport, is a century-old refinement on the 50-odd varieties of military jujutsu prevalent in Japan at the end of the last century, disciplined by the old Chinese concepts of fair play and chivalry that had been somewhat neglected in Japan. *Yawara* is another common name for early jujutsu, while *atemi* is an advanced paralyzing variant of judo.

Karate and judo are both based on "precepts of the bamboo." Aikido evolves even a step further, to evolve a new species of bamboo tumbleweed. They are all for use against a foe physically superior in size, equipment or number. All operate by turning the antagonist's own strength against himself. All are for defense. All involve a strict code of chivalry. There the similarity ends.

Judo works on the bamboo principle that though enough snow to break the oak tree may also fall on the bamboo, the supple stem will give way with the load causing the snow to be flipped off by its own weight.

Karate follows the bamboo principle that though a heavy object may be propelled against the bamboo with enough force to smash a stone wall, the supple stem will give way with the attack, then spring back to break the attacker with the cumulative force of attacker's forward inertia and bamboo's inherent strength. This strength of bamboo is duplicated in man—its strong tubular shape is bone, its resilience, muscle.

Aikido "follows" nothing. It has reduced the bamboo principles to their quintessential. Like the tumbleweed, it blows away in the breeze of the shock wave preceding any object rushing toward it, spinning like a billiard ball so as not to inhibit the forward inertia of the attacker but to let him fly on out of control to his self-destruction. It is in a class by itself. But once any degree of mastery in it is attained, proficiency in any other sport or art will improve.

Application has also made them different. Jujutsu, the forerunner of judo, came to Japan from China in the thirteenth century, at about the same time as Zen, the meditative sect of Buddhism, also founded by Daruma. Several "tricks" or throws of Chinese kempo, "fist order," were introduced and probably combined with variations on wrestling forms the Japanese have loved since mythological times. According to Japanese sacred scriptures, 2,000 years ago the two god-heroes Kajima and Kadori used a secret wrestling art to subdue the barbarians near modern Tokyo. Zen contributed to the development of Japanese chivalry and knighthood, the development of valiant warriors who were the first in the world to defeat the numerically superior Mongols of Kublai Khan. The same warriors adopted the new fighting form but as an adjunct to their weapons. They used it to capture an enemy alive or to subdue a social inferior who they did not consider worthy of being killed by the sacred sword.

Karate was developed by unarmed people to defend their homes against oppressive attacks by foreign conquerors or local tyrants. *Te* is the Okinawan form using mostly blows, chops and rips with hand and fingers. It somehow got there from China. As Sakini says in *Teahouse of the August Moon*, "We have honor to be subjugated by Chinese, English, Japanese and U.S. Marines. Okinawa very fortunate. Culture brought to us, not have to leave home for it. Learn much."

ARMORED SAMURAI USING JUJUTSU AGAINST COMMONER
From a Woodblock Illustrated Storybook, circa 1800

The Chinese pirate-conquerors allowed no civilian arms. Their successors, ruthless Okinawan warlords, continued the policy. In the sixteenth century, Japanese buccaneer barons from Satsuma, South Japan, took the island, squeezed it dry. The Japanese forbade the natives to carry even scythes unless harvesting—yet bodies of fully armored knights were found with broken necks, mangled limbs that seemed to have been decapitated from the inside with no break in the skin. Others were found with heads stove in as if with a club, yet there would be no bruise over the fracture. Limbs were mangled, bones broken or, occasionally, arms ripped out at the sockets or wind pipes torn out—all with no evidence of a weapon being used. Samurai were being ambushed in broad daylight, for what armed and armored knight would be wary when approached by a half-naked, unarmed and submissively bowing native?

By the time the Japanese jujutsu-ists noticed that the "clumsy" peasants did not simply walk, but rather stalked like cats, they had had enough of the silent revolt and sailed home.

Karate vs. Judo: Differences

Satsuma is world-famed for fine chinaware, called *Satsuma-yaki*, and on Okinawa, where the bull is almost sacred, the locals have their own real-life version of the tale of the "Bull in the China shop." Another point for karate over judo-jujutsu.

Japanese, normally receptive to foreign ideas and gimmicks, didn't take up karate because they figured they didn't need it. For exercise the samurai had jujutsu and fencing; and for chopping off arms and heads they had their fabulous swords. On the fifth day of May—the fifth month—of his fifth year, a samurai child received his short sword. They never parted till he went to the crematorium to join his ancestors. Swords and jujutsu ability were feudal age status symbols. After about 1580, the sword could be worn only by a member of the samurai or *bushi*-warrior class and skill in its use and in jujutsu were carefully guarded in secret schools, admission to which was restricted to the warrior caste.

When the feudal system was breaking down under pressure of the merchant class, just before America's Commodore Perry delivered his coup de grace, the popular woodblock-printed paperback books of the day ran picture spreads showing some basic techniques of these hitherto secret arts. These were illustrated by artists who have since earned world fame, and samples are reproduced in this volume. When feudalism was abolished in the 1870s, jujutsu masters, out of financial need, opened their dojo to all comers and developed their secret weapon into a modern-age sport. One of the greatest of these innovators was Kano Jigoro, who called his system *ju-do*, "gentle way." The old jujutsu arts found new life.

As other oriental, especially neighboring Far Eastern, nations writhed in the agony of internal conflict between the old traditions and new ways of the West, some of their "secret hand art" masters made their way to the more hospitable climate of Japan and a receptive public. Funakoshi, father of modern karate, was one of these.

But Kano was perhaps first to see a system at work. "Each man presented his art as a collection of techniques. None perceived a principle ... led me to look for a guiding principle that applied when one hit as when one threw."

Then Why Not "Bushido 武士道？"

Bushido is a word known to many outside of Japan. It means literally "Warrior Way," purported to be an ethic, a way of life. It does not mean "martial art" in the sense of being a technique for teaching. "Zen combat" refers to these techniques, these *jutsu*. The Way, or *do*, one must make for oneself.

Bushido is best remembered as having been the excuse the Japanese military presented for their actions in World War II. It was a fine old tradition, they claimed. Maybe so—the samurai as frequently shown in modern Japanese literature and film was in fact pretty much of a brute. But it wasn't a Way of Life of a people. The word itself was invented only in the 1880s by Nitobe, Christian educator immortalized on the present ¥5,000 banknote and author of the book, *Bushido*. He was suffering exile to the boondocks of northernmost Hokkaido as punishment for his Christian pacifism. He wrote the book to get back on the good side of the rising military caste, according to my teacher, his friend Dr. Paul Yoshiro Saeki.

Saeki was the first Japanese recipient of the Order of the British Empire. In the 1950–60s he was Honorary President of the Hiroshima area Bu-do-kai, Martial Arts Association. He pointed out that Bushido was not the way *of* the warrior, but a way *for* the warrior—and a bit of wishful thinking at that; being written about men long dead who never heard the word—but perhaps being written for men then in and coming to power who obviously never took it seriously. Saeki was nominated for the highest O.B.E. which would earn him a "Sir." In World War I Japan was an ally and occupied German ports and islands in the Far East. Then the army and its subsidiary trading companies announced plans to take over the fabulously lucrative textile markets of East Asia long monopolized by England, using the enlarged mill output intended by treaty for sending to Europe as Japan's military contribution. Saeki, through his exalted Imperial Court rank, insisted that if Japan were to take her place as a modern nation she must keep her word like a gentleman, or if she preferred "bushido" she must keep her word like a *bushi*—either way, the cloth had to go to the Western Front by winter. It did. Tommies and Poilus were spared freezing to death in the trenches.

Britain was grateful, but with the O.B.E. Japan was expected to add a similar award. The military were angry at the loss of money, and at his rebuff of bushido's alleged antiquity. England, to avoid diplomatic hassle with her good ally, downgraded his O.B.E. to a lower rank—a medal, but no "Sir."

There was a chivalrous discipline of sorts for the samurai. It was called "The Way of the Bow and Arrow." The Bushido madness of 1880–1945 was centered on the sword. The bow, as we shall see, is a true Zen calisthenic, one which involves all of the extension and breathing and meditation desired. And the bow is, because of its cumbersomeness, difficulty of concealment, and inferiority to other less specialized weapons, not likely to become a weapon which leads its wielder. A good blade, on the contrary, like a good gun, invites trying out, and often leads to trouble in the hands of one not properly prepared for the responsibility. The bow encourages detachment from the tool; the blade discourages it.

The word "*bushi*" means, or has come to mean, "warrior." Actually the ideograph for it (shown above) is composed of two elemental radicals, stylized stick figures, meaning "stop-sword" plus "sir," or "noble defender." But the Roman Empire also started its expansion by defensive actions against aggressive neighbors. And of course, the recent Cold War saw two superpowers aggressively expanding against each other "out of self-defense." As a title, or honorific, "*shi*" as in *bushi*, means both scholar and warrior. This concept continually "reinvents itself" thus proving its validity. Musashi stressed traditional Chinese "balanced learning … way of warrior means familiarity with both cultural and martial arts…. A true way of martial arts is to practice them in such a way that they will be useful at any time, to teach them in a way that will be useful in all things." It is, obviously, the epitomic warrior of the *Teachings of Don Juan*.

Japanese for Zen combat is *bu-do*, "stop-sword way" which translates literally as "martial arts." This does not imply the Zen technique underlying their development, that which sets them apart from occidental sports, the "guiding principle" of Kano. That principle which encourages that detachment our own sages from Athens to Philadelphia admonished:

Tao Te Ching: "The true adept seems as if inept."

Zur Khane

IV. DANCING DERVISHES
OF STRENGTH

A WITHERING CROSSFIRE from the fanatical and disciplined defenders kept the square in front of the mad dictator's palace gate clear of the revolutionary mob spewing forth from the mystic maze of Tehran's old bazaar. Frustrated, they cowered in doorways or beyond the first bends of the numerous alleys. From here all they could see of the field of battle were the bodies of comrades who had died in futile, unarmed charges against the impregnable position. Observers say the fate of the rebellion itself hung in the balance.

Then out of one of the crowded alleys roared a giant driving an unarmed jeep. He grinned and gunned the borrowed car across the empty square, between bodies, through the torrential crossfire, directly at the barricaded main gate—and headlong through it. The defense fell apart in shock. Firing stopped. The mob charged. Minutes later it was all over. Once again the fate of the Persian Empire, now called Iran, had been decided at a fateful instant by a whirling dancing dervish from the ancient "house of srength."

The first thing I did upon my arrival in Tehran during my worldwide search for man's ancient sports was to look up a *zur khane,* a house of strength.

Friends offered to take me to theirs. Not the biggest or the best known, it was however considered the most traditional and for this distinction they were willing to go a bit out of the way. So was I.

We drove out the broad new boulevards of Tehran, with worse-than-New York-London-or -Tokyo traffic, to the narrow streets and narrower dirt *kucheh*s of old Tehran, stopping at a common, two-storey building of sun-dried brick. We ducked under a low doorway—reaction to the Arab conquest of 1400 years ago by making Muslims bow before entering Persian holy space—into a large, high-ceilinged and skylighted room. We were expected. Gongs and drums rataplanned an oriental welcome and all present stood up and saluted us in throaty Arabic and somnambulant Persian blessings. They showed us to a couch of rich tribal carpets and we kicked off our shoes, squatted down and sipped aromatic tea through chunks of beet sugar held in our teeth.

In the center was a pit fifteen feet across and three feet deep to native earth, eight-sided—the ancient Iranian mystic octagon—lined in brilliant turquoise tile. Beyond lay an ordinary western gymnasium, matted for weight lifting. On the walls were larger-than-life portraits of the then Shah, his father and the ancient martyr Ali, son-in-law of the Prophet Mohammad and patron saint of Iran, champion of the zur khane.

An explosive cacophony of drums, cymbals and gongs—all played by one man seated on a pulpit beside the door—and wild shouts. Into the room streamed a line of youthful looking men, some I later noted had gray hair. They were dressed in what looked like blue-speckled, red toreador britches that I later saw were large sarongs worn in a diaper drape. They reminded me of the nio guardian statues in the Japan temple gate. They leaped gracefully into the pit, landing three-point, touching sacred earth with their right hands and then foreheads. One man, standing out from the rest only in his air of confidence, stepped to the center. The drummer-chanter struck his instruments and intoned the blessings of Mohammad, Ali, and his martyred warrior sons Hassan and Hussain. The men in the pit bellowed the refrain and their dance began.

And dance it was. The center man began a series of muscle-toning exercises to the music. The tempo slid from one paradiddle to another and the athletes moved with it through a series of squirming push-ups, legs positioned in a full split, shoulders and hips rippling in a sensuous one-two roll, now straight down, now to one side and down on first one arm, then the other. "To develop their virility," my host confided.

IN THE SACRED OCTAGONAL PIT

Between each strenuous exercise set they did a light, skipping dance or muscle-relaxing neck roll. The music whipped up faster and the men in the pit took turns at the spinning dances of whirling dervishes, whirling so fast they appeared, like the tiger in the children's tale, to be turning into butter. These were to "teach balance and relaxation." Unless the whirler is completely relaxed and centered he will topple and crash.

All the time the one-man oriental orchestra continued his symphony of strength. His voice was operatic; clear, strong and masculine. His song was epic poetry chanted to music. He was reciting some of the 60,000 rhymed couplets (all of which he had memorized) of Iran's great epic history, the *Shahnameh* (Book of Kings) of Firdosi, written about the year 1000. Firdosi ranks with Homer, Dante and Shakespeare as one of the great literary masters of the world. He sings of the battles and loves of the Persian and Aryan heroes from the days of legend, through the exploits of the historical Xerxes and Darius and the blessed foreigner Iskander, or Alexander the Great. Here in meter that makes one's pulse throb is the tragedy of Sohrab and Rustam, heroes of Turan and Iran, victor-father and victim-son. And it sings of the high morals and ethics that made men great by their adherence to them. Here is the fountainhead of European chivalry.

I had read in Herodotus, the ancient Greek "father of history," of the importance the ancient Persians or Iranians had attached to sports. He tells how children were taught riding and shooting at the age of five. Other sports then in vogue, traces of which I had seen even today in my travel in Iranian villages, were polo, wrestling, sword play (as 'stick dancing')—and inseparable from sports in all of Asia, dance. In Herodotus's day, as again when I knew Iran, Iranian women participated in these sports as equals. Competitions were held at village festivals, as still today in parts of Asia, notably Japan.

My host told me something of the history of the zur khane: "Firdosi sings of it, of how our heroes came to gyms such as these from most ancient times. The zur khane trained warriors in the days of Cyrus, two and a half millennia ago. Alexander introduced Greek calisthenics and we put them to music. The common man always took part. Centuries later Iran was humbled by the barbarian Arab and for four centuries we sat in the shadow of the humility of slavery, though our culture steadily conquered the conqueror. Then Firdosi gave us new life with the music of his words reminding us of our ancient glories and we orchestrated them. The Mongol terror swept down on us, leveled our cities—a million died in one town, as many as three million in another. We became a desert.

"Muezzins wailed from the tops of the minarets, 'Oh God, what have we mere mortals done to you to bring such hell down upon our heads.'

"But the music of Firdosi kept us alive. We decided to relive our greatness. Our men gathered in secret cells. We concealed our true intentions by posing as mystic prayer groups, to whom dance is a form of prayer, with health through exercise an act of obedience as caring for the body God has loaned us. Someone thought of using Firdosi's orchestrated poems as musical accompaniment to our calisthenic dance. We called ourselves *zur khane,* houses of strength. But in Old Persian, *zur* means also 'deception.' We were houses of deception-cum-strength—of srength through deception."

From my knowledge of Chinese and Japanese history I recalled that the Chinese had reacted to the Mongol conquest in the same way, with Taoist and Zenist mystic secret societies which developed into numerous 'schools' of martial arts—jujutsu, karate, yawara, aiki, kempo, pag, tai chi-chuan, and the Boxers—of which the modern sport of Judo is secularized and demilitarized sport adaptation. As I watched the martial dancers, a picture of a Japanese temple came to my mind. In the gatehouses of most Buddhist temples, as we saw, in alcoves flanking the main portal, are two statues of guardian gods. The Japanese call them *nio* or deva-kings; *deva* is an ancient Persian word for god, deus. They are dressed in the sarong of the zur khane, of western features and wear the topknot as worn in ancient times by Iranian and Turanian warriors.

Then the dance of strength drew to its finish. The leader raised a great iron bow with string of chain above his head and broke into a fierce yet graceful dance. Much as the Sumo wrestler does in Japan at the end of the day's bouts. Many of the dance calisthenics had seemed familiar. Then I recalled that they were almost similar to, but slightly less refined, than those I had myself learned in the practice hall of aikido, in Tokyo. It seemed obvious that the zur khane of Iran and the Taoist shadow boxing halls of China—through perhaps Zen expatriate Chinese teachers in Japan—had formed one great undercover network which had helped to overthrow the Mongols. Perhaps it had maintained its interconnections even afterwards, into more recent times?

It is the zur khane which had given modern Iran so many world champions in wrestling and weight lifting, though many of the adepts I saw were not built for either. Basic Zur Khane drills are all muscle-toning exercises, put to music. "Music is the rhythm of the Universe," said my host, "the athlete must be in tune. Health is but being in tune with your life. Poetry and music are life and health to us." Shades of Mass Oyama.

What kind of people, I asked, come to the zur khane to practice? He pointed out the athletes, one by one ... a Harvard graduate in classical Greek who had come in his Alpha Romeo, a bread salesman who had come on his jackass, a colonel of constabulary, businessmen, unemployed, students, scholars, illiterates. "We have had kings and dictators, tyrants and benefactors, but all Iranians are, deep in their hearts, democrats and the basis of strength is democracy, of democracy strength —personal strength."

I could well believe him, for the stirring couplets, the soul-piercing rhymes of Firdosi had been instilling the ethic of democracy into succeeding generations of Iranians for almost a thousand years. Notably, in the popular revolt against the madman Mossadeq several years before, it was a Zur Khane champion, "The Brainless One," who led the unarmed civilian attack on Mossadeq's stronghold mansion to overthrow the unstable tyrant.

The next morning, as I sit down to get my observations down on paper before the dawn—I've taken to the local schedule of early rising and afternoon siesta—I hear a familiar song outside my window. On previous mornings I thought it was the muezzin's call to prayer from the amplifier atop the nearby minaret. Now I realize it is most of the radios of the neighborhood turned up full volume to allow the exotic sensuous rhythms of the Zur Khane broadcast to rise over the city and greet the morning sun. I see the shadow of my host on the balcony; the silhouette of a neighbor on his roof. The bread delivery boy and the household servants are in the courtyard. The bread boy's ass brays a downbeat and shadow, silhouette and courtyard forms begin the movements of the dance of strength.

Excuse me. I think I'll step out onto the balcony and stretch.

Illustration in the chapter heading of a man in zur khane towel and striking a fighting pose, is an eighth-century temple guardian from Nara, Japan, a Persian deva king. Calligraphy is Persian, "zur khane."

寒稽古
kan-geiko winter practice

V. BUDDHA IN A COLD SHOWER

ON THE TWENTY-FIRST OF JANUARY the time period known as *Daikan*, or Great Cold, sets in and Japanese bundle up for what is traditionally the coldest fortnight of the year. That is, some Japanese bundle up—others strip down to perform some of the strangest rites of purification, the *kan-mairi* and *kan-geiko*, winter pilgrimage and winter practice. Cold is "purifying"—and invigoration is certainly a pure feeling. Or perhaps, as has been suggested, it's just that the only way to get warmer in an unheated environment is first to get colder than the environment.

Kan-geiko is for judoists, karate-ka, archers, kendo-fencers and track-and-fielders who work out every day at dawn in the open or in gyms with windows wide open, taking ice-cold showers afterward. I first did it one winter at the aikido dojo in Tokyo and came down with an almost fatal case of good health, have continued it since with archery, and modern plumbing notwithstanding, still in my late sixties take cold showers year-round. This, however, was not my first experience with playing Buddha in a cold shower, as we were to see.

A second extreme clime practice period is held during the heat of summer to sweat out the heat. Neither hot nor cold practice is limited to he-men or crazy writers. Musicians, especially young geisha, rise early and practice on their instruments on the open veranda until their hands are numb and blue with cold, or preferably until they learn how to control the "inner heat" and prevent the hands going blue-numb. In summer they will practice in the heat of midday.

Kan-mairi pilgrimage may be either Buddhist or Shinto or independent cult, but it will usually be led, if a group affair, by a *yamabushi*, an ancient order of lay monks almost always found associated with the more exotic or tantric rites of modern Japan. Wearing an animal hide seat apron, they obviously are a holdover from pre-Buddhist practices. I have heard them nightly during cold season, just after supper, honking on their giant conch shell trumpets, calling the faithful out in a procession of white-clad ghosts from the primeval past, chanting their soulful *"Zange-zange"*—"repent, repent." They wend their way through the streets of suburban Tokyo or Kyoto or alleys of the little fishing village on the Inland Sea in which I lived. They make their way to a mountain stream, with a waterfall if possible, or any body of clean, flowing water. There they chant sutras and immerse themselves.

Are they fanatics to submit to such torture?

Sinologue-author David Kidd and I hunted out a group during our first winter in Kyoto and I jotted down and preserved my first impressions.

Dave and I hiked up behind the magnificent Miyako Hotel, then grandest tourist hotel in Japan—in which we were not staying. We cut through Nanzenji Zen temple and its gigantic ancient Chinese-style gate that stands alone in the middle of a field, now being neither exit nor entrance to or from anything, a true 'Gateless Gate.' We continued on under the Roman-style aqueduct, built in the days of the last century when Roman and Greek set the style. Uphill we climbed in the dark, in silence, past the Buddhist nunnery and the temple and the little mountain shrines. We did not use our flashlights and we spoke little, and then only in whispers. There was no moon, no sound but the rustling of the pines. Dave tripped and caught himself on a rock alongside the path. He cautiously played his light on a leering figure of the deity Fudo, the Immovable One, painted on the flat, football-size stone, avenging sword upright in his right hand, bolo dangling from his left, the ever-present halo of flames around him. It was newly painted, primitively done, but with power. Then we heard them: Fudo's followers.

If you ever wondered why the hero of a Hollywood spook film doesn't turn back when he hears the music of the voo-doo cannibals, but continues on, knees shaking—let me tell you: he's enchanted. As were we when we heard mysterious, deep, rhythmical moaning. We continued on toward the sound till we saw a tiny light flickering through the trees. We climbed on till we came to a ravine, down which icy mountain waters surged toward the Romanesque aqueduct. Across the ravine, in a low shed offered before several rock wall—snake Fudo is probably of the most primitive man, the Earth deity and its snake. Many such absorbed into the Buddhism, just as pagan practices and adapted to

MAITREYA
Coming Buddha
Meditation Position

ing candles burning tiny niches in the holes. The cult of a survival of one ancient cults of worship of the messenger, the cults have been noble faith of many ancient were adopted by Christianity.

To the left stood enclosure into of icy water fell above, to flow on fence and drop in into the ravine enclosure from a wooden-fenced which a column from the cliff out under the another cascade below. It was this which came the odd sounds we soon recognized as Buddhist sutras, scriptures, being chanted by someone near hysteria.

We crossed the ravine by a small bridge and headed for the protection of some bushes. The door in the fence ahead opened and just then, from behind us, a deep voice froze us in our tracks—even though it bade us welcome.

An elderly woman stepped calmly from the enclosure, clothed only in an inadequately small face towel held up to her ample breasts. She looked our way as the man behind us ushered us out of the darkness toward the shed. We were politely invited to warm ourselves over their tin-can charcoal brazier while she stepped into the darkness to don her peasant kimono. The warmth of the coals and the hospitality soon routed all our goose pimples. The pair were the last of a

97

larger group, we learned, who had come earlier and who came every night—heat or snow the lady walked three miles each way to "commune with the one god through the intermediary of Fudo."

As we started to leave, the old man asked, "Wouldn't you like to strip down and go under the purifying water?"

"No, thank you," we politely declined, "we bathed earlier this evening."

In the succeeding four decades I was to see countless other rites of midwinter immersion. Thousands of young men and women dressed only in skimpy loin cloths march through snow and into freezing rivers up to their necks, then dance around madly until great clouds of steam rise from their bodies and all become so "hip" that some of them climb up onto a third-storey balcony and leap down onto the steaming, milling mob, unharmed. I have seen the elderly farmers of our village march straight into the Inland Sea. I have followed our college karate club as it paraded en mass into the icy mountain river. I have, myself, participated in *kan-geiko* at the aiki dojo in Tokyo; there ice cold showers substituted for the nonexistent mountain waterfall. And I have visited Mass Oyama during one of his periodic mountaintop seclusions in the winter, when mountain waterfall replaces nonexistent plumbing. There's no doubt about it, it's purifying; it's as invigorating as hell.

This is explained and taught in Japan mostly in a religious framework. But this need not be so and the religious aspect need not concern us here; the technique alone is sufficient—with or without the cold water. The cold water is included only as a test of one's composure. Thus it is a handy reference for anyone without a teacher who is attempting to master the techniques of quietude.

Meditation Positions

The first two problems are body position and breathing. The latter has been discussed earlier. It is basic to all movement and action; it is basic to all nonmovement and inaction. Body position is not the bugaboo most people think it is. The famous lotus and half lotus positions are difficult, and at first painful to assume. But it is not necessary to twist yourself up into a pretzel. Any comfortable position which allows your

GREAT BUDDHA OF KAMAKURA
"Mudra" hand positions indicate "Total stillness"

body to fall into complete rest will do. Reclining positions are discouraged as they make it too easy for the meditator to fall asleep. They are all right, however, for the bedridden, or as an aid to falling asleep. Images of Buddha are sometimes shown reclining full length on his right side, right hand up on its elbow supporting the head under the right ear—but this position indicates that the image portrays Sakyamuni-Buddha awaiting his earthly departure, his 'death' from this world. The position favored by the medieval European knight, face down over clasped hands, body extended, is not much used in the Orient as it encourages nodding off. Squatting, sitting and standing positions are preferred.

Simplest is to sit erect on a backless stool exactly knee height. Feet should be flat on the floor, back straight. Hands may be folded, backs down, open on the lap, fingers intertwined or one hand flat atop the other. In India the hand position preferred is each hand on the corresponding knee, knuckles down, thumb and forefinger tips touching to form circles, other fingers hanging loosely arched. Japanese and Chinese prefer the closed circuit of hands on lap, palms up, one upon the other. You may tuck one leg up, crossing it in The Thinker's position popular for representations of The Coming Buddha, or Maitreya, Buddhism's Messiah as illustrated (page 97). Or instead of crossing the raised leg, you might tuck it under the other and sit on it, dropping your hands into your lap. Do anything that's comfortable.

Now that you have one leg tucked up in that odd position so many children like to assume at the dinner table, you are on the way to the lotus positions. If you simply sit cross-legged it is hard to get into a fully relaxing position because the stomach hunches up. To avoid this, you should have a few inches of cushion under your behind, to prop it up higher than your legs. In Japanese Zen temples common *zabuton* cushions are bent over double and used for such props—not to soften the seat but to rectify the stomach angle.

In many ancient gardens there are zazen stones, seats carved out of a large decorative rock in the garden where one may squat and meditate upon the view. These flat spots are usually at an angle of 15 to 30 degrees; sometimes they are a step affair, the rear a few inches above the front step. Thus even if you are going to try a simple cross-legged position, use a hard cushion or a brick or a thick book to perch on. Straighten out the stomach by bringing—even forcing—your knees down as close as possible to the ground.

For half lotus, bring the left leg (right if easier, but most do left) up and set it, sole facing up, on top of the right thigh, tucked against the groin. To make this easier, make sure back is straight, don't allow small of back to hump, force it forward, spread thighs as if to air the crotch, bring the left knee down and to the rear. You can try this at first with your back flat against the wall. Now bring the right leg up and cross it normally, which may be simply resting under the left knee. This is the half lotus. For full lotus, when the second leg is brought up bring it over the opposite thigh, and as with the first, tuck the foot sole up against the groin. You are now sitting with your feet in your lap, as it were, soles facing up. Force your knees down. The first few times don't try to hold the position long. After a while you can take it until your feet fall asleep and then blood will eventually resume circulation. Everyone finds it somewhat painful; even old monks wobble when they again stand up, rubbing their ankles.

In Japanese monasteries lay "sitting sessions" run 45 minutes, a break, then another 20 minutes. For those who visit Japan and want to do temple zazen, my guidebook *Japan Inside Out* lists dozens of hospitable temples of various sects with details where, how, when and how much it will cost to visit for meditation, and in many cases to eat and sleep over.

This pretzel contortion is to pull the stomach and innards into healthy position to restore proper circulation and permit deep breathing. Ancient Persian statues demonstrate a simpler procedure using a chair—sit on the edge of the chair with thighs down at about 45 degrees and spread at least 90 degrees to each other. Set feet back under your seat. Now you can place soles of your feet together, or cross the feet at the ankles and soles point outward—the steeper more near vertical the angle of body to thighs and larger the angle between thighs, the better. Fold your hands on lap, palms up. Now whichever sitting position you take, follow deep breathing exercises as set forth earlier (pages 22–24). Bring shoulders back and down, chin in, relax, deep sigh.

STANDING MEDITATION

Mass Oyama preferred a standing position. When he did squat, it was usually simple cross-legged Turk style, not lotus, which heavy muscular development interferes with. Standing position may be a simple Fudo—the all-immovable—ready stance or anything comfortable facing straight forward. Best is simply a steady stance similar to that taken by a trumpet player or other wind musician about to solo. What do you do with your hands? For standing meditative position, bring them up, palms facing forward. A bit of tension someplace always helps, as with the odd leg positions in the squats. For this tension, force the hands back against the wrist, counter this with projecting force down the wrists against the hands. The wrist should soon feel strained, then warm, then pass over the hump and not be felt. It helps—don't ask why. This 'projection' is dealt with more in aikido.

Four Steps to Stillness

Note the chapter head illustration. It is a simple field squat which Mass liked to take when backing against a swift, strong waterfall. Any position that is comfortable and that pulls your stomach in is fine. You're in position. Now what?

Sit still or stand still. That's all. Easy posture puts mind at ease—mind at ease puts body at ease. So don't think about anything complicated or emotional. Don't think at all. Physical stillness is the first gateway to mental stillness. According to ancient sage Yen Hui, there are four steps to mental stillness —these correspond to the steps of hypnosis. The one exception is that Japanese doing *zazen* (sitting meditation) or Tibetans doing *tsowang* all agree: any position will do except reclining on the back for this position encourages sleep. Sleep + mental stillness too often result in catalepsy or trance, and these are something quite different from mental quiet. Quite apart.

The four steps to Yen Hui's four stages are:
   (1) let limbs and frame go slack;
   (2) close all avenues of sense perception: shut up,
       don't listen, don't look, don't bother, don't – ;
   (3) shake off material forms;
   (4) dismiss knowledge.

Best time to try this is at twilight, just before dark. Try taking your body temperature at various times of day and night—those times when temperature dips are best for meditation: usually twilight or predawn.

Try it on the edge of your seat on the crowded subway going home after work—better than that second martini. (A single cocktail can help, but two bring lassitude. A muddled brain isn't quiet, it's just muffled.) Or try it standing on the crowded subway if you can't get a seat. You'll find an easy test of your quietude—if you do it right you won't need to hang on to the strap or hand pole, but can stand unconcerned no matter how the train lurches or who lurches against you.

To dismiss your concentration, concentrate on a single internal focus. Try not to close the eyes, this induces sleep—so if you want to throw away the sleeping pills, then follow the same instructions but with eyes closed. Cross your eyes—this relaxes tension in their muscles, also divorces you from visual distraction, reality. If this won't work at first, then do as the hypnotist does and use an external focus—a light, the tiepin of the guy across the train, the subway tunnel lights rushing by blurrily outside. Your brain will rise in mutiny—stick to it. Mental effort comes first, then mental quiet; like getting the guy down on the mats, huff and puff to get him in fully subdued position and once attained, he ceases to struggle.

Talk yourself into it; use suggestive words carefully; words must accurately describe the stage you mean to suggest. Do not be sloppy about choice of words — sloppy word choice results in sloppy thoughts and a messy mind. Eventually you can skip words; nascent suggestion will transmit itself, be received and suggest the proper, desired result. Then no word or thought for no-word, no-thought. This is stage One.

Stage Two is another revolt of sorts in which you will engage in critical self-analysis. If you suddenly become conscious of breathing now, you may start to pant as if you have run up stairs. The chain is broken. Don't try to start again, just relax. This will happen often, each time later, until you can pass into . . .

Stage Three, cessation of thinking. In combat or at work, this state of detachment sharpens one's consciousness: one acts spontaneously. Mastery of combat drills and meditative quiet combined can lead to one's existing most of the time in this state. You now do not *re*act to danger, for there is no "re-" —you are part of any and all "act." When attaining this state in meditation sitting you do not go into trance or stage of euphoria. You remain fully conscious of yourself, but not of self. It is a selfless state. Your senses are as sharp as never before, clear, clean, unencumbered. (You feel as if there is no dust.) Breathing is almost that of sleep, even when moving.

Warning: "Degeneration to psychism is mystical practice conjoined with moral weakness." The hip wise guy is no bodhisattva. Remember, the same paradise garden the sages used for mystic experiences of love, The Old Man of the Mountain used to prepare his hipster Hashishin, assassins, for murder and hate. Some of the 'hippest' prewar Zen-nuts were Nazi: like archer Herrigel. The nutty Ford-spring-sword (see p. 127) samurai of the Greater East Asia Liberation Army of Japan meditated before they committed their atrocities. The key lies in the eyes. Shining eyes—not bulging or frenzied—of the successful loser-of-self are the same shining eyes of the young lover. Corny as it sounds, the feeling is much the same as that pleasant floating nothingness of first infatuation. The technique suggested above is also, notably, of value in bed.

Once you have gotten the hang of this meditative sitting, what Japanese call *zazen*, apply the technique to body action. True meditative technique is both passive and active. Zazen is the passive way, but merely to stop one's force is not to be still, thus not to be truly passive. One must learn to "float like a butterfly," to allow one's force to flow naturally, to synchronize with the general flow of all. The Hindu phrasing, which aiki masters prefer, is "to allow one's atman to become one with the great atman." To "blend with the universal" as the occidental sages said. Seen in this light, the mystic's phrasing is not so much romantic gobbledygook, but his way of expressing a fact for which we have no everyday words.

This detachment and resignation—the Moslem calls it '*Islam*' —is the true passivity. This does not mean that you must accept everything and not try to better yourself; it means move with the current and thus move faster with less, even no effort to "float"; it is not enough to sit on a lotus leaf. You must apply the technique to movement to control action. Control of life's action, of life force (*aiki*) is a dance. All true efficient action is—to bring us full circle—dance. The ceremonial archery performance, the sword drill, the *bo* stave drill, the karate *pinans* and *taikyokus*—all are dance, a ritual of action reduced to its quintessential movement.

By so reducing action to a dance, the body may perform naturally, freeing the inner, higher mind for meditation. Thus while the body is active, the mind may be totally freed and so purely passive. The balance of passive and active—the full union of yin and yang—brings completion. It frees the highest level of mind, the intellect, for the creative act.

舞
dance

VI. CHOREOPTIC QUINTESSENTIAL OF KARATE

*T*HROUGHOUT THE EAST, dance and sport are as inseparable as yin and yang. Spinoza, that fabulous early bridge between East and West (a suspension bridge whose soaring single span is unmatched) defined yang and yin perfectly, calling them *natura naturans,* the active and vital process, and *natura naturata*, the passive product. The English translation is substance and mode, defined further as essence and incident. Dance is the essence and sport is the incident.

It is essential that one master the dance. Once this is accomplished, mastery of the sport or combat form is incidental.

It is no accident that the primitive warrior prepares himself for battle with a dance. It is no coincidence that the dervish in the zur khane dances in training for combat. It is no coincidence that the Japanese Sumo wrestler begins his sparring with a slow dance after a musical introduction, or that the Mongol wrestler begins in the same way. The Sumo wrestler, in fact, is called Sumo-*tori* in Japanese, literally "wrestle-dancer." (Karateists, judoists are called -*ka*, members.) Siamese boxers come out of their corners to the music of a small band playing the rhythm and mood music of combat as their fists jab out, their flying feet flash out, their heads bob and batter and their bodies weave and writhe to the drum rolls and flute rides and cymbal clashes of the accelerating band accompanists.

It is that boxer or Siamese sword dancer who manages to establish the closest rapport with the orchestra who is sure to win. Indonesian temple duelists fight to music, whether boxers, fencers or whip-men. The Chinese tai chi chuan adept shadow-boxes to music (available on tape and CD) and his drill has entered the classical Chinese dance repertoire.

Throughout the Orient sword dancers twirl their flashing blades. Royal Thai dancers show off their hairsplitting timing, dueling in dance with razor-sharp swords. Rural Japanese farmers at harvest festivals attack dragons and defend maidens to the music of their ancient sword dance, performed by avid amateurs. The swordplay dance is still a popular stage attraction in modern Tokyo. There is no spectator combat more exciting to watch than classical Chinese theater fight scenes, dancers leaping, somersaulting, pirouetting to evade sword and halberd slashes. In theater or combat, it is hard to draw the line where duel becomes pure dance, or performing duet becomes dueling duo.

If one sees dancelike movements in zen combat forms, it is not incidental to technique. Combat technique is an incident of the mastery of dance, of rhythm. The archer opens his ceremonial draw discipline with a dance step, left foot left, draw right toe to left ankle then slip right; identical to opening step of the opening dance of Imperial Court bugaku dance. The entire archery rite is dance in rhythm with one's breathing.

When Mass Oyama, grand master of Kyokushinkai karate, set his basic entry requirement in the one question, "Do you like music?" he had recognized the choreoptic basis of karate.

The reason is best stated in *The Secret Oral Teachings of the Tibetans*: "Tangible world is movement, not merely a collection of moving objects.… Nothing can remain, not even for a single moment, without acting.… Every action … emits energy."

Zen is, historically, a combination of Confucianism and Taoism, or Confucianized Tao; in technique it combines the former's ritual and the latter's music. *Ritual + Music = Dance.* As I wrote in the Introduction to *Ukiyo, Stories of the Floating World of Postwar Japan*: "The 'gentle arts' are at least as numerous and probably more varied in Japan as anywhere else. Certainly, I believe, that of highest rank has been the dance. It is an essential element in all of the Japanese performing arts, from pure dance, both sacred and at the other extreme very profane

SADO —SERVING TEA

(though 'sacred' in use), through various forms of dance-drama, which also run the gamut from sacred to most profane; the combat dances, from spectator sports like sumo, whose performers are called literally sumo-dancers, to the dance calisthenics of martial arts of aikido, judo, karate, various arms drills; the etiquette dances which ritualize making and serving of tea, arranging of flowers, reception at court or private home, offerings to deity, the geisha's serving her client, artist's warming-up rites, and even that choreography of the artist's brush known as calligraphy." The dawn purification prayers of Ueshiba O-Sensei are pure interpretaive dance, as are his extemporaneous sword and stick exercises.

According to ancient texts, by blending ritual and music one may attain a state of "sitting and forgetting"—that is, quietude. First stage in this technique is to master the physical forms of the technical drills, zen combat dances. Then, when drilling by rote, allow the mind to wander (do not force it to do so), to think elsewhere.

"The method of the Oral Teachings of the Tibetans is to suggest to the inquirer various subjects for reflection: it is for him to make what he can of them." Thus, when doing your drill dance, think about something which interests you, puzzles you—but don't think of anything that might arouse emotions. Think, for example, about how the engine of your car works.

Sado – The Way of Tea

Action by rote distracts the reptilian 'primitive' portion of the brain. Another warrior discipline towards the attainment of enlightenment is that ultimate zen pastime *chanoyu*, literally 'tea and hot water' or *sado*, 'Way of Tea' (inset) which seemingly boring ("Why else serve such strong caffeine?") rite is mis-translated in English as 'tea ceremony.' This strict mastering

107

by rite and rote of often seemingly senseless hand motions ties the reptilian brain in knots while stimulating it with almost pure caffeine (so pure it has none of the usual side effects of coffee except extinguishing sleepiness). Zen monks, artists and yes, warriors, have long been its 'addicts.' Great warriors up to the very shoguns traditionally steeled, or settled and centered, themselves before combat by engaging in a ritual tea service. And I personally believe there is no *budo* as strong as *sado*. In my first six months in Japan I lived "behind the bamboo curtain" as a personal guest, a family member, of the grand tea master. I frequently heard it said, "You cannot cut a tea man" but not till years on in my pilgrimage, studying the way of battle, was I to come full circle and discover what was there from the first, the secret immutable strength of quietly sitting down to tea.

Dance in Western Sport

In all forms of zen combat, basic training consists of a series of dance routines, which are all utilized later as fighting maneuvers. Kid sister Ruby watched me start my aikido warm-up. Then she sat down next to me and acted as my shadow, doing the exact same actions. "I don't know what you call what you're doing, bro, but we call it the Martha Graham Warmup. You know," she added, "the mother of American modern dance studied Japanese dance early in her career."

My sons attended an international high school in Japan where the students performed classical kabuki theater on a near professional level. As 'movement conditioning' the kids did several hours a week of graceful classical *buyo* dance. The macho Yankee and European boys objected—but danced. And basketball players found they dribbled and shot better. All sportsmen realized score improvement.

The purpose, then, behind memorizing the rituals of performance is to free the conscious mind. Once the mind and the bodily functions have been disassociated, the reptilian brain tied up and distracted, you can forget mind and develop body: or you can forget body and develop mind. When you can do either well, you can do both and when you can do both you can forget the whole thing and just play it cool.

忍者

ninja

VII. THE MAGICIAN: NINJA

*T*HE MOON melted away behind a cloud and the shadow beneath the castle wall seemed to move, slithering across the pale white wall of the keep and straight up it and over the parapet, like the shadow of a passing night bird. But if a bird it could be called, a queer bird it was—a ninja, practitioner of *ninjutsu*, or *ninpo*, literally a "warrior wizard," a magician.

There are many tales of what these fantastic little men could do—and extant costumes indicate they were usually smallish, wiry men with broad shoulders and powerful chests but capable of great feats of strength and daring. The word *ninjutsu* is often translated as "the Art of Invisibility" because of the reputed ability of the ninja to vanish in a wisp of smoke, transform himself into a small animal or bird or inanimate object, sink into the ground or flow through stone walls. A ninja is reputed to be able to fly, or live under water like a fish—not impossible it would seem as a Sri Lankan spent hours submerged before witnesses in late 1993.

My wife's great-granduncle Nishimura was the greatest ninja in the feudatory of Aki, now Hiroshima, although not a follower of any of the five main "schools." Old folks of the family still talk of how he could sit in two separate rooms with two groups of people, drinking and talking with each (I've known bar hostesses like that), or how he could teleport himself through walls, leap over rooftops. Of course, none of the old folks had ever seen him do any of these feats of magic and the only eyewitness account of any action of great-granduncle was the testimony of nonagenarian Grandaunt Tamura.

"It happened during the War of the Imperial Restoration in 1867... or was it in the second Choshu revolt of 1874, perhaps ...?" She wasn't quite sure which, recounting it in 1954, but it was "a long long time ago" and she was a very little girl. There was a lot of fighting and the side her family was against seemed to be getting the upper hand in her area and being the daughter of a samurai of the losing side, she was sure to fare ill if captured. Her ninja uncle detached himself from the fighting and retreated long enough to get home to Grandaunt Tamura and her mother and "make us disappear from all mortal view."

"So, doubting long-nosed Yankee, here is your firsthand report" grinned my in-laws, "Our Great-granduncle Nishimura made Grandaunt Tamura and mother just disappear from mortal ken. An entire rampaging army passed them by and never noticed them."

I pressed the old woman for more details. She was reticent —as it turned out because she was more sensitive to certain peculiarities of the Japanese rural landscape than most farm folk, being a sophisticated veteran of a sojourn in the great West, as a canefield worker in Hawaii in the days of Good Queen Liliuokulani.

"Well, you see," she finally confessed, "he buried my mother and me up to our noses in the sunken human manure pots out in the rice fields and then plopped compost straw over our heads. Who would think of looking for a live human being in such a place? The enemy never noticed us, but," she added thoughtfully, "after we were rescued, everyone else did."

Great-granduncle was the master of a "school" of warrior discipline which practiced *ninjutsu* and which he called *ki-ai-jutsu*. Most ninja specialists were *eta,* or untouchables, but many samurai, or warrior class, were adept at the tricks of *ninjutsu*. He left a *torah-maki*, which is a "scroll of the ultimate laws" or rules of a group: *maki* means literally scroll, or rolled-up thing, and *torah* is a mystery word of unknown origin, implying "basic teaching" and not otherwise used except to modify *maki* and never used alone. Paired sculptures of heavenly lion dogs (see pages 76–77) or the fox messengers of the rice god are sometimes seen at the entrance to a shrine or temple, one of the pair holding a *torah-maki* in its mouth.

The family treasured great-granduncle's *torah-maki* and they loaned it to me for several weeks during which time I had my kendo master look at it, and Oyama, and aiki master Ueshiba (whom we shall meet in a later chapter). No one could make head nor tail of the meaning of the writing on the scroll. It was useless to anyone who had not been schooled in *ki-ai-jutsu*; it was meant only as a refresher, a sort of secret shorthand mnemonic memo to a fully trained adept, and only a fully trained adept could understand or interpret it. The mystic terms used had no meaning for an outsider, the diagrams might just as well have been doodles. The school of *ki-ai-jutsu* was dead and irrecoverably lost.

The above tale brings home three basic points. First is that you could fill a lot of field pots with stories about *ninjutsu* and *ki-ai-jutsu* or karate masters—deep enough to drown in, too. Second is the hint that the basic gimmick of the ninja's art is the doing of the unexpected. Third is that understanding what a lot of these old masters had or have to say is a matter of subtle semantics for they spoke in a language partly of their own making, using terms in other than their popular or common dictionary sense. Sometimes, as with our Great-granduncle Nishimura, they did this to conceal the secrets of the craft from outsiders, but more often because they did not have dictionaries and were using a personally evolved or limited vocabulary which has since become extinct. Often this was because they tried to explain self-discovery in scientific, or rather alchemical, terms, which they themselves did not fully understand. Other times they were only communicating words learned by rote which had had meaning to their teachers, but which they themselves never properly understood except as mnemonics descriptive of specific actions.

The "Secret" Teachings

These teachings were almost always "secret." But their secrecy was due, as Alexandra David-Neel states in her *Secret Oral Teachings of the Tibetans,* to the fact that these teachings were "reserved for certain class of disciples." Or they may have been secret "in the sense that only especially perspicacious minds can attain them" for, as David-Neel says elsewhere, "it is not on the Master that the secret depends but on the hearer." This all boils down really, to the simple fact that

"The Only Secret is that There Is No Secret," for, to return to David-Neel, "Truth learned from others is of no value, the only truth which is effective and of value is self-discovered ...the teacher can only guide to the point of discovery." All of which I was made personally aware of when I introduced the Japanese ceramist Kato Tokuro to the pottery world of Persia. He was, without doubt, the greatest potter of this century, among other things a great scholar of the history of the art, and teacher of Pablo Picasso. In Iran, he offered to scout out promising talent, if any, among young apprentices and to take at least one to Japan for training in the latest techniques and to teach him his great repertoire of glazes. "You mean," I said in surprise, "you would reveal your great secrets?"

"Secrets?" he laughed, "the sole cause of secrets in craftsmanship is the student's inability to learn!"

One of the arts developed and used by the Japanese ninja and his Chinese ancestor, was that of *sai-min-jutsu*, what we would term in English, hypnosis. Medical tracts in Chinese, dating back to the period when Marco Polo was in China, describe in detail a technique for inducing hypnosis in a patient for the purpose of curing psychosomatic ills and relieving painful symptoms. Such tracts give greater credence to legends which can be interpreted as indicating that certain "wizards" used the hypnotic art in other ways, not clearly described. This scientific art was lost to mankind for centuries until its rediscovery by the European Mesmer and only recently has it been redeveloped to a level which might compare with China of the thirteenth century. All sorts of magical powers have been, and still are, attributed to hypnotists—to magneticians or Mesmerists or whatever they have been called in the past—often to such detriment that the name for the technique has had to be changed on several occasions. This parallels the great powers attributed to the ninja.

The scientific hypnotist, Paul Schilder, discussing in *The Nature of Hypnosis* points out that "it appears to the subject that ... the hypnotist holds great powers over the subject's physical functions; in other words the hypnotist is for his subject a magician, a sorcerer. In the first place we are taking for granted that the hypnotist does not possess such magical faculties. Subject must have a specific motive for attributing them, such as the desire to possess them himself, and he attributes them to the father image to copy." As Schilder brings hypnosis thus down to earth, I hope I have brought *ninjutsu* back down, too.

None of the many self-acclaimed modern ninja I have met have given the slightest indication that they possess any special powers, though they are popularly attributed with many. One famous ninja near Tokyo, featured in an article in a prominent American men's magazine, claims, as do many, to be "the last master of *ninjutsu* alive." But the only art he practices, outside of a cockeyed form of karate, is the use of dirty weapons—highly impractical to carry around (certainly nothing he could get onto an airplane) and overspecialized to the point of being themselves highly vulnerable—of a coarseness and primitiveness that would make even an inner-city thug flinch. Many of the *ninjutsu* tools preserved in museums were never practical and they have been preserved in mint condition for centuries because they were only used once, if ever. Such devices include foot clogs with built-in springs to enable the wearer to jump over rooftops, round sandals a foot or more in diameter meant to enable the wearer to walk on water, and other Rube Goldberg type of contraptions. Onetime use of most of these could well result in one less ninja.

What is a Ninja ?

If all this then is what a ninja wasn't, just what was he?

He was, first of all, a practitioner of a variety of the combat arts so far discussed: this was his basic training. He was, as a relatively unimportant aside, a master in the use of specially devised "dirty" weapons—or anything that might come to hand as a weapon just as the modern master karate-ka. (Favorite lethal weapon of a Persian teacher of mine was a cheap plastic ballpoint pen carried in his shirt or handkerchief pocket and used like a *yoroi-toshi* armor piercer.) He was, building upon his basic conditioning, a master of stealth and of deception. Very little that he did was strange to our knowledge. Where the ninja differs perhaps from anything we have known in the West is in his organization of this knowledge into a separate discipline of education. He was, first and foremost, a super spy, and his skills were used almost exclusively to this end. One Tokyo ninja, who also claims to be the "last living" practitioner of *ninjutsu*, was reportedly teaching CIA agents.

But then again Hollywood is full of Orientalist martial arts supermen who have "trained the CIA" and Royal Storm Troops and the Shah's personal bodyguard and its ilk—which possibly helps account for our lousy intelligence record.

Deceptions were defined according to Taoist category, whereby all actions and objects are composed of one or more of the five primal elements—earth, fire, water, wood and metal. Each of these "elements" can overpower one or more of the others, and in turn be overpowered by others. Thus the ninja would decide which category his problem fell into, and then use a superior elemental technique. Most of this classification was merely a handy mnemonic for remembering what to do in particular set situations—rather like saying that if someone is in "hot" pursuit, a fire problem, use a water solution: if there is a pond around, jump in and hide.

Ninja Tools

The ninja usually carried a long smoking pipe rather like a cigarette holder with an upturned bowl. Generally farmers or shopkeepers sat around puffing such pipes and it made a handy disguise-prop for a ninja who wanted to disappear by sitting out in the open among the locals. But it also made a perfect snorkel when he wanted to hide in a well or a pond or even a manure pot. However, if such a water solution to the problem was too obvious, the escaping ninja could expect his pursuers to look for him in the nearest well or pond. In this case he might emulate the great conqueror Taikun (after whom our 'tycoon') Hideyoshi of the late sixteenth century, who grabbed up a large stone and dropped it into a well and then faded off into the shadows. When his pursuers rushed up to the well, he slipped out behind them and backtracked to freedom.

The Earth category of *ninjutsu* tricks included most of the elements of camouflage, or becoming one with the earth. To blend with the scenery, to squat immovable among the rocks, or stand immovable as another tree in the forest, to burrow noiselessly through rice fields or shrubbery, this was the secret of the ninja's reputation for being able to transform himself into some animal—mole, frog, ground spider, field rat.

His costume was designed to make this task easier. Basic dress was, as illustrated on page 109, a black or somber-colored affair complete with tight black cap, face mask, black tights and rubber-soled sneakers with black puttees. But we know all this from thriller movies of the 1980s, and newsreels of Special Forces. If armored, he wore either black mail hood and shirt, or black-lacquered leather plate armor, featherweight but arrowproof. His blouse was a loose-fitting kimono-type, the better to carry tools in. His sash could be easily unwound to use as a climbing aid or form a carpet across the loose gravel usually set out "decoratively" around important houses, but dangerous for the noise of passage across it or the tracks one might leave in it. His scarf was of fine tough cotton, useful rolled as a garrote, or flattened over stagnant water as a filter to drink through.

Actually, his costume was basically that of the *kurogo*, the little man in black of the kabuki theater, the stagehand who sneaks out on stage during the play to move scenery, help the actors with costume change or remove no longer needed articles. You really don't notice this little man even though he may remain onstage for a whole act, right out in full view of the audience—he seems so much a part of the furniture. And when he does move, it is so swiftly and unobtrusively that he escapes notice.

The Ninja Walk

The main lesson to be learned from the ninja is his walk. He scurries sideways, like a crab, but the basic trick is his lightness of foot, which must first be learned facing forward. The ninja walk is the "Indian walk," toes first and pointed straight ahead. The way the ninja practices it is a foolproof test.

He wets down the wooden or stone floor thoroughly, then spreads a long roll of the paper used for *shoji* sliding panels; a light, porous paper, translucent and tough when dry but easily torn when wet. This paper is not easily available outside Japan, so you might use a soft toilet tissue or paper towel. Test it, wet it and see if it tears easily. Then wet down a wood, linoleum or other hard floor. One which tends to become slippery when wet is best, as it makes walking even more difficult. Lay the paper in a long strip, making sure it is well wet through. Now try walking, barefoot, along the paper without tearing it, or crumpling it. When you master this walk you should be able to pass along the whole length—20 feet at least—without even crumpling the paper or leaving any trace of passage. Next, speed up your pace, gradually, until you can run along the paper without leaving a crinkle.

Most of the ninja's sneaking around would be down narrow alleys between buildings, spaces too narrow for normal passage, or flattened out against a wall to stay in its shadow. This calls for a flattening technique to compensate for the width of his shoulders. Thus ninja learned to move sideways, and at great speed. This odd gait is actually very easy once mastered and can propel you speedily over great distances with little fatigue.

Stand back against the wall. Now crouch slightly, in an exaggerated bow leg, knees pointed aside. Now turn your head to face the direction in which you wish to move, and lower the shoulder in your facing direction. You are in an exaggerated fencing position, lead toe at 90 degrees to body trunk, or pointing in the direction you intend to move, and rear foot facing at least 135 degrees away. Now bring your rear foot forward and place it down ahead of the lead foot, toes still pointed back so that the toes of the two feet now face. Shift your weight and now bring up your other foot to the original position.

Practice this moving flat along a wall, but do not touch the wall. You should be able to move quickly, quietly and with ease down a passageway only a fraction of an inch wider than the depth of your chest. Your step should be at least a yard a pace, and your speed at least that of a double quick time march. When you have this down pat, try it crouched lower on your haunches—both to strengthen your thighs and calves and to move in low shadows three to four feet high.

The ninja never swaggered. A modern karate-ka, or judo-ka or aiki-ka or archer will never swagger. If he does, you know he can't be very good. His walk is light, straight and swift, yet unhurried. This is the secret of remaining unobtrusive, of "disappearing" by remaining unnoticed. A master of this walk finds it easy to become a human chameleon, to blend with any motion around him, or motionlessness. He will walk into a group of teenagers and saunter along with them, into a group of old folks and adjust his pace to their faltering shuffle, or he can walk down a quiet street, alone, and never be noticed. People may look at him, but they will not see him. He is, to all effects, invisible.

The "Invisible" Tibetan

A friend of mine is a Tibetan rinpoche—that's a high-ranking lama who in his previous incarnation attained full purity and the rank of Bodhisattva, about-to-become-Buddha or so-called "Living Buddha." His lamasery in Chinese-occupied Tibet was under persecution, and fearing for his life—important to him only as a repository of sacred knowledge—he decided to escape to India. The trip over the mountains to the border was accomplished without incident. But the border was something else: fenced with razor wire, patrolled by armed men with dogs. The only way through was past an armed kiosk manned by trigger-happy passport checkers. He had no papers. Neither did most of the normal border traffic of traders and peasants. But they did not have the status-look of a well-educated gentleman, potential opposition leader, an obvious Living Buddha who by his movement and airs stood out like a ballet dancer in a football mob.

He told me, "I just had to get through. It was imperative. So I thought myself into a state where I was sure I was invisible, one with my surroundings, undifferentiated from anyone around me. And I calmly walked ahead, past the guards who peered into everyone's face, even mine, and walked on into India and freedom."

I, for one, much as I like and admire the rinpoche, sincerely doubt that he was physically invisible. He was just esthetically invisible, socially invisible. Unable to be told apart from peasant, caravaner, mountain bandit. He was not so much "invisible" as he was a human chameleon perfectly emulating his surroundings.

I have made slightly less dramatic use of this ploy in sneaking into the Shi'a holy of holies in Mashhad, Northeast Iran, or mixing with the anti-American rioters on May Day, 1952, on the Imperial Palace Plaza in Tokyo—and it works. I've even participated in meetings of fundamentalist Christian missionaries in Kyoto and not been spotted.

The main magic of the ninja was and is the magic of his walk. Once this walk is mastered, the rest is easy.

The rest is a walkover.

火渡り

hi-watari
fire-walk

VIII. FIREWALKING MADE EASY

*T*HE FIRES OF BELTANE are no longer kindled all across Europe with the coming of spring but, as happens with fires, some of the embers have blown away and set fires elsewhere —across the world atop sacred Mount Misen off the shore of Hiroshima on the scenic shrine isle of Miyajima, one of Japan's prime beauty spots. But where the Misen "Beltane" differs is that when the fire has been reduced to glowing red coals, the onlookers don't go home, they slip off their footwear and walk across—as I did.

Twice every year—at noon on fifteenth April at Mount Misen's base and November below its peak—a great pine log bonfire is kindled from torches lit from a sacred eternal flame originally struck by Buddhist Saint Kobo 1200 years ago. The ceremony is called *Dai Goma*, Big Goma, as distinguished from Small Goma, the common ceremony of offering kindling of personal name slats and incense at the small fire altar found at the feet of the main images in most Shingon Buddhist temples. This Tantric Shingon sect of Buddhism is the most closely related Japanese sect to the Lamaist sects of Tibet.

The firewalkers of Miyajima are not specially trained fakirs, nor are they graduates of $3,500 yuppie seminars. They are for the most part simple farm wives, with a sprinkling of men —farmers or shopkeepers, an occasional writer—or writer's wife, for it was my wife who induced me to walk the first time by first walking herself. Firewalkers are led by a group of conch-shell-honking yamabushi, an ancient order of lay-monks or Buddhist dervishes who follow their own peculiar tantric rites, for the most part in secluded mountaintop temples of mixed Shinto-Buddhist elements called Shugen-do.

The ceremony atop Mount Misen begins between one and two p.m.* with a blast from a conch shell trumpet heralding the procession of Shingon priests, monks and yamabushi from the small Temple of the Long-Nose Goblin of the Double Ax atop one of Misen's twin peaks, down to the saddle between the peaks where the main mountaintop temple stands. Then follows an intricate series of sutra recitations, to Fudo of Immovable Strength and the Jewel in the Lotus, led by the priests in their various purple, red and yellow robes, indicating rank as in Catholicism. A yamabushi on base drum, another on conch trumpet, a monk on cymbals and lay nuns on rattles and bells start up a syncopated beat which the audience of country folk take up, chanting, *"Wan-mon Shingon Dai Nichi Nyorai Fudo Myo-O, Wan-mon Shingon..."*

The Yamabushi

A yamabushi dances out, whirling dervish-like to the music, sprinkling the area and people with purifying salt (extra dash for the foreign barbarian). Then, if it is spring a group of children dressed as yamabushi, if autumn a low-ranking yellow-robed adult yamabushi, dance out, shooting colored blunt arrows to the seven sacred directions—cardinal four plus northeast, northwest and skyward, which usually lands near the fire pit (see illustration on page 121). Onlookers scramble for these to take home as talismans for their family altar. A senior yamabushi, noted by his cardinal-red or even bishop-purple robe, unsheathes a razor-sharp two-handed sword and dances, whipping it, slicing air, jabbing at the great stack of timber and kindling with a loud ki-ai spirit yell to exorcise the evil spirits in the fire, those wood spirits who cause burns. Then the five-foot-high stack of logs is lit, again as part of a dance, by two torch-wielding yamabushi. The stack literally explodes into flame with a crackling roar as the accompanying chanting of the crowd rises in pitch and volume and approaches the ecstatic.

* For full calendar of where and when to firewalk, see Appendix.

The chief yamabushi, a large-eyed man with seemingly un-Japanese high-bridged hooked nose, sits at the head of the ten-foot by five-foot fire pit, dressed in royal purple, presiding over the scorching inferno and barely a yard from it. His hands now dance about his rosary in a progression of the mystic hand symbols of the Shingon kabala; now exorcising with his sword; now feeding the flames new kindling, resembling 12-inch rulers, each inscribed with the name and age of a supplicant, present in person or in proxy.

Onlookers hold photos of loved ones who could not come, to gaze at the fire. Rosaries are handed to a yamabushi who suspends them and other personal articles—baby's kimono, maternity girdle, pair of drawers of a bedridden invalid—from his sword over the fire. Old religious articles are consigned to the flames, too sacred to be desecrated by any other disposal.

The pitch of ecstasy of supplicants' chanting rises. I close my eyes and the sound of the fervid voices suggests upon my mind the picture of wildly dancing, crazy-eyed dervishes—but there is here an order about the emotion. I open my eyes and look at the crowd. The actual picture does not fit the sound track: the faces of the people are radiant with tranquillity, their bodies perfectly motionless except for hands snapping rattles or bells in accompaniment to the musicians. I have never seen such stillness outside of a meditation chamber.

At last the flames flicker and die down. The bed is raked smooth. Chanters cease their song, then bend like a sea of grain in a wind as they remove their *geta* (wooden clogs) and *zori* (sandals), their *tabi* (sox). The purple-robed yamabushi stands deathly still, gazes into the glowing coals to center himself, intones a prayer to accompaniment of a finger-dance of mudra hand signs done in secret beneath his flowing sleeves. Then he steps out and walks across the glowing coals. A deep sigh, a moan, rises from the crowd, becomes a chant. Yamabushi, lay nuns and local "witches" follow in order. (The regular priests abstain.) Then ordinary onlookers start across. It takes four to eight steps in the coals to get across. The priests warn: do not run, walk slowly. Nervous walkers get burned, hop off the coals limping painfully. The calm remain calm, and unharmed. The coals are hot, too hot to stand near for long as a bystander or photographer. But our color slides clearly show bare feet trampling upon glowing embers.

— arrow fired
straight up

My wife and I have walked a dozen or more times. We made most of our crossings in the position of honor behind the yamabushi—in among the visiting "witches." Fazl Fotouhi, then of the Hiroshima (Miyajima is its suburb) United States Information Library also walked, as did Sandi Martine-Mori columnist for the *Mainichi Daily News* and Robin de Clive-Lowe of Prentice-Hall. In the spring of 1960 my wife and I coached a group of American GIs from nearby Iwakuni Airbase across— who later wrote it up in *Pacific Stars & Stripes* as an original discovery. In 1970 we led our two teenage sons across. None were burned. Robin limped a little, true, and stayed home for a few days, but he stomped and we think hit a splinter. We've been back a few times since, sometimes walking.

Basil Hall Chamberlain in his classic book *Things Japanese,* describes a rite performed over 110 years ago at which walkers first stepped in salt, as he believed, to "insulate" the soles: nothing like this is used on Misen. A *True* magazine writer critiquing a commercial firewalk seminar in California in 1964, claimed perspiration protects the feet of firewalkers: the priests of Misen warn those with sweaty feet not to walk. Women who are menstruating or pregnant are also enjoined, but for reasons of ritual purity.

This commercialized fire walking seminar makes our mouth water with the realization of the fortune we passed in not accepting talk show ace Long John Nebel's invitation to do the firewalk on his TV program in 1964. I was simply not sure of how to prepare the fire bed and determine when to walk. A bit more research could have solved that problem. The seminar was run by ICAN, Institute for Communication Alternatives and Networking. "Coals to Newcastle," literally and glowing at that—in 1987 they even brought the seminar to Tokyo, a 3-day/2-night affair for ¥60,000 (then $300), including hotel. F.I.R.E. of Twain Harte, California advertised in *New Age Journal* in 1994 for $3,500 for a 7-day seminar in USA. In 1987 ICAN claimed that 30,000 had walked with no burns. We've only led twenty or so.

So here's your —

$3,500 Instant Firewalking Seminar *FREE*

Collect yourself. Breathe deeply and slowly, as Oyama Masa-tatsu taught us. Meditate. If sitting at a seminar or in a festival spectators' bleacher, fine, just close your eyes. If standing in line for the fire pit, close your eyes and do standing meditation as Oyama taught for under a waterfall—like the yamabushi and Fudo-followers are doing in front of you. If you have trained in any of the "mind control" disciplines, then go down into *alpha* level. What the hell, just walk.

Quick steps invite burns, those who step slowly pass safely: thus guilty consciences bring burns, while the faithful pass. You needn't believe in Tantric Buddhism to walk—just keep calm, go slow and roll flat-footed from heel to toe. This way no part of the foot is in contact long enough to burn, whereas when running the ball of the foot is actually in one place longer and rotates to drill through the thin topping of inert ash. Alternatively, some yamabushi stamp down hard, flat-footed—this momentarily suffocates any flame beneath your foot. The danger with this direct approach however is that you run a risk of getting a glowing splinter in your flesh. Whichever footwork one prefers, the main prerequisite is complete calm and passive control.

Like cool ... which is then quickly followed by a feeling of high elation. That is, a "high."

Hokusai

刀道

sword-way

IX. KENDO: WAY OF THE SWORD

HUNCHED OVER A BOWL OF NOODLES in an early seventeenth century counterpart of a trucker's drive-in beanery for palanquin bearers and human workhorses, his clothes were tattered and patched, caked with the dust of the road. The stubble on his chin and pate and his ruffled topknot were in sharp contrast to the magnificent pair of swords at his side.

The trio of rogue samurai who swaggered in figured the swords would look better on one of them. Perhaps, if the blades were as fine as their lacquered scabbards and sharkskin hilts suggested, they should sell for enough to retire the three in luxury. Top swords in those days could fetch as much as a year's rice allowance for 100,000 commoners. They bandied lewd remarks loudly hoping to goad him into drawing first so they could legally draw and cut the bum down.

He ignored them. His chopsticks dipped delicately and rhythmically into his lunch. Three flies buzzed around him. As he chewed he sighted in on the flies. His chopsticks snicker-snackered in the air. He caught first one fly on the wing, crushed it and threw it down, then another. He snapped the third and in the deathly silence could be heard, retreating in the distance, the rapid patter of three pairs of sandals.

Miyamoto Musashi (1584-1645) was Japan's greatest swordsman. Delinquent son of a fencing master, he spent much of his adolescence tied to trees or locked in rooms in punishment

123

for some misdemeanor or other. At age 13 he killed his first man in a duel—a rival fencing master who had slighted his father. He came under the tutelage of several of Japan's greatest warrior-monks; later set out as a knight-errant and to find his father's killer for a vengeful showdown. Unlike other knights-errant, he remained on this vigilante pilgrimage the remainder of his exciting life. His biography in Japanese fills several blood and thunder volumes. Television and radio series portray him as 'The Lone Ranger' of Japan. His personal philosophy, penned late in life, *Book of Five Rings*, became an American yuppie businessman's bible when translated in the 1970s.

Despite, and partly because of, his stormy beginnings he epitomizes "*Zen, ken, shu*—禅刀習 Zen meditation is the sword, is the brush." (Alternate rendition: Zen=Sword=Learning.) His life was one long meditation; detachment from self attained through constant activity; detachment from everyday reality by grappling with it directly, unselfishly. He originated new concepts in fencing, developed the two-sword Nito style, and was never defeated. And, in my opinion, with the brush he stands as one of Nippon's greatest painters; unparalleled master of the sumi-e, simple black-ink style.

Musashi trained with the brush to develop a master surgeon's delicacy with his blades. And his bold swordsmanship gave an incisiveness to his brush line that sets his art apart, as nearly impossible to counterfeit as a Benvenuto Cellini silver. Musashi painted a whiff of breeze, catching a breath, echo of a laugh. He could switch from single-hand fencer to two-hand slasher like Rostapovitch conducting and just as rhythmically.

In one painting, a bird alights on a reed and we see the reed has just begun to bend, as much from backlash from his braking wings as from the first sampling of his weight. The viewer is drawn into the scene, gasps in synchrony with the bird's wing action. The painting is spartan in use of only the quintessential lines to portray the bird; the reed is but two brush strokes. The whole thing probably took only as much time to brush in as the bird itself would have taken to alight.

Another painting by Niten—Musashi's brush name, similar to that of his style of swordplay, Nito—shows a rear end of a horse, its head turned as if looking backward, and its teeth showing as though just having finished a laugh, which you can almost hear fading away behind you. The painting and the laugh were begun together and finished almost together.

"When I stand with my sword in hand against a foe," wrote Musashi, "I become utterly unconscious of the enemy before me or even of my own self, in truth filled with the spirit of subjugating even earth and heaven." With his brush in hand Musashi, in truth, subjugated even earth and heaven.

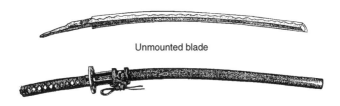

Unmounted blade

SAMURAI LONG SWORD
(Note that it is toted cutting edge upside)

With his sword in hand, Musashi fought through some of the great battles of Japanese history, at Sekigahara and the siege of Osaka. On his pilgrimage countless ruffians witnessed the moment of truth at his blade. Musashi himself died peacefully in bed at age 61. He was a retainer of a Kyushu lord, and during his early days in that southernmost of Japan's four main islands, he learned European fencing using two rapiers, from the Portuguese, Dutch and English around Nagasaki. This skill he wedded to the Japanese weapon—or weapons, for the Japanese had for centuries carried two swords, one a two-handed sword with a blade of 3 to 4 feet and the other a single-handed of between one and two feet, each with its own separate use (even a longer third down the back). The result was the Musashi two-sword style (*ni-to-ryu*, and for his brush paintings, *ni-ten*).

But you are about as likely to find Musashi tradition alive today as you are Musashi himself. The raison d'etre of kendo ceased with the recruiting of modern armies in Japan a century ago. It might have survived as an ivory tower mysticism, except that the military distorted it to fit their own fascistic tastes. One such survivor of the real sword-way it was my privilege to study with.

Nakamura Sohei, red-belt ninth-rank judge, was my kendo teacher, my personal sensei. He stressed that kendo has no practical use whatsoever in combat. Indeed, the kendo of the past several decades would have been equally useless in the days when the sword was worn and used. The bamboo weapon bears no similarity in balance to the real steel. The forms taught bear no resemblance to any that could be used—they are, to begin with, linear and any karate-ka working on circular principles, or any aiki-ka, can make mincemeat of a modern kendo man, turning his own sword against him. Nakamura-sensei always stressed this point even before and during the Pacific War and was extremely unpopular with the fascist military. But as he could lick any of them in a kendo match, which earned him the high proxy military rank of full colonel staff officer, there wasn't much they could say against him openly. They could only sidetrack him into relative silence.

Similarly, he mourned the loss of countless fine antique swords carried off to war in the scabbards of pompous little farmer-descendants of the original owners. In the 1930s he was traveling in Korea, then a Japanese colony. In a low-class, hard-seat train with his beard and grungy traveling clothes, he looked very local. A uniformed army major and two orderlies entered the crowded car and rudely shoved an elderly Korean and his family out of a cubicle. Nakamura called the man down. Unheard of. Who had the audacity to scold an officer of the celestial emperor?... the capital crime of *lèse majesté*. One could lose one's head. Nakamura reminded him he was a bushi, with a code of conduct as gentleman. The trio fumed and went to draw swords against a middle-aged 'peasant' with a walking stick—who turned out to be an 8-dan! Nakamura cackled. His stave cracked against swords, sending them flying. Then he tossed the trio out of the slow-moving train, gathered up their beautiful *Nihon-to* swords. The major's was a fine antique in GI scabbard, criminal waste. He found an army camp, called on the commandant, a lieutenant-colonel, almost his equal—8-dan was a brevet colonel— lectured him on code of conduct, reported the trio, and turned in their "confiscated" swords. He never learned what became of them.

The mad cult of the sword in the Japanese army was a recrudescence of primeval shamanism. In most ancient times, when possession of a fine blade meant near invincibility over Stone Age savages around, worship of this magical weapon is understandable. A sword of the '*tachi*' or hanging-from-the-belt type, not 'samurai' style, is one of three imperial regalia. The original is treasured at Atsuta Shinto shrine in Nagoya. Emperor Akihito keeps a replica of it at home, with the second treasure, magatama curved jewel. The third, the mirror, is the treasure kept at Ise Shrine.

Rites of its creation were magical: extracting of iron from stone, constant treatment with fire and water and more fire to make damascene steel and shape the final blade. (Common reaction to complaints of hard knocks, "It takes lots of heat, hammering and cold shock to forge a good sword—and a good man.") The magicians who performed this miracle of alchemy since the 8th century were treated as priests. Their science was, justly, a religion and their religion was pragmatically scientific. I have seen this rite of smithery performed in modern Tokyo, at the forge of Inami Hakusui, who preserves it and still, on rare occasion when a really fine blade is required —as for a United States naval officer's dress sword—invokes it to purify the smith and place him in that mystical state of detachment essential to performing a creative act—Hemingway called it "Getting the juice flowing." A few other smiths in rural areas also continue the tradition.

No blades in the world compare with them. Modern technology has yet to equal swords turned out by the top eleventh century-smiths, artists in the science of steelmaking laminated to 10,000 layers. But this is not the sport of kendo. Nor were they the swords carried by most pompous phony-samurai officers, who could not afford a real *nihon-to* 'samurai' sword. Nor were there enough good blades available. Most general issue army swords were re-forged automobile leaf springs— best were from American Fords, Chevvies used coil springs.

Equipment 道具

The costume of the kendo-ka is a cotton blouse and an ankle-length divided skirt. (In the illustration, by Hokusai over a century ago, the skirt is not worn. Moderns prefer it, however, as it is chic.) He works in his bare feet, or in *tabi* (sox). The helmet is an iron face grill similar to a catcher's mask, with leather or heavy padded side and top flaps. A towel is worn under the helmet. Breastplate of bamboo slats covers chest and stomach. A short padded or leather-plate kilt covers the groin and genitals. Forearms and backs of hands are covered by shell gauntlets from fingers to above the elbows.

The breastplate may also be finer slat or wickerwork over which lacquer-impregnated linen and numerous layers of lustrous urushiol lacquer are applied. The armor I wore was my teacher's, a superb piece of art in speckled gold-splatter lacquer with delicate arabesque design. Most kendo gear was seized by the United States Occupation Forces and burned. Nakamura concealed his antique armor, "I didn't allow our own military nuts to ruin my kendo—why should I let your nuts do so?" It was, and is, one of the finest sets in use. It was my sublime pleasure to use it when studying with him.

The "sword" is bamboo, 16 inches (41 cm) of handle and 30 inches (77 cm) "blade." The latter is split lengthwise several times, with a cord lengthwise inside maintaining spinal tension, and the "petals" bound together. The result is to deprive it of its terrible striking power. The split also enables the judge to estimate the cleanness and power of the blow by its sound.

Higher rank kendo-ka who have sufficient control over their weapons to be able to pull punches like karate-ka fence without armor using solid loquat or oak shaped like real swords, with hilts of water buffalo hide. A samurai kept such dummy sword by his pillow. A blow from it across the shoulder blade will totally incapacitate a night intruder—or anyone else—leaving him alive long enough to answer questions. Also, it will not mess up the clean house as would a good sword slashing an artery. The balance on this wooden sword is like that of a real sword. In solo shadow fencing and warm-ups it is far preferable to use this than the split bamboo.

A slightly modified version, without water buffalo hilt and with less curve to the blade, is sold as a walking stick in many parks and scenic spots in Japan. In less halcyon times, it was a good idea to carry one.

En Garde

The basic forms of present-day kendo are few. The rules of a meet are arbitrary in the extreme—and vary with the various *ryu*, or schools, of which there are perhaps 4,000 today, mostly one-man affairs. They differ mainly in nonfunctional

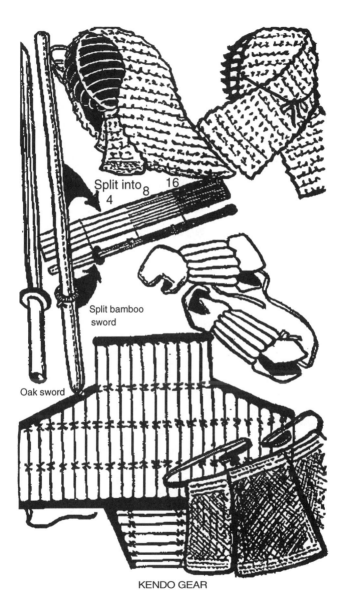

Split into 4 8 16

Split bamboo sword

Oak sword

KENDO GEAR

KENDO DRILL "A"

and nonessential calisthenics and theatricality. True kendo is simple and clean—as are all martial arts.

The basic overhead slash is considered a good calisthenic in karate and other defense arts. The footwork in kendo is of value. Perhaps if the karate and aiki principles of movement were applied to kendo (or reapplied) with some occidental open-mindedness, a fast and worthwhile competitive sport might result. In karate or aiki dojo in Japan you will often see a kendo-ka shadow-dueling, applying empty-hand principles to his sword—especially the movement in circles. These dojo maintain full armories of other weapons for defense drills against them. In the ranks above novice, as we saw in Oyama's karate dojo and would see in various aikido gyms, other traditional weapons are taught.

The basic warm-up in kendo is also taught in karate, using a heavy cudgel. I have seen Japanese baseball players in front of the dugout doing it with bats, first one bat then several. Stand as illustrated, feet at 90 degrees but hips facing forward. A right-foot lead is usual, however Nakamura-sensei made me practice it with either, also alternating hand grips. Stance should be with 70 percent of your weight on the rear foot, or as the Japanese call it, a 3-7 stance. This is the modern kendo en garde position.

KENDO DRILL "B"

En garde . . . lead foot step back . . . crouch and slash
. . . stand and . . . advance and slash

Inhale. On exhale, raise lead foot and jump between 18 inches and two feet forward on to it. Simultaneously with your advance, swing arms down in a chop, bringing elbows almost straight to lengthen your reach, while rear foot slides forward to toe against lead heel. Sword should be stopped, with a sudden stop of air in your exhale, at about imagined opponent's head so that should you miss, you would not swing through to the floor and be left wide open. All martial arts stress that attack must never leave you open to opponent's attack. Now, skip back, rear foot first, inhaling, bringing arms back up to en garde. Repeat this on a one-two, one-two count, forward-back, forward back.

Be careful not to slash down with a wrist action. Arms are not straight but slightly crooked. Chop is with your whole arm. Keep your body erect, do not lean forward.

Faster step is to execute above, but recall weapon so quickly that chop-recall-full-exhale-inhale are completed on a single skip forward-return, single count—in continuous action after chop, recall weapon on retreat. Repeat this as fast as you can, one-two, one-two. Nakamura-sensei had me execute this, changing the angle of advance slightly each time so that my footwork rotated me like the hand of a clock, clockwise, then counterclockwise. Also kneel on your haunches and execute the drill in this squat crapshooter position, again revolving.

The Grip

Now that you have the heft of the weapon, look to the proper kendo grip. The strength of the grip is with the small and ring fingers—a pistol grip—with the middle and fore, relaxed, providing control, projection. Strength and control is similarly distributed between the rear hand (usually left) and forward hand (usually right, but lefties lead as you wish). The rear hand is back near the butt, the forward up near the hilt.

On the chop, Nakamura taught me to let the forward hand slide back to the rear, extending my reach, with a slight clockwise twist to the wrist so that the heel of the hand bore its force to the sword. On the recall, the hand slid back to stop near the hilt. This movement adds a forward slice to the overhead chop, which in using real sword adds cutting power.

Hands and arms should be equally balanced so that you can release either hand at any time and use the sword one-handed for an attack with recall to a two-handed grip. Ambidexterity is essential. A one-hand attack can outreach a two-hand, can even outreach a spear or lance as in the cavalry.

Touché !

The score-points in kendo are: the crown of the head, above either temple, forearms and sides of the torso. In collegiate kendo, the right side only may be hit. There is also a point below the Adam's apple which is made with a lunge, but this attack is discouraged as the protection at this point is inadequate and accidents—sometimes fatal—occur if the target fencer cocks his head back any, or stands less than erect. It is not permitted to point an opponent here when he is on the attack. The reason for this is that when his arms are raised, his helmet rises, sometimes baring his throat. No one, it seems, has thought to try and improve the traditional armor; a rather simple feat if undertaken.

Basic bout consists of two fencers chopping at these points. All attacks are made with the whole body. Your hands and arms are no more than your sword, merely an extension of the body. The force of your attack comes from the rear leg.

Basic defense is a skip backward, out of range, with tucking the hands in closer to the forehead to pull them back an extra few inches. Then immediately counterattack to oppo-

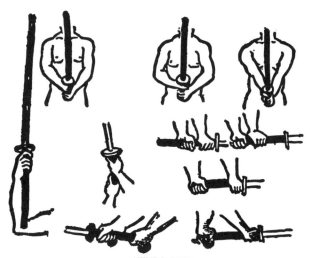

KENDO GRIP
(*Left*) Proper handle length and correct stance
(*Center*) Correct grip, top and side view
(*Right*) Common errors in stance and grip

nent's crown while his sword is forward and his crown open. Of course, you are both open to neck lunges, but hitting this point is illegal in this position. As the attack always stops at head height, another defense is a quick crouch onto your haunches, with a slash at his open right side. Another is to wheel back on left foot out of his line of attack and either crown him as he passes or hold your sword horizontal and slice his open side. This is not as easy as it sounds.

Basic parry position is to hold the sword on a vertical forward plane but tilted right 30 degrees across your face. Then bring your fists down, right in front of left shoulder, left under left breast.

On footwork, advance is always lead foot first, retreat rear first. Movements to right, at any angle, are with right foot first. Those to left, left foot first. On attempting one hand attacks, the advance is with the corresponding foot—left hand slash with left foot surge forward, right hand with right foot.

Most of the above is quite cursory, for anyone taking up karate or aiki will find the principles the same. Aiki and

133

karate may differ, but either is adaptable to kendo, the choice being up to your temperament. Kendo fencing, while quite simple, is excellent for timing and reaction conditioning.

The Short Sword 短刀

By far the more wicked of the two swords is the short sword. This is not studied by modern kendo-ka until the third rank (*san-dan* blackbelt equivalent) is attained. Even then, most kendo-ka ignore it.

Actually, the real samurai sword was used like a short sword. This despite its length, for the balance of a Japanese sword is superb. I spent one boyhood summer in 1939 with my uncle in the Royal Northumberland Hussars in Sherwood Forest, as mascot to one of the last horse cavalry units in the British army. I recall that a punitive discipline was to have a trooper stand at attention, holding out fully extended the hideously imbalanced British cavalry saber. Next day he'd be one aching muscle from toe to eyeballs. A Japanese two-handed sword of equal or slightly greater blade length (and far superior cutting edge) is not any trouble to hold in this manner. The balance of the Japanese sword is perfection. Used one-handed, the long handle acts as a counterbalance to wrist action and it can be manipulated almost as easily and speedily as a short sword. The bamboo fencing sword lacks this weight and subtle counterweight, is not as light, thus fast, in handling even though it is light in poundage.

When two swords are used, the basic en garde position is long sword in right, short in left (reverse if you prefer), hold hands forward about eye height, blades extended cutting edge out and the two crossing each other like an inverted scissor. Short sword should overlap long by no more than four inches. I have seen a few oldsters, like Nakamura-sensei, carry this off—he would shift swords, shift leads at will. But I have not seen any younger kendo-ka try this *ni-to-ryu*, two-sword style.

Other en garde positions are possible. Even with one sword there are many in the 4,000-odd styles. Some prefer to stand wide open, sword held down to the right side more like a golf club. Others may hold it high to one side like a fly rod. Some one-handed to one side, either high or low. Overhead as outlined above, however, is standard to modern collegiate kendo.

The Lunge

KENDO: ATTACK

135

KENDO: PARRIES

I-ai 居合い抜き : The Quick Draw

The Japanese movie industry grinds out the oriental equivalent of the cowboy western—samurai "eastern" or *chambara*. The name chambara is onomatopoeia for the sound of swords clashing. The formula for the chambara is that of the western —the real old-style western in which no guy, good or bad, cares about a girl. Recent '70s and '80s easterns have added female *ninja* warriors, dressed in tight tushy-hugging shorts and revealing kimono blouse, with absolutely no precedent in historical fact.

The showdown always comes about in the classic cowboy manner. One man goads another into drawing first. To draw meant to attack. For a guest to draw in a lord's castle was punishable by death—the classic kabuki play *Chushingura*, Vendetta of the 47 Ronin, evolves around the tragedy of the young country-bumpkin lord at the shogun's court being goaded into drawing his *tanto* short sword by the lecherous (for his young wife) old protocol chief. To draw and kill a man who had first drawn on you was self-defense. Thus as with the Hollywood cowboy, a fast draw was essential. And he who draws first, invariably loses.

The Japanese swords were worn tucked into the sash, cutting edge up. Thus a draw and first slash was a single action, rather than our style of drawing from a hanging scabbard and winding up into attack position. The art of the fast draw, I-ai do, was assiduously studied. It is still demonstrated by top kendo men who, having mastered the bamboo bats, take to toying with real blades.

For dress or visiting, even in ceremonial armor, carry sword tucked curve down, showing one's peaceful intent by lack of, being one additional step short of, readiness.

A full I-ai draw involves draw and cut and quick return. The contestant is pointed on the effectiveness of his cut through a bamboo pole or sheaf of straw—and the speed and cleanness of his return. No good I-ai man will look at his scabbard on the return. Don't try it with a blade, and I will not here attempt any instruction. A novice trying a quick draw is more than likely liable to return the blade through his side or stomach in unintended hara-kiri. The principle of the return

137

is the same as the game in which you close your eyes, and try to bring your two forefingers in to a quick touch.

A contest to demonstrate the ability of Japanese swords and swordsmen to cut clean is held at Kurama-dera, Temple of the Long-Nosed Goblin, near Kyoto every June 15. At this rite bamboo poles up to six inches (15 cm) in diameter are attacked by swordsman who must try to hack through with one, or as few as possible, slashes.

The story is told that at a meeting between Richard the Lion-Hearted and Saladin, opposing leaders of a Holy Land crusade, Richard showed off his sword and sword arm by hacking through an iron bar. Saladin countered by dropping a silk handkerchief across his Damascus blade, allowing it to halve itself. The Japanese sword combines both these qualities. But this has little connection with contemporary kendo.

Naginata 長刀

Those Wild Samurai-Women's Weapons

The *naginata* is used in the modern college coed's counterpart of kendo. Originally a warrior's weapon, it was early adopted by their grass widows for defending the hearth, is today almost solely a lady's calisthenic weapon. The *kata* or movement forms of the naginata are pure dance. They are circular, not linear. At the occasional matches between naginata and the bamboo swords of kendo, the odds are all with the fair sex.

The naginata itself resembles a pole with short scimitar on the end. Those used today are about seven feet long of solid oak. The girls at first wear kendo armor and shout *kiai* like kendo-ka on the attack. But they soon learn enough control—something kendo-ka rarely, if ever, learn until third rank—to do away with the leather and bamboo armor and go at each other unprotected.

In use, the naginata is a combination blade and pole weapon. Even in warrior days, a man armed with one had a terrific advantage over a swordsman. It can outreach a sword, has far greater sweeping leverage. And a favorite naginata trick, when an opponent evades the blade, is to whip the butt end around and use it like a stave in a vicious one-two of uppercut then overhand jab. The peculiar Japanese infantry bayonet drill was developed out of the ancient naginata, and with their longer rifle and bayonet, it put the Japanese infantryman on

ANCIENT COURT LADY
WITH NAGINATA
After an old woodblock print

at least equal footing with his taller Western opponent. Today, however, its use is restricted to developing young ladies' posture.

A few naginata basic positions are shown. Slices with the weapon are not made by slicing downward with the lead hand—which again may be either as here, too, ambidexterity is developed. A slice is made by using the lead hand as a fulcrum and snapping up on the rear hand. The result is a much faster snappy slash, faster than a swordsman's. The result also is that it is very easy for the naginata wielder to avoid telegraphing her attack so that the effective speed of the weapon (time between *visible* start of attack until it is delivered to target) is phenomenal.

There are three schools of the "long blade," sometimes called halberd. 'Ten-do,' or heavenly way, centered in the Kansai district; 'Shinkagé,' or new shadow, centered around Tokyo in the Kanto. Participants in both these schools wear the standard dress kendo garment of kimono and hakama or split skirt.

The 'Shizuka' School preferred ancient court ladies' long dress, a costume out of some twelfth-thirteenth century novel. This school, extinct, cannot concern us here.

The Bo Stave 棒術

The ultimate stick weapon is the common stave, *bo* in Japanese, around which weapon the jutsu or skill of *bojutsu*—or more formally *jojutsu*—developed. It is the ultimate stick weapon because it is the most effective, yet the simplest. It is not apparently a weapon and can be carried about without attracting attention, or requiring permission. The hiking stave bought and carried by pilgrims and tourists who climb Mount Fuji every year is the long bo of six feet. Many other mountain tourist areas sell the short four-foot-long variety.

Leading teacher of bojutsu postwar was master Fukushima, in Kure, near Hiroshima. Bojutsu is also taught in Tokyo in the main aiki dojo and in Oyama's karate dojo, where also, a modern version adapted to a walking stick is taught. The essence of the technique of using the bo is the projection discussed in detail later under aikido. It is not much used as a clubbing and lunging weapon, as was the stave in Merrie Olde England and modern India, though anything goes in combat. Clubbing and jabbing and lunging are linear or at best angular attacks. The bo is used on circular principles.

The weapon itself may be four or six feet long. The best ones are made of oak, the most beautiful from red oak or the heart of old white oak. Next hardest and preferred wood is loquat, which some prefer to oak for its supposed magical qualities. The four-foot model is the more difficult to master. It is called the formal bo and here the purportedly magical loquat wood is preferred. The six-foot bo was carried by Japanese police in the 1860s and 1870s in addition to a sword, paralleling our own police billy and pistol. Police later switched to the four-foot model. Postwar Japanese police carry Yankee-style pistol and billy. They did not like the billy and for some time after the war older police agitated for a return to the bo. Indian and Pakistani cops, especially riot police, make good use of their similar *lathi*. The bo is especially effective against Japanese thugs, yakuza, who during the '50s and '60s liked to romance at playing samurai and used swords as their weapon of choice. The tough loquat will repel all but the most expert sword slash.

The bo was eliminated actually because of the Japanese police kick for kendo. Kendo is a bodybuilder. It is used by karate-ka and others as calisthenic. It is useless as a means of defense or fighting, for which the thick-skulled police-state mentality meant it. (The kendo bamboo sword is ill-balanced, as we discussed above, unlike the real in every way; the rules of the game are even more unlike real combat.) The delicacy and grace of dancelike movement necessary to mastering the bo did not fit in with the coarse caricature of rugged masculinity that the prewar police-state mentality, driven by macho feelings of inferiority, tried to effect.

Spears: Yari 槍

These differ from the naginata in that spears are purely a thrusting pole weapon. The naginata is a sword extended from a stave and combines techniques of both. The spear is basicly much simpler, though sometimes it could be a highly specialized weapon. There were five main *ryu* or schools of the yari spear. Each school had its own form of spear, which in turn dictated its limits and special uses and thus in turn required specific jutsu or techniques.

The *su-yari*, literally empty-spear was a plain iron-tipped pole. This was used as a thrusting weapon, never as a projectile.

Kagi-yari or key spear was so-called because it had a key, or oversized fork tine, extending from one side and parallel to the tip. This was used for parrying and if the opponent's weapon, especially a sword, could be caught in this fork, it could with a twist be held fast or the opponent disarmed with a further twist of the shaft.

Jujyo-monji-yari or cross spear had a cross bar just behind its foot-long steel tip. This was used to fend or drive back the opponent's weapon.

Hozu-in Ryu school of spearmanship was named after the Hozu-in or Hozu Monastery where it was developed. Their

BO STAVE BASIC DRILL

142

BO STAVE DRILL *Continued*

VARIOUS POLE WEAPONS

blade was shaped somewhat like the naginata, with a three-foot cutting edge. It could be used for limited slashing as well as thrusting. It sometimes had a small key to snag swords.

Eta-yari, or pariah spear, was simply a fifteen-inch crude blade attached to a pole. It was used by guards (who were never samurai, but rather lowest caste untouchables) at crucifixion execution grounds for mercifully dispatching the writhing crucified criminal by a stab and twist to the throat or decapitation.

Kuda-yari or sleeve spear is a bear hunter's weapon. The most thrilling and sportsmanlike method of going after a bear is with a spear. But a bear handy with his claws can give a more than sportsmanlike hard time to a spearman. A cylindrical sleeve, like an auto engine valve, four to six inches in diameter and a foot or more in length, was slipped over the spear pole. It could ride back up the pole to the handle easily, but the spearhead prevented its coming off over the point. The sleeve sat behind the point and when the spear was thrust within claw range of the bear he would grasp it and try to wrestle it away from the spearman, his claws easily finding good purchase in the wooden cylinder.

A strong spearman could wrestle a bear and maneuver the spear point into position then thrust the spear through the cylinder like a billiard cue. There are still some hunters in the wild mountainous north of Japan to whom the greatest thrill life offers are the bear hunts with this weapon. Such hunts are necessary periodically to cull the population. These hunters disdain the rifle as unmanly—and unaesthetic, noisy and impersonal.

The best modern conventional yari groups are functioning in Hiroshima.

Hoko: Halberd　鉾

This is the true halberd, a longer and thicker pole and much longer blade than the naginata. The blade alone was as large as the biggest sword. Its use was simple. The butt was planted on the ground, and the pole held vertical.

The halberdeer parried his attacker simply by holding himself at arm's length from his halberd and moving around so as to keep the halberd between himself and his opponent. To attack he stepped forward and pivoted his blade onto the horizontal.

The last traditional expert in its use died in the late 1950s.

In the feudal period, before Commodore Matthew Perry opened Japan to Westernization, each feudatory in Japan had its own local police force fully apart from professional samurai warriors. These cops were usually untouchables, pariah, also called *eta*. Swords could be worn only by warrior class samurai. These low caste cops were equipped with a billy, effective in subduing unarmed troublemakers in the same way that our modern one is, but especially useful in disarming a swordsman as well.

Back in the mid-1950s our village mayor was a 90-odd-year-old multi-lingual scholar who had first visited the US as interpreter for the head of Japan's delegation to the Chicago

JITTE

Columbian Exposition of 1892. He took the train from San Francisco to Chicago ($75). All the Pullman cars had crossed rifles on the bulkheads at each end of each car—in event of Indian attack. But what impressed him most were the hardy American "samurai" women who paraded through the cars every morning on their way to wash up, carrying samurai jitte! Some time later he learned they were curling irons.

The jitte, pronounced "jit-teh," was more the size, shape and material of a butcher's knife-sharpening rod, except that it had a tong on one side which, with the rod, form an off-balance fork. Standard kendo parries were mastered to deal with any sword slash or thrust, except that in such attack the sword would be parried into the grasp of the fork. A slight twist of the jitte handle would immobilize the sword.

Jitte may still be found in antique shops today. The steel was often of the finest, with inlay and damascene. Handles were, like those of good swords, often covered with sharkskin. Some jitte do not have the side tong, instead have a sword hilt. These were carried by police officials of rank permitted to carry swords. Such jitte were weapons used only against unarmed troublemakers, with the sword available to counter a troublesome swordsman. These are smaller, lighter, fancier and obviously meant more as a baton of rank, but still usable when needed.

There were formal jutsu of jitte. Each daimyo, or feudal lord,had his own master with his own secret techniques.

Post–World War II Japanese cops still liked to carry old jitte on their own, which they preferred to the pistol and unwieldy billy club for harmless subduing.

Some jitte had a rope attached to the hilt so it could be used as a bolo to hurl after fleeing criminals, or thrown at a good swordsman with whom the jitte-man did not dare close

Naturally, jitte was often ineffective against a good swordsman. Jitte squads were backed up by men carrying a specialized pole weapon—

Sleeve Tangler: Sodegarame

This Rube Goldberg-looking blunt pitchfork was thrust at flowing sleeves of kimono. Once its tines intercepted loose cloth, the poleman needed only twist his weapon. The tines and the horizontal spikes on them entangled the sleeve, immobilizing even the best swordsman and holding him beyond swords' length of the arresting cop.

Armor Piercer: Yoroi-Toshi 鎧通し

When knights wore armor, the sword was limited in its effectiveness. The weight of the armor of course limited its use further. To deal with armored knights in infighting, a fine steel rod-dagger or spike was developed. With specially trained thrust, incorporating karate-type projection, or ki, it could pierc both the leather and iron-leaf armor, and the joints in any plate armor. It was carried in the sash like a short sword. The higher development of kendo and its resultant maneuverability, plus the introduction of firearms, obsolesced armor and with it, the need for this specialized weapon.

Scythe-Ball-and-Chain: Kusarigama 鎖鎌

The great variety of feudal period weapons can be attributed to the same sort of mentality that results in a modern Los Angeles teenage slum gang having such a fascinatingly differentiated ordnance: from switchblades and sawed-off pool cues and bicycle chains to zip guns, blackjacks and you name it. Except that in Japan there was sure to develop a school and esthetic of any weapon, no matter how outlandish. There was a flamboyant discipline even of the outlandish import, the medieval Euro-pean blunder-buss. If the feudal age had lasted a few dozen years more there might well have been a jutsu of the bi-cycle chain or garrison belt, even for the broken beer bottle.

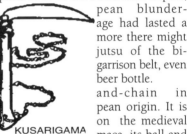

KUSARIGAMA

The scythe-ball-and-chain in Japan is of Euro-pean origin. It is an improvement on the medieval European *fundo* mace, its ball and chain extension used to lasso a sword or bolo a roundhouse wallop to split armored skull or unhorse a knight.

The kusarigama also had its jutsu, and many individual 'secret schools.' Some scythes have long handles, some almost none. Despite the scythe, it was no peasant weapon but for samurai. It supplemented the sword. Some specialized in it, however. In samurai movies, these are usually bad guys. The scythe is always held in one hand, the iron ball (sometimes spiked or knobbed), whirled on the chain and hurled.

The chains varied in length from three feet to over ten (1 to 3+ meters). When long, they were carried looped and held loosely in the scythe hand like a lariat. It is the only projectile weapon which is not spent upon discharge, for, if it misses its target, it can be instantly reeled in and reused.

Its most famous exponent was Yamada Shinryukan. He was hired and set off with 37 spearmen to knock off a noted swordsman, Araki Matayemon. Araki accepted solo battle against the lot, but retreated to a crowded bamboo grove where the spears and bolo-chain were useless. So ended the career of Yamada Shinryukan.

148

IRON FAN

Kusarigama technique is taught in karate—not because it is of any value whatever in combat (Oyama said it was useless), but because it develops speed of observation and reaction. And it's fun. It is usually begun after the second rank black belt is attained.

Iron Fan: Tessen 鉄扇

We might consider it the height of effeminate affectation to see a stalwart warrior lazily wafting a folding fan. But a supple wrist is not a limp wrist, and wafting a two- or three-pound iron lever against air pressure is not my idea of either a lazy or effeminate mannerism.

The folding fan is an item of formal dress. It also gives you something to do with your hands. Sometimes, you even use it to cool yourself. Japanese etiquette calls for carrying a fan on formal occasions. Entering a home, one goes on one's knees, places one's folded fan a foot or so before the knees horizontal to them. The hands are placed flat on the tatami-matted floor, fingertips just short of the fan. Then one bows,

149

FENDING OFF THROWING SPIKES WITH IRON FAN

the depth according relative respect. In feudal days you would have left your swords at the door with your coat and sandals. In case the host might have had evil designs on you with his sword, you need not have felt fully unarmed. Your fan, with its iron ribs and frame, could be used for parrying a sword.

Used as a fan, as I use mine, it is a good exercise for the wrist, even if it is only one of the moderns of six- to eight-ounce weight. And modern iron fans are made. It is still a practical defense weapon, used on principles that can be readily adapted to other everyday items—such as a rolled-up newspaper, in the use of its jutting heel; a ballpoint pen or pencil in the use of it with extension for thrusting. Because the fan is balanced and weighty, and iron-hard as well, it doubles as a bludgeon.

The antique iron fans still to be found in curio shops have iron ribs extending the full length of the fan. This feature increases the fan's use while open—it can be thrust at the opponent's throat, in which case a rib, often pointed and sharp, would probably pierce his throat; or thrust at his eyes, in which case two ribs would straddle his nose bridge and gouge his eyeballs. The modern fans no longer preserve this delicate feature, but they are alike otherwise.

MODERN U.S. YAWARA STICK

ANCIENT VAJRA, OR KONGO
MONK'S LIGHTNING BOLT

Lightning Bolt of Shiva: Kongo

Kongo is a part of the Buddhist mass paraphernalia. Recent models—made during the last 300 years—are of brass, usually do not double as weapons. Ancient ones of soft sandalwood did double as weapons. They had the advantage of being totally useless to anyone not trained in their manipulation.

To understand how the kongo was used we had to go to San Francisco. In this exotic town the modern police in the 1950s were using an atomic age variant of the sacred bolt, invented, or adapted, by an American of Japanese origin, *yawara* master Frank Matsuyama, a 5'2" [155 cm], 115 lb [52 kg] minisuperman. Here is how Marvin Lee described this yawara stick in the late lamented *True* magazine:

> In as few as four one-hour training sessions, a rookie can be taught how to cope with attack from front rear or side and how to bring in a recalcitrant offender. These maneuvers take only a few seconds' time and raise not so much as a bead of perspiration.
>
> The yawara stick looks like a miniature dumbbell, 6 inches [15 cm] long, 6 ounces in weight. It is made of plastic. It is fashioned to be held in the palm of the hand and grooved to fit the fingers. The yawara stick can be used in either hand, ready to strike forward, backward, up or down and at any angle. The

billy stick—limited to a forward down-hitting motion—requires loss of vital seconds in combat to set it into position.

Biggest surprise to the rookie on first acquaintance with the yawara stick is its power. A light tap in the right spot with this weapon has more effect than a super slug from its far heavier predecessor. One particular demonstration of the yawara stick dispels any skepticism in the rookie classes. The instructor plants a man on a chair, tells him to hold on, and asks yet another trainee to pry him loose. The pryer struggles, and, if he's stronger, eventually gets him off. But usually, his terrific exertions get no results. Then, yawara stick in hand, the instructor approaches the immovable subject. He taps the knob of the stick on a nerve back of the knuckles of a hand that's gripping the chair. The hand lets go immediately. He then quickly grips the man's thumb against the yawara stick. The slightest squeeze when the thumb is pressed against the grooved stick causes too much pain to be resisted, and no injury inflicted.

This is a prime example of how these ancient specialized weapons and disciplines can be adapted to modern need. Even preposterous, exotic weapons might find new uses.

The Pen Is Mightier

The lightning bolt of Shiva was the yawara stick of the medieval Buddhist priest, iron fan the yawara stick of the samurai. The pencil or pen can be your limited-use yawara stick. Study the pressure points in the karate section; they are the same ones used with the yawara stick. Study the grips suggested for use with pencil or ballpoint pen. Your pen can be mightier than a sword, even if you never use any ink or put it to paper.

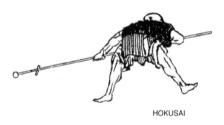

HOKUSAI

Musashi's Water Scroll (*Book of Five Rings*):
"Center your mind so that there is no imbalance, no difference between ordinary mind and that when practising martial arts
. . . . learn to be unmoved in mind even in the heat of battle."

152

弓道

bow way

Hokusai

X. KYUDO: WAY OF THE BOW

WHEN THE MONGOL HORDES of Genghis Khan attacked, they'd first lay down a rain of arrows lobbed from the phenomenal distance of 300 yards. By the time they got within range of the defenders' bows, survivors among the defenders' archers were headed for cover. In 1274 the Mongols invaded Japan. They stood off at their usual safe range and fired. But this time, the Mongol general, watching the battle from what he thought was well beyond bow range, was shot dead by a Japanese sniper's shaft right through his helmet eye-visor. The Mongols boarded their ships and went home. (They came again seven years later.)

In 1960 Japan was awarded the honor of staging the 1964 Olympics. The Japanese were to select the sports they would sponsor. Archery was eliminated. Traditional style archers, descendants of the sniper who had dropped the Mongol general, howled. But my old friend and first teacher, Onuma Hideharu, master bowyer and master archer of both traditional ceremonial and warrior styles and our own western style as well, sighed in relief, "Your western archers with their glass and metal bows with hi-tech counterweights would have sliced our time-honored traditional bamboo longbows to splinters."

What then is the value, or even the use, of Japanese archery? Another story from the second Mongol invasion of 1281: When the shogun or generalissimo of Japan, Hojo Tokimune, was reviewing his archers, he was appalled at their poor performance. A century earlier in the wars that had brought his family to power, archers had performed prodigious feats, both of accuracy and single-weapon firepower which became literary legends and classical subjects for painting. Now, whether ahorse or afoot, their form and accuracy were as poor as their overconfidence was inflated. The shogun knew a battle would be disaster. He met with his advisors, including several high Zen priests who had fled the Mongol conquest of China and migrated to Japan. The basic problem was to make the cocky samurai drill till they could master their weapons. Zen priests developed a ritual from their repertory of meditative tricks. The cocky samurai took to it and drilled. Their archery was soon fit to go against the invaders—who complied by landing in force after seven years of threatening.

The Japanese longbow has since been acclaimed as the ideal tool for Zen meditation, the very embodiment of Zen philosophy. The simple truth is, Zen tricks of technique can be applied to anything. The Japanese Zen ritual of the bow and arrow is the clearest example of this adaptability; perhaps the easiest for us to comprehend. *The Zen of Base and Ball* or *Zen and the Art of Motorcycle Maintenance* are at least every bit as valid as (or more than) *Zen in the Art of Archery*.

The Japanese bow was long a formidable weapon. It is like none other in the world. Most in use today are about seven feet four inches long to almost eight feet. In ancient times when many Japanese were taller, they ran to nine feet as extant antique bows testify. They differ drastically from the old English longbow. The Japanese are recurved—which means that when the string is undone, the released bow stave springs back to curve the opposite way and when strung the bow forms two curves, one above the hand grip and one below. Far Eastern bows are all this shape, but with Chinese and Mongols, usually only three or four feet long.

The Japanese bow is also the world's only "lopsided" bow —the top half is bigger than the bottom half. Earliest pictures of the second century show it was always thus. The upper limb, the portion above the hand grip, is over twice as long as the lower limb. The main advantage here is that while the British longbow is purely an infantry weapon and cannot be used from horseback, the even longer Japanese weapon can be—and still is—in the sport of *yabusame*.

ORIENTAL LONG DRAW ON ASSYRIAN SEAL, 1400 B.C.

The Japanese bow is a compound. That is, strips of wood, laminated—the English longbow was a single stick, a "self." The Japanese bow seems also to have been a self until about 1,000 years ago. Europe's oldest is a six-foot longbow self with flat and rounded faces found at 10,000 feet on the Italo-Austrian border on the 5,000-year-old body of the "Iceman."

Chinese records of 3,000 years ago refer to barbarians to the east as "people of the longbow." In the third century of our era "Horse-archer People," ancestors of the Imperial family, crossed from Central Asia. In the fifth century, a Korean king sent a gift to Japanese mikado Nintoku—a great iron shield. The pragmatic Japanese asked his favorite archer to test the shield. His longbow twanged. Luckily, there was no one behind the shield. Some Japanese armor-piercing arrowheads resemble chisel-head arrows Eskimo, or Inuit, long used on large game.

In the eleventh century the first star archer, Minamoto Yoshiie, hung three sets of iron shingle armor on a tree and put a single arrow through the lot. His descendant, Minamoto Tametomo reputedly put an arrow through two sets of similar armor except that his had a pair of enemy generals in them, both of whom joined their ancestors forthwith. He later sank an enemy samurai-laden sampan with his bow and arrows. Yet a century later, the descendants of these oriental William Tells were worrying Hojo and his Zen priests because of their inability to hit the side of a pagoda from the inside.

155

Ritual or ceremonial archery itself has a long history. The Persians who conquered most of Greece shortly before Alexander the Great, had a strict training discipline in archery —which with horsemanship and poetry were hallmarks of the gentleman, or knight. The Chinese book *Li-Ki*, purportedly edited by Confucius some 2,600 years ago relates:

> The archers, in advancing and retiring, in turning or making any other movement, were obliged to conform to ceremonial rules. He whose aim was straight, and carriage irreproachable, held his bow and his arrow with care and with a firm hand.
>
> In seeing him hold his bow and his arrow with care and with a strong hand, one might say in advance that he would strike the goal. By the drawing of the bow can one know the virtue and the conduct of men.

A witty Persian poet, Sa'di, at about the time of the above-mentioned Mongol invasions of Japan, wrote:

> From bowstring starts the shaft,
> but, who is wise,
> Looks to the bowman
> to learn why it flies.

And that wise old man of the east—east Pennsylvania —Benjamin Franklin (who read Confucius and Sa'di as well, proclaiming the latter to be 'lost scripture') admonished George Washington's Continental Army to remember the archer's weapons, which "are good weapons, not easily cast side."

The How of Archery

Archery in Japan even today is called a way, *-do*, rather than a *-jutsu* or mere technique. To some it is a way toward hoped-for enlightenment; but to most of the millions of longbow archers in Japan it is rather a strict calisthenic discipline. It is more than just technique because its discipline, once perfected to any degree, is of value in improving other techniques.

If enlightenment or *satori* is attained, it will be incidental to, independent of, and more than likely despite anything that I or anyone else writes or explains to you.

The greatest editorial hoax to come out of the 'Exotic East' was the highly emotional autobiographical record of a pseudo-sage German's supposed attainment of self-enlightenment by the way of the bow: Herr Stalagmeister Eugen Herrigel's *Zen in the Art of Archery*. That book is a perfect example of how one can misinterpret a subject completely by concentrating

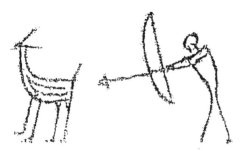

JAPANESE ARCHER ON ANCIENT BRONZE
3rd Century hunter with typical non-symmetrical longbow

on the exterior trappings, or by intensity of striving. Herr Herrigel returned to Germany after his highly publicized 'enlightenment' to become an ardent, voluntary, nazi concentration camp director—as was his wife, who also attained to ultimate bliss through the way of flower arrangement. One might wonder of what skin Herr Herrigel made his archer's glove, or what Frau Herrigel used to fertilize her flowers.

To paraphrase Thomas Cleary in his *Japanese Art of War*: Disciplinarianism, as civil militarism disguised as Zen martial arts, served to counter Western libertinism. In short, it was a fashionable disguise for fascism, and so is today at times. Elsewhere he discusses: "There is a clean distinction to be made between the Zen of Spirit and the Zen of Power."

It is a basic point made by most teachers: enlightenment that is actively sought is impossible to attain.

The Japanese archers I have known do not seek it. Some I have met seem, however, to have attained it to some degree: the man, my lawyer, to whom this book is dedicated was one of these, as was certainly my first teacher, Onuma Hideharu. To them, it is a calisthenic discipline, in spiritual sense, not sport. It is as such that it is of value to us prosaic westerners.

The discipline of the bow is epitomized in a ceremony, an elaborate ritual. Another teacher of mine, an American disciple of Hegel, witnessing Onuma's demonstration in a classical Persian garden, dismissed it as "Much ado about nothing" —as we shall see, Spinoza would have disagreed.

Naturally, samurai in combat did not go through all this rigmarole in a quick-draw duel. The purpose of elaborate drill was to make him master of his weapon, to make him and the weapon virtually one. This concept is not at all strange to us, however new or exotic this specific example may be. Much of this can be adapted to our own archery, with value.

The most immediate value of the oriental form of archery, bodybuilding, is derived from the physical peculiarity of the weapon. The western bow is drawn until the bowstring touches the front of the archer's face. Oriental bows, whether Chinese, Mongol or Korean recurves of less than three feet length or Japanese longbow of almost eight feet, are drawn back till the bowstring comes well behind the archer's ear. One can easily compare draw positions and see how the elbow of the draw arm of the western archer forms an obtuse angle with the line of the shoulders, a position as inefficient and uncomfortable as it is unaesthetic. (See p. 164.)

In oriental full draw the entire pull is shifted directly onto the shoulder of the draw arm with resultant forming of an efficient, unbroken straight-line vector. In this position the chest can and should, ideally, be extended and the shoulders thrust apart in a healthy and lung-expansive posture. The oriental draw acts then in the same way as our coil spring chest developers and other similar bodybuilding apparatus.

The ancient English longbow which put an end to the era of heavily armored mounted knights, was also drawn full back. There is no reason why our modern bows should not be. We adapted the Mongol bow to our fiberglass and metal production technique as the 'Turkish recurve,' but we shortened the draw to what we were used to. Restoring it to its full draw would restore the calisthenic value of the bow.

The greater the effective length of the arrow (that is, not the length of the actual missile, but the distance between the front face of the bow stave and the string at full draw), the greater the thrust and thus the greater the penetrating power —even at the same pull weight. Onuma pierced an iron plate with a 30-pounder. Never attempt to draw your western bow to this distance, it wasn't made for it, stresses are different.

If you wish to try the full draw with a western bow, and thus use it according to the following Japanese ceremonial forms, then compute the length of your arrow according to the oriental formula, as below, and then order a western bow to fit this arrow length and draw—something like ordering

CHINESE FORMAL ARCHERY
WITH SHORT BOW

off the rack an oversize jacket. If you wish to use the western or Mediterranean two-finger release rather than the oriental thumb release, then you may reduce the arrow length by two to three finger widths. This, however, will breed new problems and is not recommended.

The superior accuracy of the western archer is due entirely to technological superiority of our modern equipment. There is nothing in oriental technique inferior to our own, and much that is superior, despite the fact—and possibly because of the fact—that practically everything is done the other way.

Equipment

The basic tackle of a Japanese archer consists of his bow, four or more fletched arrows and one unfletched, one glove, quiver, spare string roll, resin pad, and nock-shaper blocks. He may also wear a special kimono similar to that worn by kendo fencer or aiki adept, but many modern Japanese forego the costume for slacks and tee shirt. All of the tackle are articles of extreme utilitarian simplicity and, except for the small pad and blocks, also great beauty.

The *bow* when strung forms the most beautiful of any bow curves. With its handgrip about a third of the way up from the base, the small arc of the lower limb stands in normal, mortal proportion, the great sweeping arc of the gigantic upper limb stretching heavenward like a cathedral spire, the two together seemingly linking the archer and his striving.

This bow shape is peculiar to Japan. It may have originated in Manchuria or eastern Siberia and have been brought to Japan by the horse-archer invaders of the early Christian era. The bow of the Ainu, the aboriginal white Japanese, is the common balanced self of more conventional size. The oldest Japanese bows are selfs, single staves. For at least a thousand years the bows have been composites.

One of the oldest Japanese longbows is a self kept in the Shosoin Imperial Repository in the former capital, Nara, put into storage in the year A.D. 752. However, it does not fire arrows. The string nock is a small cup—the bow was in fact a glorified slingshot. Mongol children today still use similar, short pebble bows to hunt small game. Arrows are expensive.

Modern-engineered western bows surpass the ancient Japanese-style weapon. But it took twentieth century atomic age engineers to discover what oriental bowyers have long known. The excellent *Fawcett Archery Handbook* says: "When engineers approached the subject of bow design they found that the area between the belly and the back was 'dead wood.' The bow in shooting is subject to two distinct and equal forces. The back must sustain a tremendous amount of stretch, while simultaneously the belly undergoes an equal amount of compression. (The belly is the face of the bow inside the curve facing the archer: the back actually faces front, that is, away from the archer.) The center area remains inert, serving only to hold the back and belly in position.

"In redesigning bows it was necessary to eliminate bulk in the center—the deadwood area—for lightness."

The English longbow had an almost triangular cross section, pointed to the back. Our western bow was redesigned to have a rectangular, or even trapezoidal cross section. Japanese and Mongol bows have been like this for centuries.

Here belly and back are strips of bamboo, perhaps the most resilient of natural materials. Bamboo of three-year growth is best, older or younger being more brittle. The deadwood center consists of five full-length strips of wood. The middle three are bamboo, cut from alongside one another off the same growth. Their round surfaces are shaved flat and they are set at ninety degrees to the sandwiching belly and back strips. The outer pair are of the even lighter waxtree, a brittle and poison-sapped wood.

Some bowyers further lighten the center by a five-piece combination of waxtree-bamboo-waxtree-bamboo-waxtree. They are glued together with fish glue and bound at critical points with rattan strips. The ancient bows had more rattan binding than the moderns; due to inferior glues they required more weaving. At either end of the bow nocks for the bowstring are of wood set in between the sandwiching bamboo and bound in with rattan. The grip is of deerskin, hardy and sweat-suppressing. The wood is usually lacquered ('japaning' or urushiol, not European lac), clear in ordinary bows but often deep-coated black or red in the more beautiful ornamental 'dress' weapons of masters.

The Japanese bow thus may not match various western bows for specialized uses, but it is a fine all-around bow offering the "sweetness" of the longbow at short range, and the long cast of the flatbow, for it is in fact both.

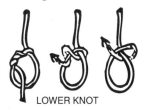 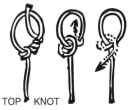

LOWER KNOT   TOP KNOT

The *string* is hitched to the bow as illustrated. The upper knot is tied in advance. The place for the lower knot is determined by running the string along the concave face of the unstrung bow and marking it where it crosses a rattan binder near the butt which is fixed at this point for this measuring purpose. The lower-end hitch is then tied. Slip the top knot onto its nock. Brace bow, convex face up, against point on wall about eight feet up, push down to bend it back —remember that when strung it will bend in the opposite way. With bottom nock against inside of right knee, press down on handgrip with left arm. Now nock bottom of string.

Test *fistmele* (distance between bowstring and stave at arrow nocking point) by placing your head between string and stave. Face should pass between, but not your ears. If too much fistmele space, string is short: un-nock and twist string a few turns so as to unwind it (note direction of twirl). If too little fistmele space, shorten string by twirling to wind it.

Nocking point on bowstring should be reinforced, thickened so that arrow is tight fit, so that it has to be lightly thumped into nocking. Old bowstrings are saved, unwound and cut into four-inch lengths. Resin the bowstring, wind on piece of flattened out, shredded old string, being careful to wind this outer layer in opposite direction to string's normal wind. Take the two little wooden blocks and roll the padded string area between them to tamp it down. Test nock an arrow.

Arrows are also of bamboo, probably the finest arrow material known until our recent developments. It is said that "the bamboo was created with the arrow in mind." The type of bamboo used is neither too rigid nor too flexible, with enough range of either quality available to suit any individual need. Fletching is similar in appearance to the native American, or untrimmed full feather, though there is some slight trimming done. There is also a selection of fletching styles for distance requirements. The ancient arrowheads had a "tail" and were hafted into the arrow shaft, like a sword blade into its handle. Modern target tips are hollow and cap onto the shaft as ours do. They are similar to those that western archers sometimes use for firing into earthen butts.

The single unfletched arrow, the *bo*, is used in form drill for firing into a *makiwara* straw butt (p.181) at five-foot range.

The proper arrow length is measured by extending the bow arm—the left—straight out horizontally to the side at shoulder level, fingers outstretched. The distance from Adam's apple to middle fingertip, plus two to three finger widths, is the arrow length. Thus longer by slightly over half the breadth of your shoulders than the length required for Western archery.

The practice arrows are usually an inch or two longer yet to allow for possible overdraws at first. But I found this measurement slightly short. I had bought a set of cheap arrows, slightly long, for practice and a set of five good arrows, straighter and more finely fletched, for competition, cut to my exact length. A few months of archery drill and my left arm length had increased by an inch and a half, my right by almost an inch. I found myself in danger of shooting myself in the left hand. The arrow measurement allows for less than an inch to extend beyond the bow as any arrow beyond the bow face lessens the efficiency of the flight. When I eventually ceased regular practice, my arm length shortened again.

162

A glove is worn on the right hand to draw the string. Western archery uses the Mediterranean release, holding the string with middle and forefinger below and alove the arrow nock. All Far Easterners, except some primitives, draw the string with the thumb, the so-called Mongolian release. Most Orientals use a ring on the thumb, of horn, ivory or jade, usually of great beauty. (I have a collection of antique rings I

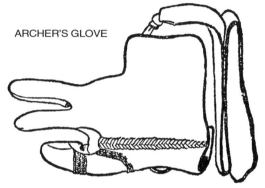

ARCHER'S GLOVE

often use, a Sung era Chinese jade excavated in Iran is my favorite.) Japanese use a glove covering thumb, middle and forefinger. It is made of deerskin, but the thumb is a hollowed deer horn, usually with a notch at the base of the thumb just above the crotch closest to the forefinger. The glove is bound around at the wrist with a band of deerskin, purple dyed for holders of ranks, similar to the black belts of judo and karate.

No glove or pad is worn on the bowhand as the string does not slap the inner forearm. The string should slap the outside of the arm, but not with enough force to matter.

Chinese sometimes wore a broad jade ring, matching the right-thumb ring, on left forefinger for the arrow to ride on.

Quivers are generally of woven rattan, lacquered, and little more than long slim baskets used for carrying arrows to the range and for storing them. A quiver is not used when firing. A spare arrow is held with the ring and small fingers of the right, or draw, hand. Two other spares may be stood against the groin in informal shooting. A special quiver is worn on the back for *yabusame*, archery from horseback. This is, in effect, the traditional medieval warrior tackle.

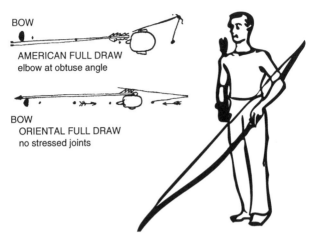

BOW

AMERICAN FULL DRAW
elbow at obtuse angle

BOW

ORIENTAL FULL DRAW
no stressed joints

STANDING NOCK: ONE – FACING TARGET

The *string roll,* shaped like a large yo-yo, holds three spares. It is of lacquered rattan, often matching the bow. The string is of the bark of a variety of hemp. Japanese prefer thin string, often replaced. The resin pad, for rubbing down the bowstring, and the pair of small wooden blocks for shaping and compacting the reinforcement on the string at the nock point, are other accessories.

Dress ceremonies are occasionally held in which the participants wear ancient suits of armor or court costume. These are often shown in tourist brochures. Few archers but antiquarian buffs would own such paraphernalia. For special meets one would wear a dress kimono, which can be a standard formal kimono.

The sleeves get in the way, but this is taken care of either by a band tying them in a tuck, or by slipping the left sleeve off and holding the bow bare arm. Many student archers wear a simple cotton kimono with short sleeves and traditional *hakama* split skirt, similar to the kendo or aikido costume. This is cheap and comfortable and the sash is an aid to proper breathing. Most training is done in shirt and slacks, though the standard kimono-style *dogi* is preferred. Girls usually wear a special leather or canvas breast cloth to bind themselves in, though very few Japanese girls really need it.

STANDING NOCK: TWO

The Ritual of the Bow

There is a long formal ceremony used in competitions and in tests for the *dan* or rank. More casual meets do not use the whole thing, nor do archers at practice or just popping away at a target. But even those portions eliminated in informal shooting contain valuable drills in, or tests of, balance and manual dexterity which you may find of value or interest. I will describe in detail the formality I went through in taking my own tests for my ranks. The ritual varies slightly with the various schools, but not in any significant way. The principal schools or systems are the Ogasawara and the Heki. All others are offshoots of these.

Both of these date back to the Mongol invasion period —earlier actually, but in that era Zen meditative discipline was infused into them. The Ogasawara family set up the Zenist archery drill in Kamakura by shogun's order 800 years ago. Ogasawara further developed along ceremonial lines. In the sixteenth century a reaction set in, leading to the expansion of the old Heki style for immediate practical use.

Most younger styles are offshoots of the Heki school. But as archery became more and more used, as Spinoza admonished it should be developed, as "a means ... devised for improving and clarifying intellect," the military schools moved

STANDING NOCK: THREE

back to the ceremonial system. All ceremonial schools are today essentially the same. Only the military style, Heki, differs. Onuma of Asahi Archery in Tokyo was a master of Heki-Sekka system—by birth, for his wife's and his families have been archer-bowyers/equipment makers for centuries.

He recommended I study ceremonial Ogasawara, in which he also held highest (nonhereditary) rank. He claimed Heki military technique is a snap after one has the ceremonial down pat, but the reverse order doesn't work. Similarly he considered the ceremonial discipline of great value in training western archers, even adapted part of it to training American children in Japan and Japanese Olympic aspirants. I studied the ancient Ogasawara system, later took instruction with a Chikurin teacher and finally took my test under Honda rules.

We now go through the entire ritual, noting those portions which are basic. The brief warrior form is outlined at the end.

The Approach

Take the bow in your left hand, as illustrated, string outside against the back of the forearm, top of the bow dipped forward and down, as a color-bearer dips the flag, except that the point stands in line with your body center, your navel, and close to but not touching the ground. Your bowhand, the left, is resting naturally against the front of your hip, knuckles

STANDING NOCK: FOUR

Next
see
p.174

in the soft flesh, palm up. Hold two arrows by their points in the right hand, which you position to match the left. The arrows will stand out behind the elbow, under the arm, forming a fantail with the butt end of the bow. Stand heels together, toes comfortably apart. Pull the shoulders back and down, chin in but not so as to puff out the neck. Compose yourself. Start the deep breathing. Now walk slowly to a position several paces back of the firing line. Compose, and we are ready to begin. Your turn to shoot.

This affair of shooting now concerns you alone, and all else, everyone else, must be banished from your mind. I have always used a simple yoga trick to clear the mind when preparing to address the target. I look at the target then slowly cross my eyes so as to blur everything. I hold this position several seconds, forcing my breathing slower and deeper, towards my scrotum, then allow the eyes to relax. The target falls into focus first and the rest of my field of view composes itself in perspective about it, but less sharply. My range of vision is also at its widest possible and the other senses keened.

Shuffle forward to the firing line. Take slow, sliding steps, toes straight forward now, heels raised slightly but balls of the feet slipping along the floor—the Japanese archer is in his bare or stocking feet, but this holds just as true if you prefer

167

to wear soft-soled slip-ons. When you get the knack of this catlike walk, your feet will not slide along the floor, but waft along a sheet of paper's thickness above. This is the karate-ka and kendo fencer's walk, a dance step literally (used also in the noh dance and kabuki, in tea ceremony and religious ritual) from which it is easiest to dance into any position if attacked. Stop at the firing line.

In full ceremonial competition, you will now kneel. However, if following the abbreviated form, face right, but in the reverse foot action to the western military maneuver. Slide the left foot forward at right angles to the right, left big toe in front of the right one, and without turning the hip now pivot the entire body on the right foot turning it into final position alongside the left.

The Kneel and the Nock

Now we test your composure. Without composure there is no balance. This action is followed only in the formal competitions and rank tests. Even then, all but higher rank archers are allowed, even expected, to cheat a little. However, I have found Americans can do it better than young Japanese and I have always done it correctly, while almost all the low rank Japanese chisel. The action is simply to kneel, bending both knees together, keeping heels together and your trunk erect. Go down steadily, while exhaling. Don't thump your knees to the ground but touch them down gently—perhaps pause before reaching bottom and ease down, like lowering into a too-hot bath—and sit on your heels. Try practicing this alone, heels and seat against a wall—if you pitch forward, you're wrong. Good party entertainment. Few Japanese can do this even if they are permitted to first slide the left foot three inches forward, placing the left heel against the right instep before dipping. Do either. Just don't fall.

Now on your knees, pivot to be at right angle to target. Place weight, without moving your body, onto your right leg. Pivot left leg on its knee, move foot out 90 degrees left. Shift weight to left leg and pivot body and right leg in a kneeling right face. Raise the left knee slightly (necessitating bringing the left foot forward a few inches) till the thigh is horizontal.

Simultaneously, bring bow up vertical, butt on the ground inside and alongside the left knee. Twist it slightly clockwise,

KNEEL AND NOCK: ONE

bringing your right hand over and, while holding the arrows with the ring and small fingers, take the bowstring with the thumb and forefingers about four to six inches above the ground and complete the rotation of the bow to its normal ready position, stave left, string right. Return right fist to right hip, arrows tucked under elbow, and breathe deep.

To nock the arrow, raise right hand to left hand height, next bringing it out and left across the bow till the bowstring touches your right upper arm. Now grasp your lower arrow with the left forefinger, releasing the arrow from the right hand, careful not to drop the spare which is still held by the pinkie and ring fingers. Bring right hand back to grasp the nocking arrow at its butt end with right forefinger and thumb. Twirl it so that the nock notch is vertical, and the feathers are positioned like an airplane's tail—one vertical atop, two near horizontal on either side. Slide arrow leftward to nock position, arrow butt being stopped an inch before coming into line with the string. With right thumb below arrow, bring bowstring back to drop into notch. It should be a tight fit and require a knock with the back of the deer horn thumb to plunk it into its berth with a musical twang of the bowstring.

Stand the spare arrow on the ground vertically, on its tail several inches right of your right knee. Holding its head, looking down at its feathers, twirl it by the head till the horizontal feathers face you and the vertical faces away. Now

FACING TARGET   90° TO TARGET

KNEEL AND NOCK: TWO

bring it up as before as if to nock it—but tail forward, head
at the string but extending beyond. Grasp it at bow with left
(bowhand) middle finger. It will now sit an inch or two
below and parallel to the nocked arrow, in reverse, the vertical
feather is down, arrowhead protruding four fingers to right
(rear) of the bowstring, at which crossing point you lightly
grasp it and bow string with your right thumb and forefinger.

Gaze straight ahead. Breathe deeply. If your balance is
good, drop your left knee and bring your left foot alongside
the right. If not, stay as you are. Now rise, gracefully, steadily,
inhaling slowly deeply, to a standing position. Exhale. If you
can do this, you are, on all oriental standards, collected,
composed—just plain Cool.

The Stance

You now turn your head to face your mark, to sight your
entire being in on it. You concentrate upon it, judging distance,
height, sensing windage, feeling your own point of reference
as behind the navel. Better yet, you meditate upon your target.
Advance your left foot, toe pointing toward the target, and
plant it firmly. Shift weight onto the left, bringing the right
foot up in a dancelike step against the inner left ankle, then
without a pause slide it to the right along a line continuing
from the target to the left toe and rearward beyond the right
foot, planting it in a wide stance. Your ideal stance will be
with toes set apart the same distance as your hands at full

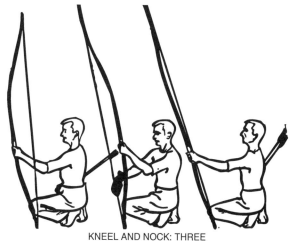

KNEEL AND NOCK: THREE

draw, which means two or three finger widths, an inch or so, less than your Japanese arrow length. You may feel insecure in holding this wide stance at first; it will pull on your thighs and leave you sore the next day. Fine.

Knees must be straight, back straight, buttocks pulled in, shoulders back and down. A good equestrian seat, and the position is rather a seat than a stance. When you can maintain this properly relaxed, a friend—as my teacher often does—may poke against your chest or back and not move you. If he can upset your balance, you are not relaxed and not breathing correctly. Push the kneecaps back, try pointing them in toward each other slightly. If you experience a feeling of delicious floating, as if you might levitate any moment or receive enlightenment on a gold plate floating down a rainbow, then start all over, you're all wet—though not alone.

If your stance is firm, place the bow butt against your left kneecap, slightly inside or wherever it will anchor comfortably. Move your empty right fist to your hip position, knuckles down again. Breathe deeply—into the pit of your stomach, into your groin, into your genitals, to your toes. Look at the bowstring at the nocking point, raising your eyes up to follow along the bowstring, slowly, absorbed in its spiral, then down again. Raise right fist, palm up, grasp the spare arrow at the

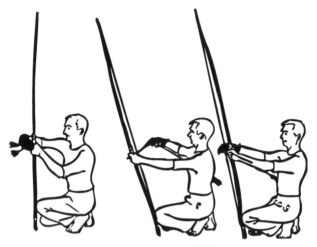

KNEEL AND NOCK: FOUR

string with pinkie and ring fingers. About three inches of arrowhead will protrude between ring and middle finger. With a counterclockwise twist of the forearm, exhaling, sweep arrow out and around and down under the right arm, returning your right fist to the hip position. Tilt the bow on your knee slightly to the right, so that your gaze falls midway between stave and string. You are now ready to draw.

For short form, eliminate the entire kneel: approach firing line (p.167) and turn, take stance, rest bow butt against knee and proceed to nock as above. In simple shooting, you need only nock the firing arrow, retaining the spare in your right hand. Then prepare to draw.

The Draw

Let's digress a bit and clear the air. Japanese did not, traditionally, rate their bows in pounds or kilograms of pull, but by thickness of the stave. (Pounds of pull is now in use.) This to all purposes amounts to the same thing. General adult beginner bows run about 27 to 32 pounds of pull. A heavy bow may run slightly over 40 pounds. In ancient times there were greater bowmen and thus greater bows. The first bow I ever tried was a western style of 70-pound pull (I weighed about 130) and I fired off half a dozen shafts. A few weeks

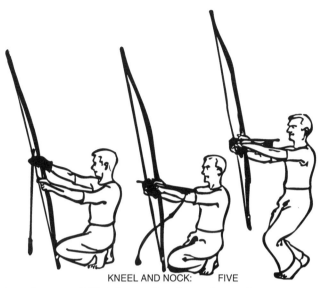

KNEEL AND NOCK: FIVE

later I met, and fell in love with at first sight, my first Japanese longbow. It had a pull of about 35 pounds. Shown how to draw it, I was handed the bow and an arrow. I pretty near wrenched myself in half, but to no avail. I could not draw it. I have yet to meet a westerner who, without training, can draw a Japanese longbow of even beginner weight back to full draw, unless he be a hunk of muscle greatly outweighing the bow—or trained in aikido, tea-way or dance. And this is where the value of the Japanese draw lies, as a toner of muscles our modern living otherwise lets atrophy. Come to think of it, few if any Japanese can draw one at first, either.

You can draw a very heavy western bow because you can brace your bow arm stiff against it, then hunch up and heave on the string. Many archers are over-bowed, as they call this using too heavy a bow, because they think there is a direct correlation between one's bow weight and one's virility. Many top American western-style archers warn against this over-bowing. The oriental archer has long known that the bow must be matched to his muscle tone. Overbowing is inefficient. The shaft does not release true, clean, and thus loses power. The archer's muscles are strained, unnecessarily, foolishly.

173

KNEEL AND NOCK: SIX – DRAW

Onuma ran some tests many years ago. He found that he could pull a Japanese bow of some 65 pounds without trouble, and heavier with some strain. But he obtained just as much or more effect in accuracy, distance and depth of penetration with lighter bows. He found he got the best results in all fields with a bow of just under 40 pounds. With this he could put an arrow through an eighth of an inch of iron plate. The heavier bows, like the lighter bows, bounced the arrows off the same plate, or even shattered them. He found that a man of 35-pound bow capability equipped with a 35-pound bow got far better results, all else considered, than a man of 40-pound capability armed with a 50-pound bow. This holds equally true for the western bow. And in oriental long draw archery the man who overbows himself is in for some painful mornings after.

Getting back to the drill, I left you standing, legs set thigh splittingly apart, right hand in front of right hip, left hand holding bow, staring between string and stave. I hope you

THE DRAW
Right: Perfect Draw by a Master

have been doing deep breathing, for that generates strength
—and you are going to need it, available in a smooth flow.
Raise the right fist an inch or so, spread the thumb and two
gloved fingers. These, fore- and middle-fingers, shall work as
a unit, just as the ring and small fingers do. Move the arc
formed by thumb and forefinger to catch the bowstring inside
it at a point on the string halfway between nocking point and
bow butt. Hook the thumb groove onto the string. Close the
finger arc, holding the thumb down with the two gloved fingers. Twist forearm slightly counterclockwise till forefinger
almost touches string—this to keep the groove on the string.
Slide thumb up string, inhaling, feeling to keep the string
nocked, against the arrow.

The thumb release is a clean release, with none of the
synchronization problems of our own Mediterranean two-

finger release. Howard Hill, then the world's greatest archer, Onuma and I had an archers' afternoon in Tokyo many years ago. Howard said Mongolian thumb release is superior in being basically clean. However, he thought it useless for heavier bows. He thought all oriental bows as light as those in general use today. But the samurai of old used bows with pulls up to a hundred pounds. Mongols had even heavier special purpose bows of fantastic pulls for use as siege mortars to lob gunpowder bombs. All were pulled with the thumb. It stands to reason, anyone who drills for years up to a heavy bow will in the process build his thumb up enough to handle his bow.

Now, right thumb set—be careful not to pinch the arrow with the forefinger. Keep right elbow raised; take care not to let it sag. Set your grip on the bow with the left hand. Grip is with middle and ring fingers mainly—not with kendo-style pinkie and ring finger, nor with western middle and forefinger. Forefinger is free, relaxed, and will point crooked, standing away from the bow. Hold the bow only tightly enough to keep it from slipping through the hand. When properly drawn, you should be able to release the left fingers from around the bow holding it only by the pressure of the thumb crotch, and still get a perfect release. Push out with the thumb in order to set the wrist with a straight line along the inside of the wrist and out the outer edge of the thumb; and another straight line along the top edge of the wrist and down the back of the thumb. The heel of the hand does not touch the belly of the bow at all, but leaves a space "big as an egg."

The western grip has the thumb bent back against the wrist and the grip is with the top fingers of the hand. In kyudo it is rather with the bottom, and with heel and thumb ball both pressed against the bow back.

Both hands set, turn your head to face the target. Exhale. Commence a drawn-out inhale as you begin to raise the bow, raising both hands simultaneously, almost to full height. Stop just short of full extension to retain a slight crook at the elbows, forcing your shoulders down. You will find yourself leaning forward slightly; fine, but beware of bending at the waist or sticking your seat out. Pause, and hold the breath for a few seconds. Now full draw commences on a slow exhale. The first few times you try it you will probably need help to pull the bow and string apart even if using a 25-pound bow.

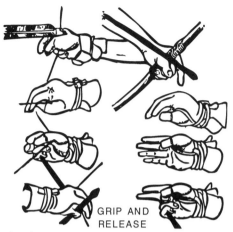

GRIP AND
RELEASE

(*TOP*) ARROW POSITION IN GLOVE AND BOW HANDS
(*MID-LEFT*) GLOVE HOLDING BOWSTRING
(*MID-RIGHT*) GLOVE AFTER RELEASE
(*BOTTOM*) GLOVED PINKIE HOLDING SPARE ARROW

The two hands are drawn down, drawing the bow stave and string apart in the process. The bow hand describes a convex arc with a radius of the full left arm. The arrow hand describes a concave arc coming down to the right eyebrow across the right ear and about to the shoulder so that the arrow crosses the mouth as a reference point. Both hands come together on exhale. The only breathing instructions I have seen in western archery suggest an inhale on the draw, which goes against all oriental breathing discipline, and does not make sense. On the draw, there is no action of pulling. The left hand thrusts the bow out, the arrow arm thrusts out, strength concentrated in its crooked elbow, forearm hanging free but drawn taut by the draw between elbow and bowstring.

Right elbow pulls its shoulder out and down. Left hand pulls its shoulder out and down. There should be no hunching up, rather a stretching out, a surging outward, to pull the shoulder blades out flat. In some systems, or 'schools,' there is a slight pause when the right or arrow hand comes down to the level of the hairline. In others, an uninterrupted arc is preferred. This parallels the two varieties of yogic breathing: one suggesting holding the breath when about half exhaled

177

then resuming exhale, the other calling for a steady exhale. As your breathing drills progress, you take longer at the draw, its duration being decided by your breath control.

When full draw is attained, you hold the position without releasing the shaft. The left elbow, bow arm, was pointing downward. If you have stretched your arm out correctly you will find the elbow cap has been rotating clockwise about 90 degrees and is now pointing outward. On hold, exhaust every last wisp of breath—stretch, surge outward at the target, project yourself at the target until mentally (some might prefer the term psychically) you are hitting it as the arrow. In the hold, you and the bow and arrow will form five crosses: bow stave and arrow, bow hand and bow, thumb of glove and bowstring, your jugular vein and arrow, your backbone and shoulders.

As you simultaneously stretch the arrow arm out, surging the right elbow out to the rear, the right wrist will rotate clockwise slightly, bringing the downward facing palm inside-up to face the right shoulder. Somewhere on this slight rotation, the groove becomes disengaged from the bowstring and release occurs. Fore- and middle fingers have been held against the thumb just strong enough to reinforce it, not heavily enough to hold the string in check. In the perfect release, the bow in the left hand will rotate fully, the string swinging around and slapping against the back of the bow hand. In ancient times when heavy bows were used, this could be a smart slap and a leather or armor shield was worn. But a bow of under 45 pounds will do little more than flick flies away.

The shooting is not over. You follow the arrow to the target—visually if you are a prosaic Occidental, psychically if you prefer, but follow it, holding your open released pose, perhaps holding your exhausted breath, the last wisp of which wafted out drawn out by the vacuum in the wake of the arrow's release. Your arrow hand will be out almost, or completely, straight back, thumb up, fingers extended but not fully. This follow-through is of utmost importance, as any golfer or bowler will understand. If the form of your follow-through is off, then something must have been off in your main action. Allow hands to droop slowly, not drop, to your sides. Allow the lungs to draw in air naturally. Bring your right foot halfway in, then your left.

You are ready to nock your second arrow.

MILITARY QUICK DRAW AND RAPID FIRE

Military Quick Draw

In the Heki or military draw, the simple single arrow nock
procedure is followed in the same spread-leg stance. But instead
of bringing the bow above the head, it is brought forward
toward the target to the full length of the left arm and slightly
down, butt just above the ground. Then raise it to just above
eye level and draw on the following slight downswing. This
is quite similar to our own western draw. Hold your arrow as
in the ceremonial form, with other arrows standing with heads
against groin or laid on the ground. Nock-draw-fire as fast as
you can, but maintain rhythm and form.

You may shoot from a kneeling stance, following either
ceremonial or military draw. On your left knee and right
foot.

Indoor Arm's-length Drill

For drilling, the simple firing procedure is followed for several weeks with target set off at the tremendous range of four to five feet. This is to develop form and to avoid the common beginner's disease of becoming all involved in hitting the target and getting results, making points. Musicians who have had to drill on scales and exercises and been forbidden to try picking out a tune will understand this discipline. I shot at the butt set at a range so close that I could touch it with my bow tip from my firing position. I shot at this range every day for six weeks before being rationed out the privilege of trying two shots every other day or so at a target at 15 yards. When I had my form fairly set, I was allowed to set cigarette butts on the five-foot-distant target and try for them.

Howard Hill in the garden of the old Imperial Hotel in Tokyo popped away at cigarette butts barely beyond his toes. He said if you can hit them at that range you can hit them at long range. Oriental archers agree. All archers begin a warm-up at the indoor five-foot range using unfletched arrows before moving to the full range. Dojos have a mirror set up alongside the short firing line so that archers can study their own form.

Ranges used for competition are usually of 33 yards, 30 meters. There are some of about 60 and 128 meters. In cities or private yards where space is limited, ranges may be only 15 meters. Contest ranges generally are shorter than those in male western archery shoots, but the Japanese archer considers the 30-meter range ideal for training, that ability to hit the target at this range means you can hit it at any you can reach. And he is concerned with hitting the target, once he gets his form down pat. The slouch form of the Hokusai sketch next page is not recommended. And once the form is pat, hitting the target is no great problem. One need only sight.

Aim

Aiming is done to the left of the bow, predominantly with the right eye, the left filling in for depth of field. If your release is clean and the arrow flies true, then sight so that the left edge of the bow cuts the target cleanly in two. The rattan winding on the stave just above the handgrip acts as a graduated sight. You must, of course, adjust height of your shots according

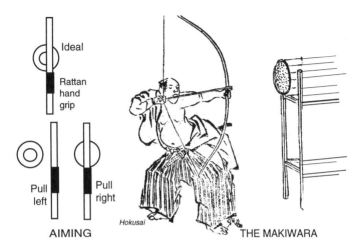

Ideal

Rattan
hand
grip

Pull
left

Pull
right

Hokusai

AIMING

THE MAKIWARA

to distance, weight of draw, your efficiency, etc., just as with any bow or gun. If at first your arrows fall to one side of the target, persist in this sighting line-up and try to find out why you are pulling the arrow to one side—almost certainly the right. If you cannot find an error in your form to correct, and all else seems to come off well, the arrows release clean and fly true, then adjust your sighting: if firing off to the right, adjust to what is called "eclipsing the moon," to cover target with the bow so that the view of the target with the weaker left eye superimposes its hazy image on that of the bow stave. If for some reason, a rarer fault, you pull to the left, then compensate by uncovering the target completely.

These instructions were worked out under supervision of my teacher, leading woman archer Ogasawara Tsuruko, 8-dan, and subsequently checked by Master Onuma against photos I took of myself in a mirror (reversed in printing) going through paces. From these I made these drawings. In 1966 I moved to Iran. Master Onuma stopped off in Iran as our guest on his return from Europe in 1967, and gave several demonstrations in Tehran (in the garden of a study group on Sufism, and in the imperial household garden) and in Shiraz in the garden of our Asia Institute of Pahlavi University which on short notice drew an immense and for unruly Iran appreciative, to the point of being mesmerized, audience.

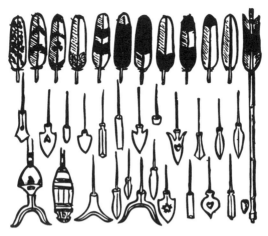

JAPANESE ARROW DETAILS

(*Top*) Natural feather patterns. (*Bottom*) Arrowheads:
(*Left*) Howler heads for psychological sound effects;
double-tips are "bowstring cutters" honed like small knives
(*Far Right*) Western-style for straw targets and dirt butts

The Bow of Ritual

The perfect release is less seen than heard. It is literally music to the archer's ear. Archaeologists are at odds whether man first invented the bow and from it developed the harp, or first invented the one-string harp then started shooting his violin bow around. Whichever, a Japanese longbow is a musical instrument and there are few musical notes more pure, more clear, more penetrating than the twang of a perfect release on a clear winter morn. An archer will buy a bow by its sound. A formal meet of master archers is a string ensemble. Perhaps significant is that both ancient Chinese and Persians considered music and archery to be arts necessary for the gentleman.

One of the first ceremonies a Japanese imperial prince participates in shortly after his birth involves the carrying of a longbow to the imperial bassinet, where a chief courtier strums it, symbolically imbuing him with both valor and rhythm.

It is his downbeat to begin the dance of life.

YABUSAME AT KAMAKURA

(See Datebook, page 277)

Archery on Horseback

Archery is also performed on horseback, a sport called *yabusame* (ya-boo-sah-meh). Again form is stressed and the archer is scored more on form than on hits—though the latter are expected as a matter of course. In ancient times, dogs were run onto a course and knights galloped after them firing arrows with "boxing glove" heads—still a bit rough on Fido. Another variation was to fire at the hoofs of a fellow horseman galloping ahead. The version still played at certain shrine festivals requires a gallop down a course of 250 yards, draw arrows from a back quiver, nock and fire at three targets during the run. These are about 10-inch squares set on end like diamonds atop a bamboo pole at about mounted-archer shoulder height and ten yards or less off to the side of the run. A run is made from each end so that left and right side shots are fired. The usual costume at major *yabusame* runs is the lovely Mongol period Japanese warrior outfit with sweeping, wide-brimmed "oriental cowboy" hat.

183

Varsity Archery

Archery is a major coeducational college sport. Most colleges have clubs and their own ranges. Neighborhood Youth Associations usually have ranges and sponsor clubs. Large companies also field teams. Meets are held, particularly in spring and autumn. The greatest is at Sanjusangendo Temple in Kyoto on May 3, moving to the Imperial Palace range on May 4-5.

This is for holders of fourth ranks or above. Examinations for lower ranks are held in April and September-October in the regional clubs, and higher ranks are influenced by performance at the Sanjusangendo and special meets.

A winter pastime, as in all sports and arts, is *kan geiko* or cold period drill. Archers rise before dawn, bathe in cold water (cold shower will do), and at dawn's first light begin peppering away at the butts as fast as they can nock arrows. At Sanjusangendo there is a contest on January 15, the end of New Year, to see who can hit the target with the most arrows within 24 hours. The range was only 128 yards, but overhang of the long temple along the side verandah of which this ancient range is set requires that the arrows never rise higher than 16 feet. The all-time record was set in 1686 when an archer sent 8,133 arrows the full length of the verandah, out of a total of about double that many released. Today the range is 60 yards and competition is open to all comers, regardless of rank.

In Japan, bow and arrow symbolize the flight of time and arrows are sold as talismans at Shinto shrines on New Year morning. Lovely as decorations. They are peculiarly without tips—is the passage of time thus pointless?

Hokusai

184

Hokusai

O-Sumo *

XI. SUMO

THERE IS NOTHING AS THEATRICAL as Japanese sport. Even flamboyant kabuki has a tough act to follow in sumo, a balletized wrestling match between biped hippopotami. It is the only fight staged not in an arena but in a theater in the round.

And, like true theater, sumo has its on- and off-seasons. On-season are the six 15-day *basho,* or grand tournaments in Tokyo, Osaka, Nagoya and Fukuoka. Off-season is lesser tourneys in the ancient capital of Kyoto or other main cities, and in recent years, overseas. But mostly, off-season means one-nighters—more accurately one-afternooners—or *jungyo* to smaller cities and towns, fishing villages and mountain hamlets. There the earth mound squared circle is raised on a riverbank or empty lot or shrine courtyard. Then pageantry and ceremony return to their original home of two millennia, to the days before the invention of fight promoters.

A couple of champions with their stable of novitiates and apprentice pugs toured the mountain shrines and seaside fish markets around the Inland Sea, where my wife and I were savoring a two-year honeymoon. The advance men posted their appearance in a suburban slum outside Hiroshima.

A sloping mound about 2 feet high and 18 feet square was raised on a riverbank lot on the edge of the slum, near a bridge which led across to the Korean ghetto. A post was raised in each of the four corners of the mound to support a flat-topped canvas roof, draped with purple bunting adver-

* Traditional sumo-style calligraphy from banzuke announcement

185

tising milk chocolates and caramels. Each upright was wound with a different color cloth: red, white, black, and green representing respectively the four cardinal directions, south, west, north and east. Atop the flattened square mound a circle of 15 feet in diameter was marked off by three inches of what appeared to be thick straw rope half imbedded in the dirt, but was actually the visible edge of large old-style straw rice bales. Two breaks in the rope, opposite one another between the north-and-west and south-and-east posts marked the "corners" for the fighters of the West and East teams into which all sumo tourneys are arbitrarily divided.

On the big day an area around the ring for twenty yards out was roped off and straw mats spread, on which for a small charge ringsiders could remove their shoes and squat in comfort. Out beyond, standees were free, compliments of the local merchants and the sumo guild. It didn't seem a financially solvent operation, but these tours are also to break in new fighters, do a little scouting—possibly recruiting— among local amateurs, and spread the popularity of the sport, while keeping the grapplers in shape. It is not only concert musicians who believe, "If I miss practice one day I know it, if I miss two days my colleagues know it, and three days the world knows it." The red ink would be made up by the guild, royalty-paying sideline industries, and supporting fans and local merchants, after the fashion of feudal finance.

The Korean ghetto across the river and the slum around was evidence that Art and Sport know no caste. Sumo to an oversized poor boy in Japan may mean the only way to a full belly and possible fame.

Sumo economy is the traditional Japanese economy: feudal, paternal. A full rice bowl for everyone: chicken in nobody's pot but a few chicken parts and giblets for all. The sumo novitiate gets plenty of simple food and a seven-foot square of floor on which to spread his bedding at night in return for opportunity salted with a generous portion of head detail, floor scrubbing and all the old boot camp routine except the short haircut—his hair is left to grow. If he beefs up and regularly wins a majority of bouts he will have his hair tied in a simple topknot with grand ceremony. From here on in, as he climbs the ladder of rank, his topknot gets more ornate as his seat in the barrackslike dressing room moves farther from the door of the *heya*, or privately run 'family' stable, closer to the top ranks. And he gets paid—nowhere near the scholarship dole of an American football player at a second-rate college, but nowadays handsomely when he attains the second top rank, *juryo*. Invitations to attend parties, whether autograph signing by and for them where they make *tegata* ink prints of their immense hands, or guest stints at embassies or corporate PR parties involve fat fees relative to their rank.

Sometimes from the fans come fame and wealth. Charge accounts are presented, gifts flow in. Fans fight for the privilege of buying their favorite his expensive *mawashi*, the ornate brocade loincloth and apron, the sumo wrestler's dressing gown. And, in olden days at least, there were the geisha who sent their bills to other fan-clients and often gave far more than the generous, puny, wealthier fans paid for.

Sumo fandom is universal and in days before movie stars and television, the glitter from their fans' money and light of their eyes was a footlight shared only with kabuki actors and courtesans. But if the kabuki actor and woman of the Pleasure Quarter appear in more woodblock prints than the sumotori, it's only because the beauty of his art is less pictogenic. Nevertheless, the beauty of his motion and the sounds accompanying are only matched in kabuki in the great plays.

Television raised the commercial value of sumo. Even on the noncommercial nationalized network, NHK, advertising signs in the arena are clearly visible. In late afternoons and evenings coffeehouses with big screens serve regulars only; giant screens in public baths invite cleanliness; aisles in front of TV counters in department stores and along 10,000 streets are crammed with "prospective buyers." In mountain villages Yagi antennae (a wartime Japanese invention spooked away by the US Navy) on thatched roofs designate the local "Terebi Teateru" which are SRO—Squatting Room Only. By the final days of the 15-day tournaments, it's standing room only in the big communal tubs, appliance salesmen face all sets towards the window and join the crowd and village TV theaters open up the "balcony" by spreading mats in the farmyard.

When Commodore Matthew Perry 'opened' Japan to foreign intercourse in 1854, his landing was celebrated with exchanges of gifts (the Americans wrote that they were shortchanged) and mutual entertainments. A performance of sumo was recorded for the first time by an American observer, officer J.W. Spalding of the steam frigate *Mississippi,* flagship, in his memoir *The Japan Expedition,* published in 1855:

On the 25th (of March, 1854) ... there was a landing ... for the reception of presents from the Japanese....The Americans were entertained with the contests in the ring of some Japanese athletes. These men were of great stature and much obesity, but their limbs displayed none of the angular muscularity, of a Monsieur Paul, lifting his cannon or resisting the draught of horses, or of the pugilistic activity of the American Tom Hyers or Sullivans, who could no doubt whale them with little difficulty. These men are in the pay of princes, and have such designations as "Giant of the North," &c. Their hair is gathered upon their head, as others of their country, though not shorn, perhaps to prevent their Samsonian qualities being affected. In front of their person, which is otherwise unclothed, they wear a scarf, with the insignia of the prince they serve upon it. They commence with an exhibition of their strength, such as throwing with each hand over the shoulder, or lying on the ground, and somerseting with large straw bags containing two hundred pounds of rice each. Then came the trial of the ring, not more than eight [?] feet in diameter and made of rice straw. Before commencing the combatants squatted and rubbed their knees, as if to assure themselves of their strength, and then rubbed a little dust [salt?] under each arm, something like an infuriated cow, when she throws it on her back, and then with a grunt they closed, and though the claret was occasionally drawn, and great welts were raised upon the shoulders, yet there did not appear much of that bellicosity, descriptions of which have graced some of the columns of the papers of our own country, since the infusion into it of Bill Poole blackguardism. The effort was to get one another out of the ring, when the effort ends. After being sufficiently amused by this *intellectual* display, the commodore and party returned aboard.

An amusingly shallow observation, except that he notes "there did not appear much of that bellicosity...of our own country."

The excitement at the main Tokyo arena was matched by the local audience at that riverside lot near Hiroshima. Ringside filled up with young sports dressed in the calf-high split-toed sneaker of the day laborer and their baggy pantaloons with red and white calligraphy-decorated indigo denim happi-coats. Old men passed around magnum bottles of sake and shochugin hawked by bent-over old ladies. Families opened tin lunch

The Japan Expedition

SKETCH DETAIL FROM PERRY EXPEDITION, 1854

boxes and nibbled at rice balls, dried sour plums, brine pickles and dried fish. Kids hounded parents to buy sweet-soy sauce-coated broiled cuttlefish strips; Japanese "jelly doughnuts" of sweet bean paste in pancake; or western exotica candy cotton, ice cream or the advertised caramels which pay for the show.

The formality of the great Tokyo arena was absent, though the partying aspect of both was identical. Sumotori—literally sumo-dancers or more commonly *rikishi* or powermen—strolled back and forth between stage-in-the-round and an awninged-off area set aside for them. Kids in clusters followed them at a respectable distance, into the roped off paid-admission area past guards blinded with the myopia of remembered youth. Occasionally some squid-chewing squirt got out of hand and an usher would ask in full mock-brusqueness of his one-day authority to see his ticket and banish him for all of five minutes to the free standing room. But never was the unguarded private dressing area violated (except for an occasional peak under the awning even I was finally tempted to risk). Japanese are not modest. It's just that this was also the sumotori kitchen area, and kitchens rate inviolate privacy in Japan.

An announcer in baggy haute-couture-colored knicker-bockers, seemingly off the kabuki stage, mounted the mound.

189

Then, like a Persian muezzin on his minaret calling the faithful to prayer, he sang the names and ranks and stable affiliations and all-important hometowns of the *rikishi* who would appear. He was not as out of place as he seemed, for kabuki evolved from Shinto shrine allegorical dance-plays performed on just such a mound, but without the rice-bale ring. In earlier days, when art and sport were even less differentiated than today, both shared the same stage as part of the primeval community's offering of entertainment to the harvest gods.

Our first wrestlers that day were a pair of bushy-haired novices—programs start with the bottom, playing to sparse audience and climax with the champions, for whom the seating area is packed. Good-natured catcalls disparaged clumsy standing-split preliminaries and they got on with it even before the announcer left and the more ornately dressed referee got to center ring with his wand of authority, resembling an oversized distorted Ping-Pong paddle. One went down and the winner returned to his break in the circle, bowed as the fan was waved over him in victory. Another pair of sumotori gargled from the buckets at the east and west corners—so-called but actually south and west—threw salt unconcernedly into the ring and at some of their fans at ringside, entered to the operatic announcement and lost little time getting to it, not having sufficient rank for ritual. The referee kept up a steady choral accompaniment with the song of his trade like a speeded-up recording of a sonorous old army sergeant singing cadence.

Referee declared a *gonin-nuki*—sumo king-of-the-mountain fracas in which the gladiators, clustered around their water bucket like apes in a Tarzan movie who they didn't seem too distantly evolved from, jumped in against the winner as soon as someone hit the dirt or broke the ring. The ref had a hard time making his song heard over the babble of rikishi arguing for a chance to get in next. Obviously the house wasn't big enough to take seriously yet. Then too, the wrestlers had to keep moving to keep warm in the brisk climate. The audience had their sake bottles and happi coats to keep them warm.

Two Goliaths squatting front row ringside and dressed in yukata—light cotton kimono dressing gowns—join in the kibitzing, but the novices seem to pay attention to them. One stands up and slips off his yukata revealing the heavy canvas 'undress' jockstrap of a rikishi and well-developed paunch of a champ, though the little hair fringing his bald pate was cut short. It was retired *yokozuna*, grand champion, Terukuni, whom I had rooted for in Tokyo's Kokugikan a few years earlier. When a sumotori retires, his topknot is cut off in a ceremony, formalities depending on highest rank he attained. A rikishi loses rank if he fails to win 8 of 15 bouts in two successive basho—except that a yokozuna feeling demotion in the wind usually retires. There is not one of grand champion rank but many, though there is only one grand championship, or *yusho*, awarded every basho. A rikishi may win many (record was Taiho's 32, retired 1971) but he is never "toppled" as each new tourney starts afresh, and titles or other prizes won go toward reckoning his rank and order of appearance.

Once retired he may become an *oyakata*, trainer, and start his own *heya*, or stable, as Terukuni had done, and more recently the beloved gentle Hawaiian giant, Jesse, fighting as Takamiyama, now called Azumazeki Oyakata. One duty of an oyakata at basho is to act as a judge, though obviously neither as a referee nor announcer as these are always tiny men to contrast with the sumotori's immensity. Honored professions in themselves, their ranks similar to those of rikishi are reflected in the ornateness and colorfulness of their costumes. Most likely, if he never made it up into the top ranks, he will go into the restaurant business and operate one of the many concessions in and around the great Tokyo arena which control the market for tournament tickets. All these are affiliated with the guild.

Some say Terukuni didn't retire because he'd had enough of the mound. He really stepped down because he was going bald so fast he was going to lose his treasured topknot and no one would know he was a grand champion.

Lilliputian Sumotori

Terukuni gave a playful shove that downed five novices at once to clear the ring. The announcer called attention to an important proclamation:

> The all-powerful Guild would generously relax its monopolistic control over the sport for a time and all non-Guild sumotori under age 13 (the limit of childhood by samurai rating) were cordially invited to challenge the great Terukuni.

A score of kids mobbed the registration clerk of the East side to give their names. Lower rank rikishi stripped them down and wrapped them in small loincloths, took off their sneakers or sandals, explained the rules, including the one about no greasing the body, and wiped their noses. The referee swept the ring with studied ceremonial swipes of his witch's twig broom. Terukuni danced his splits and deep knee bends gracefully with serious ritual while his tiny challengers fell all over each other in emulation, gave the ring its best salting ever and almost drowned one of their number in the water keg. The purification rites were declared sufficient (there wasn't any more salt and someone had tipped the East bucket).

It was soon evident that the guild had erred. Their champ was no match for the first contender who charged head on, butting Terukuni's flabby gut. Goliath winced, visibly hurt, his face contorted with each butt and he was forced closer to the ring border. His 320 lbs couldn't withstand the repeated smashes by the hardheaded, 40-lb David. The Champ's arms windmilled as he tried to keep his balance, heels back to the rope. In one last superhuman surge of energy he flipped his ponderous paunch up like a belly dancer at the onrushing mite who went airborne and headed for a set down. David got to his feet, tears of laughter streaming down his face and, bowing, exited like the true champ a good loser is, to the raucous plaudits of the admiring adult audience.

It took skill for Terukuni to drop him like that without at least snapping his neck or knocking him into the next chapter of this book. While undoubtedly the funniest, this is also the most brutal of sumo attacks and the ranks aren't decimated by it only because it's almost impossible to deliver in full against an evenly matched opponent. It's often used lightly to nudge an opponent into position and one of the funniest, if rare, sights in sumo is to see two great rice-belly behemoths sparring gut to gut with these abdominal lunges, like bull walruses in their mating duel.

Terukuni used every trick in his repertoire to keep his record inviolate against the army of tykes and handled them like a mother bear batting her cubs around—not hard enough to hurt, but enough to educate. One with a wingspread of possible three feet tried to grasp him around his waist. Terukuni raised the spare tire hanging over his canvas belt and dropped it again, contracting his abdominal muscles and pinning the toothpick arms completely in folds of flab. He walked him to the edge of the ring, raised his stomach to lift him over the inch-high border and dropped him to ignominious defeat.

It was forty years ago that I saw my old favorite Terukuni amuse his fans this way. I was to see shorthaired retired Chiyonofuji, the incomparable "Wolf," as well as all-time heavyweight 525-pounder Konishiki do the same act two generations later. Played in London in 1991, it was again a house-leveller.

But Terukuni met his Waterloo when he called for a match pound for pound and took all on. One sly six-year-old had studied the belt of a novice while his fellows of the tyke team watched the bouts for pointers. When the whole team swarmed in, he took a long detour around to the back of the grand champ and worked on the bow holding the 42-foot-long loincloth-girdle in place. He'd studied well. The Champ's eyes and mouth popped and the audience roared as he grabbed for his demeanor and stepped out of the ring to defeat.

The referee waved his fan and sang the paeans of victory over the whole team, while the defeated, but still grandest of champions, fanned his modesty and had his wardrobe retied.

History

This sport dates back to legendary epoch of the Gods when before Emperor Suinin in A.D. 720 Nomi no Sukune of Izumo beat Taima no Kehaya of Nara. Similar wrestling styles exist in Korea and Mongolia. Tomb murals in ancient North Korean kingdom of Kokuryo, fourth through seventh centuries A.D., mentioned earlier in our martial arts history, show wrestlers, somewhat less well-fed than modern rikishi. This sumo-look-alike was used at the royal court as divination to foretell harvests. Similar belt-wrestling was known across ancient north Asia into Europe, with one still in rural England, probably of Viking origin. In Japan it was also divination. In medieval time it was a martial art reserved to the warrior class and each local lord kept a stable of rikishi. It was the best way for a strong peasant boy to earn promotion to samurai. In the peaceful shogunal age of Edo, 1600–1860s, as Perry saw, it gradually became a professional sport and, supported by merchants, evolved into what it is today—Japan's most popular spectator sport.

In the 18th and 19th centuries woodblock color printers sold large quantities of full-length portraits of popular rikishi as 'pin-ups' (facing). But eventhough sumo is commercial and spectator, it is definitely a budo, a zen combat or martial art—for the very reasons that I consider judo is not. Note that judo, created by a wondrously powerful little man, Kano Jigoro, slim and less than five-feet tall who could toss sumo giants, now has weight classifications. Sumo is limited professionally (except in school teams) to men 75 kg (165 lbs) and over, all of whom fight each other. Its 1996 smallest major wrestlers are barely 100 kg, 220 lbs, and they meet, and on occasion beat, top weight 240-265 kg champions—quarter tonners!

There is obviously more than beef and brawn involved—as we'll see. On several occasions a rikishi visiting America has gone shoulder-to-shoulder against an entire varsity football line several times his weight and pushed them back. Certainly not mere brawn. Though the smallest weighs the same as Mike Tyson.

Still based on feudal structure, start is as unpaid apprentice, to live a monastic life in a *heya*—do all menial tasks for group, shop for food, cook, clean up, wait on seniors, scrub their backs in bath. Apprentices start practice at 4 A.M., don't eat till noon, main meal of *chanko-nabé* after seniors finish. Compared to this, English boarding school is libertarian, marine boot camp is boy scout camp. Like sport elsewhere, it is the best way out of the pits for poor boys, who may start at 15 after compulsory middle school (sons of champions may start at home barely out of diapers, like Wakanohana and Takanohana brothers). With more and more college graduates from varsity teams choosing it as a way of life, it has become a respectable profession.

The stereotype of rikishi as big dumb pugs does not hold, what with sumotoris-become-billionaires like Otani Yoneichi (fighting as Washiodaka), illiterate country boy, whiz at mental math and total memory who quit in 1915 after injuries to found steelworks and later Otani hotel chain. By late 1930s his private home was the immense baronial estate with garden that is now Tokyo New Otani Hotel.

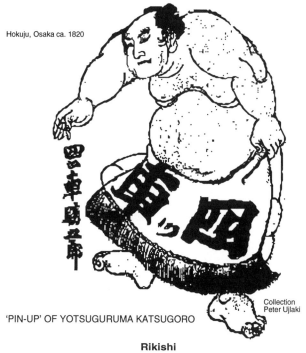

Hokuju, Osaka ca. 1820

Collection
Peter Ujlaki

'PIN-UP' OF YOTSUGURUMA KATSUGORO

Rikishi

'Power-men,' since 1988 record highs, now 854, all listed on seasonal *banzuké*, calligraphed poster. Lowest is: *jonokuchi* at 'arena mouth,' 112; *jonidan* 'step #2' at 356; *sandanmé* 'step #3' 200; *maku-shita* 'curtain-below' 120 and *juryo*, literally '10-units' (ancient weight and coinage unit, like lb/£) junior pro rank fixed at 26; top *makunouchi* or 'curtain-within' pros 40. Latter two, collectively called *sekiwaki* and with whom basho are mostly concerned. Makunouchi are again subdivided *maegashira*, 'before pillar' or seniors, about 25; with *sanyaku* top three, for each of East and West *komusubi* 'champion 3rd class'; *sekiwaki* 'champ 2nd class'; then *ozeki* 'champ.' Top is 'grand champ' *yokozuna*, of whom in 1990–91 there were four and '92 none, '95 again two, eligibles rising. Certificate of new ace reads "You are recommended to yokozuna rank on account of your *dignity,* competence and skill."

Juryo and makunouchi rikishi wear traditional oiled top-knot, *oi-chonmage*, get personal *sukebito* servant, regular salary —very modest for all but top ranks, but even then no basketball-star bonanza. Sponsors help, top bouts earn individual purses, advertised before bout by pantalooned ushers parading banners around ring, and handed out in envelopes to squatting winner after bout. Popular stars used to make good fees in TV and periodical commercials, but guild banned it as demeaning to their professionalism (how we miss their homey humor).

Yokozuna are not demoted, but if performance drops resign with great pomp, the treasured topknot is cut off in a grand *dampatsu-shiki* ceremony. At hair cutting retirement rite there is performance of satirical sumo, *shokkiri*, by makushita juniors.

I drew cartoons of sumo for the leading Japanese sports daily in the mid-1950s, one showing the 'impossible' situation of a wrestler whirling another around by his topknot—then over a quarter-century later saw just this act in 'comic sumo' or shokkiri and learned it is actually done to mid-rank rikishi by their stable master at daily practice.

These are not mugs, but gentle giants and disciplined craftsmen. Their whole world is arbitrarily divided into East and West camps. Not a fixed team designation, rikishi move from one to other each tournament, but East- anything is senior to its West- counterpart. Each rank has a number with top men ranked "East/West maegashira number-X (to maximum 16)." Rank is raised or dropped each tournament, even back down to juryo or even makushita. Rank determines monthly base salary (pre-juryo no fixed salary), paid by Sumo Association. Add to this individual bout prizes and fan gifts.

Non-Japanese Rikishi

Being used to a less-regimented lifestyle, most can't seem to make it. One reportedly half-Russian, born and raised Japanese in postwar poverty-stricken north, made it to the top—concealing his parentage. Japan-born Korean Rikidozan quit midway to become pro-wrestling star. Several Americans, Hawaiian, have made it to top: pioneer Takamiyama to komusubi (#3) retired '84; Konishiki ozeki (#2) May '87 ('96 maegashira 10) and Akebono to the celestial height of yokozuna (#1) 1992; Hawaiian Musashimaru to ozeki, 1993. Juryo 1996 has Hawaiians Daiki, Sunahana and Yamato, Mongolian Kyokushuzan.

SHOKKIRI

J.G., Daily Sports, Tokyo

Fallen to makushita Hoshi-tango and Hoshiandesu of Argentina, Sentoryu of Missouri and Ryudo of Brazil.and risen to it are Nanfu, Takamio of Hawaii, and Mongol Kyokutenho. Sandanme Waka-azuma, Kita-azuma and Azuma-kaze of Brazil and Kyoku-tenzan of Mongolia. In jonidan is Takao of China; and jonokuchi has Kuni-azuma of Brazil and Maetaiko of Taiwan.

Some years ago several promising Pacific islanders quit, took sport to Samoa. One Caucasian Canadian in entry division undefeated several seasons, but couldn't take limitations on his love life and quit for grunt and groan never to be heard of again. Argentine brothers Hoshitango and Hoshiandes poetic names are ideographic homophones for obvious Argentine names; 'family name' Hoshi is 'star,' for Star of David, with Tango not the dance but scenic Japan Sea area north of Kyoto. Mongols and Chinese find stringent life as much culture shock as Americans. Yankee hopeful African-American Sentoryu from "Sento-Ryuis," Missouri could model for a statue of Atlas.

No new non-Japanese 1995, vs 10 in '87: perhaps chauvinist reaction to success of Hawaiians; perhaps problem of lapses of above-mentioned "dignity" (one doesn't emote about defeat or victory—no "Oh, shhhucks" at loss, nor high five wins).

In the US some fat wrestlers formed a "US Sumo League." They wear short pants and eliminate all ceremony, thus missing much of the soul. "Form without Essence."

Weight Classifications

They just don't exist (except in amateur collegiate sumo). They do in modern judo, a postwar desecration. Which is why, to repeat, I don't consider judo a martial art, but do so consider sumo, as I will explain.

New hopefuls enter Osaka Spring Tourney, March. These fight from 2nd day, every other day, except collegiates with

197

good record who may start as juryo. Smallest must be 173 cm/ 5'8" and 75 kg/165 lbs, but most run 100 kg/222 lbs and up. A few underheight implanted plastic under scalp—one for over 3 inches looks like a comic conehead. All-time scale-tippers are Hawaiian Americans: recent retiree 'Jesse' Takamiyama (High-View-Mount) 200 kg/440 lbs and protege 'Sally' Konishiki (Little Brocade) heaviest ever at 265+kg/qtr ton and Akebono (Dawn) tallest so far at 204 cm/6'8", 235 kg.

Jesse had all-time record for consecutive bouts without absence thus most coveted perseverance awards; changed name and citizenship (required) to become stable-master Azumazeki.

Tournaments and Jungyo

Held in Tokyo mid-January, May (which emperor may visit), and September, with others in Osaka, March; Nagoya, July; Fukuoka (Kyushu) November. Each, of 15 days, begins Sunday nearest 10th of month, ends Sunday. NHK TV covers them live daily 15:30–18:00, earlier (shorthaired novices) on cable TV. NHK replays highlights 23:00. There is well-done English commentary on satellite TV, and carried by Hawaiian TV. UK formerly had good coverage on channel 8—who knows?

Tokyo's Kokugikan also hosts college championships in November, amateur playoffs in December. And for the aficionado, its Sumo Museum should not be missed (open to public year-round, but during basho to ticket holders only).

Smaller tourneys, *jungyo*, are held all over the country and may be stumbled on, as I did in Hiroshima, above, where champion may play shove-of-war with whole classroom of jock-strapped toddlers, to general hilarity. *Jungyo* road tours of 2–3 weeks are held after each main tournament except January (too cold), with entourage on one-night stands in town halls, tented fields, etc., organized like road circus complete from *gyoji* referees and *oyakata* (retired champions, now trainers) down to *yobidashi* announcer-sweepers and souvenir hawkers. Start 8:00, go till 16:00 when camp struck. Rikishi earn no points during tours, must be goaded to avoid slacking, but playing hometown of even lowest rassler sees him 'helped' by mates to elevate his 'face' at home. Lower ranks, as usual, perform all necessary services on tour—from cooking to packing and cleaning.

HAWAIIANS
Major Contenders

J.G., Daily Sports, Tokyo

Basho In the Kokugikan

These giants clash and crash most often at Kokugikan, 'National Sport Pavilion' in Tokyo's olde-Edo Ryogoku district, built exclusively for sumo, but usable for musicals and other major events. This impressive structure holds 11,500 spectators and has been sold out every performance since 1988. Albert Hall, where London sumo sold out for five days, seats 5,500.

The great Tokyo coliseum is modern steel and concrete, its flat roof collects rainwater to flush the toilets and air-condition in Tokyo's jungle-heat summers. But its air is still that of feudal era. During tournaments we enter through alleys lined by eating stalls run by retired rikishi, and into the arena. A diminutive feudal throwback in oversized pantaloons, the *yobidashi*, now ascends the earthen *dohyo* and operatically announces the next match. Also ever 'on stage' is the referee, or *gyoji* who always inherits a special personal name that goes with his rank. This ref and five judges, who are retired champions all in black kimono seated around the mound in the front row, will change every several bouts.

Two rikishi lumber forth, seemingly nonchalant but deeply concentrating, each rinses his mouth from a bamboo ladle at the team bucket, much as a worshipper does before entering a Shinto shrine, scatters salt as purification, does crotch-splitting calisthenics in a rite which makes as much good sense as good theater. These splits are a hint of how lithe these immense athletes are—most can sit indefinitely in a full 180-degree split, thighs and calves jutting out from opposite sides, flat to the ground.

The Bout

Fighting arena, *dohyo*, is a squared circle, literally: a truncated pyramidal mound of special pounded clay 54 cm/21" high by 5.54 m/18' square, with circle 4.55 m/15' diameter outlined by 20 buried rice bales rising ankle high out of this base.

Burial under its center enshrines an earthenware offering vat of kelp, nuts and cuttlefish. This circle is halved by breaks, gates, as in a Tibetan mandala and designs on prehistoric painted pottery—representing the four-quartered world atop the celestial mountain. At center are starting lines, two parallel white lines of 90 cm/3', some 120 cm/4' apart. Whole is roofed with *sajiki*, a Shinto-style *shinmei-zukuri* roof, remnant of primeval Shinto shrine where this sport was originally held. Now suspended from ceiling dome, until late '50s it sat atop corner pillars, against which rikishi were often injured. *Dohyo*-ring and *sajiki*-roof in Kokugikan can be stowed away at push of a button (in other arenas less easily) allowing unencumbered use of hall for concerts and exhibitions.

Tournament begins by 9:00 A.M. with shaggy-head teenage *mae-zumo*, 'pre-sumo,' novitiates. At 11:00 longhaired lower four apprentice divisions through *makushita* grapple. They are busy growing hair long enough to knot as pompadoured and salaried *juryo* rank. Juryo parade in *dohyo-iri* grand entrance at 15:00. Makushita fight alternate days for best of seven, sekitori professionals juryo-up, fight daily for 15 days.

In *dohyo-iri* processional entry, East first then West, in fancy embroidered aprons like walking art exhibition or fashion show of Goliaths, each is introduced by costumed announcer in sumo-operatic voice. This repeats when the even more ornate *makunouchi* professionals parade an hour later.

The latter's exit is followed by yet greater pomp of *yokozuna dohyo-iri* as each grand champ enters with personal escort of two rikishi, one with broom as *mi-harai*, dew-sweeper, and *tachi-mochi* ceremonial sword carrier. Each troika is in matching *keshomawashi,* great decoratively brocaded ritual aprons costing some $25-30,000 each but which supporters vie to present.

For bout, apron worn at *dohyo-iri* entry procession is left back stage. Rikishi strips down to broad silk *mawashi* belt, 10–13 m/32–42 ft long by 80 cm/31" wide, wrapped around waist folded in two, but in six where cupping genitals. Simple *mawashi* silk fighting jock runs $10–15,000 also fan-sponsored. It is decorated with separate silk-cord tassels which often fly off during contest. Fighting belts range from exquisite colored silk for seniors, who choose their own hues, down to blue denim *aizomé* cotton for lowest ranks. In early days of US Occupation, late 1940s, boxer shorts were also worn to shield US officers' coy wives of view of brawny broad buttock.

Yokozuna wear great 13 kg/29 lb white rope bow *yoko-tsuna* 'horizontal knot' exclusive rank chevron, bedecked with five *gohei,* zig-zag-fold paper tassels. Trio mount mound on west, face east, squat, and so that champ can show he's unarmed, he spreads arms, claps hands, turns palms to all. Then struts to ring center, faces north, emperor's box (North Star), performs purification *shiko* so dearly associated with sumo: legs spread in horseman stance, arms and hands dance with the grace of great power, one leg raises—some to ballerina heights, Waka-Taka brothers 135°—stomps down with great force exploding simultaneously with crowd's spontaneous cheer, three times. Any other yokozuna follow and repeat.

Then makunouchi ranks fight in reverse order. Yokozuna last to fight—if more than one, meet on final days. A sixteenth may be called for end of last day to break any first-place tie.

As fast as boxing or karate or judo are, so sumo seems slow. Yet with all its initial slowness, it has in essence the same spontaneity of action of lightning-fast hand to hand. Where boxer or judoist may keep up a barrage of feints and engage in considerable sparring, the sumo wrestlers go through their sometimes tedious preparatory ceremonies of leaving and reentering the ring, casting more salt to exorcise evil influences (butterfly in stomach), let their arms wave seemingly completely detached in gracefully choreographed shadow-boxing or go through their ballerina exercises of great standing *shiko* split-kicks to the side, deep knee bends and readying to start from their down-on-knuckles crouch. They steel themselves for the tremendous exertion to follow.

Then stare evileye at opponent to "uncenter," to rattle him. 1980s star Chiyonofuji (53 successive wins, 1,000+ total, top of century), aka 'Wolf,' pure muscle, handsomest yokozuna ever, half heaviest's heft, noted for stare best described in US teen term 'stink-eye.' Lovable Hawaiian Takamiyama could curdle coconut milk. This *shikiri naoshi* in bout Wolf vs. Jesse was always an Oscar-winning face-down performance of sneers. They revived it as a native art form and most everyone does it now, despite frequent reprimands from the referee.

This psychological, almost psychic, duel goes on for one brief preliminary face-down for lower ranks, gets progressively longer up-grade—limited since present generation TV, but until 1950s yokozuna might take a quarter hour to start. Medieval-costumed ref takes center stage. He raises lacquered ancient Chinese battle fan to signal end of prep time as rikishi in corners accept towel to wipe off, gather more salt. Crowd claps, tension builds. They stoop one last time, knuckles touch clay and they go at each other spontaneously. Start must be simultaneous or the ref may recall it, and a premature start before the opponent is set can result in a fine of ¥50,000 ($500). Rikishi collide head-on with speed and force that would snap a normal man's neck with whiplash. And the occasional loud "bonk" indicates a literal "head-on." Aikido Master Tohei discussing martial arts with a member of the imperial family noted that the greatest speed of action in any sport is not in aikido nor even karate, but in this sumo *tachi-ai*, starting clash. If simultaneity fails, either may pull back, or be sent back by ref, and they restart. If they really "spontane" they may both start early before the ref turns his feet outward and raises his fan up to signal "time"—in which case it is bound be a great bout.

Each bout averages 4–5 minutes at top ranks, just 2 minutes at juryo. Akebono's actual fights spring 1995 averaged 3.7 seconds, leaving the giant panting and drenched with sweat, so total was his involvement. Most of this is preparatory ceremony—sip water, toss salt in purification, stamp out bad luck with characteristic high side kick, *shiko*, to center oneself and make "centering" energy flow.

Hokusai

Sumo as box office is matched only by the annual high school baseball tournament. Unlike pro-wrestling, sumo is strictly ad-lib and legit. The highly formalized, well-scripted pageantry of its curtain-raising sees the script thrown away once the referee marks go. It is wrestling reduced to its quint-essence, all promotional hogwash and ballyhoo removed. Every bit of its medieval pageantry is harnessed to contribute to psychologically preparing audience and combatant for the contest. Centering. Studying each other as they engage in what seems to be telepathic sparring before the unsignaled, simultaneous charge and grapple.

This is what, in my opinion, sets sumo apart as a zen combat form, a true martial art. In sumo it is not the beef that forces the opponent down, it is skill and true power. In judo it is leverage and tricks. (Tohei jibed, "To defend against a judo-ka, just slip out of your shirt.") But sumo involves that mysterious power of centering, *ki,* which Mass Oyama first introduced me to before the temple gate guardian statues. With rikishi getting ready to go, there is none of the jittery, jack-in-the-box jumping around of the boxer. The rikishi seems in an almost hypnotic state, oblivious to the crowd. A meditative, zen meditative state. For those with "mind control" techniques experience, it is an alpha-generating state.

Here is where, whether watching on TV or in the dohyo, I like to play bookie, bet who will win. The rikishi who shows superior centering by doing his squats without a bounce, remaining totally still, no flinch in his stare-downs, unwavering in action or inaction—he gets my bet. Betting ¥100 a shot, in an afternoon I end up several hundred yen ahead. Never yet a net loser. It is especially accurate in juryo or lower, but quite effective and better than odds even between yokozuna.

Spontaneity is the keynote, nonevident as it may seem at first. Even, or perhaps especially, during the clinches when both opponents stand frozen, interlocked like some oriental Rodin sculpture, is the spontaneous action of a high-speed sport in subtle evidence. Not a muscle twitches. Not a movement is apparent. Yet each rikishi is constantly alert for the slightest shift of an iota of balance, for the slightest indication of an instant's relaxation on the part of the other. With no movement, there is no inertia to overcome when a move is to be made and so action is truly instantaneous. Like gunslingers facing down in a cowboy movie.

Each slaps the other's hands away from grabbing arm or belt to try to gain one of 70 listed throws, lifts and pushes. Loser is first to touch the clay of the dohyo with any part but soles of feet, or touch clay (covered with layer of dry sand the better to show footprints) beyond straw circle. Bar only closed fists (but open-hand slaps occasionally score brief knockouts), blows to privates, and eye gouging. It is all out, no holding back and full steam for several seconds or a few minutes—but no bawdy free-for-all. One UK sumo-scribe writes: "Ring decorum and sportsmanship are of the highest order, making even cricket seem somewhat rowdy by comparison."

Professional rikishi are classified by win-lose record. I have seen petite 98 kg/215 lb Mainoumi best a foe over 500 lbs. With "bellicosity" abolished, as Perry's scribe noted, and allowing one fall only—even a step out of the ring, or touching ground with anything but the sole of the foot—there is little chance for serious injury. Yet it is a wonder that rikishi are not seriously injured more often—their *gambare* philosophy will not allow even the most painful injury to show on their faces. One will hobble out under his own power even on a broken leg. Little less wonder is rarity of injury to front-row *sunakaburi*, "covered with sand" seats. But as they contend 90 times each year, plus countless jungyo matches and hours daily of all-out practice, there is a lot of bandage tape used.

Usually honest, fixes are rare—especially since rash of dives, called *yaocho*, in '60s imperiled its reputation. They weren't gambling instigated, but rikishi 'lending' win to be repaid by reciprocal fall later to keep majority of wins and avoid demotion. Konishiki seemingly took several early in his rocketing career to calm racist colleagues who can't accept success of any gook—here this includes us honkies, brother.

On rare occasion when pair grapples to stalemate, ref will call *mizu-iri*, water-taking break, to resume after next bout. I saw record in Tokyo autumn 1955 when it took 3 rounds to conclude match. '88 saw rarer three successive ties by simultaneous fall, at which ref decides. If any doubt about decision, five black-kimonoed judges in front rows may call for confab, *mono-iri*, mount dohyo—and correction of ref's call goes on his record. TV gives instant replay from various angles after each bout, and a sixth judge sits in a booth watching TV controlling tape playbacks. Equally rarely judges will call a tie, which then has to be refought. Note that ref carries in belt a short sword, very real and razor sharp—just in case he makes a bad decision and thus has to commit *seppuku*, or hara-kiri (no one has so far). Day ends about 6 P.M. with graceful longbow dance (rite shared with Persian *zur khane* grapplers).

On the last day prizes are awarded with, of course, pomp —parchments with each gigantic silver chalice or bowl. Most wins in 15 bouts gets literally a truckload of awards, from Emperor's Cup to some so obviously self-serving as to be meaningless. 'Fighting spirit' goes to fast-riser who dumps yokozuna; one for best technique, etc. Dumping a yokozuna also earns a *kin-boshi*, gold hat (simple victory is *shiro-boshi*, white hat). Top winner then gets open car parade through city, and later returns to hometown, usually a farm village or slum, like some triumphant Caesar. Only return of victorious high school baseball team from the annual Nishinomiya championships can match it in hoopla and TV coverage.

All rikishi are under contract to Sumo Association, which controls their lives.* Pay ranges from subsistence room and board in kind as initiate to Yokozuna Akebono's 1996 monthly ¥2,234,000 ($22,010) plus allowance of ¥200,000 ($2,000) per basho; lower ranks proportionate, juryo start at ¥820,000. Then ¥5,000,000 ($50,000) to basho winner (Chiyonofuji won 25x), ¥35,000 kensho for each bout won, plus private prizes awarded by supporters whose advertising banners are paraded around the ring, each worth ¥50,000 less 40% to guild. Fans may invite to parties for *orei*—Chiyo's famed autograph parties where he stamped his palm print in red seal ink on art boards and auto- graphed them earned him ¥1,000,000 ($10,000) each time.

From old woodblock print

CLOSING BOW DANCE

* If visiting Tokyo, stroll fascinating alleys of sumo district, visit Sumo Museum in Kokugikan arena when *basho*, seasonal championships are not scheduled, or visit the various *heya*, or "stables" and see live practice. Also visit a sumo restaurant for a meal of *chanko-nabé* and put on some weight. See my guidebook *Japan Inside Out*.

合気道

unite spirit way

XII. AIKIDO — LUKE: 4-28

I STARED IN UTTER DISBELIEF and all that came to mind was Luke, 4–28:

> And all they in the synagogue, when they heard these things, were filled with wrath. And rose up, and thrust him out of the city, and led him unto the brow of the hill whereon their city was built, that they might cast him down headlong. But he, passing through the midst of them, went his way....

For the burly American military policemen, when they had heard my descriptions of the tiny old man's physical prowess, were filled with disbelief, so we had come up in the elevator, and had led the old man onto the flat roof of the building whereon a gym was built, that they might cast him down. But he, passing through the midst of them, went his way, laughing.

And as in John: 10–39:

> Again they tried to arrest him, but he escaped from their hands.

The tiny old man was Old Master Ueshiba Morihei, O-Sensei, then nearly 80 years of age and with about one pound of weight to show for each year on his four-foot-ten frame. He had the thin, silken-white beard of an ancient venerable out of a Zen painting, and an incessant baby grin that was infectious. "They" were five United States military police of the 825th MP Company stationed in Tokyo and loaned to me for the demonstration. Their conglomerate weight was over 1,000 pounds. All had studied judo or karate, and for several repeat performances of the attack, had the assistance of half a dozen Japanese judo and karate black belt holders and kendo-ka armed with oak swords. No one even touched the Old Man, until he let several of them collectively grasp him in any way they wanted, then "escaped from their hands" and floored them all simultaneously. We took high-speed movies at 64 fps and made blowup prints. As I was sure they would, they showed nothing but a smiling old man moving unconcernedly amid intense, charging GIs, seemingly unaware that he existed—implying that Ueshiba was, in effect, moving in a different time continuum, an alternate reality.

A Christian missionary saw my photos and said they undoubtedly explained the minor "physical" miracle of Jesus' escapes. Old Master Ueshiba, a Shinto mystic, answered, "In learning aiki you must make yourself pure. He who was already pure intuitively knew aiki from the beginning."

Aiki has been around for centuries, perhaps millennia. Elements of it are, in a sense, combat yoga. Old Master Ueshiba had studied it for almost 70 years with a scientific thoroughness unexpected outside of an occidental research laboratory.

The key to modern judo throws is leverage. But the judo-ka uses only the primitive leverage of the bar on a fulcrum, where weight must still be countered with weight—unlike even sumo, which has no weight classifications; Ueshiba emulated the balance wheel of a watch, where the force of regulated motion balances mass. The karate-ka breaks bricks with his bare hands, not by sheer strength, but with a mental trick which overcomes the natural mental block against striking harder objects: he "aims" at the other side of the brick letting the brick get in the way of his forward motion, just as a smart boxer with a good knockout punch aims not at the chin but at the back of the head of his opponent, letting the chin just get in the way. Ueshiba uses the same projection idea in all his movements, but in circles rather than straight lines. Motion in a straight line cannot be controlled readily. Motion in a circle can be controlled and redirected by shortening the arc in a spiral, or opening it toward a tangent.

By trial and error and reason he eliminated the unnecessary.

But this was not enough. Again as if out of the Bible, "a little child led him." A good jujutsu-ka can hold his fist closed so tightly that none can open it. This trick normally

UESHIBA MORIHEI

takes years to learn. Yet, Ueshiba saw, so can any baby do it. Who can open a baby's fist? Who can bend a baby's legs to make it sit when it would lie or lie when it would sit? The jujutsu trick was evidently not a matter of learning, but of unlearning. Ueshiba had discovered the subconscious.

To an amazing degree, the development of aiki theory parallels the development of western, particularly Jungian, psychology, but while the psychiatrist attempts to push the conscious aside to reach or release the subconscious, the aiki man, in effect, brings his conscious and subconscious into rapport—calling them the mental and spiritual. He does so to a degree that seems mystical yet he completely avoids the superseriousness of other worldly mysticism, always laughs when in action. He does not retreat from the world but uses his knowledge to make life more palatable and compatible.

Aiki, like judo, jujutsu, karate, kempo and the many other oriental wrestling forms, is an art of self-defense. Unlike karate and kempo, it includes no blows. Unlike judo it really includes no grips or throws. It is often referred to by American adherents as "The Honorable Art of Getting the Hell Out of There." It has been reduced to such basic essentials of self-defense that a 'proper' aiki match between two aiki men cannot be held. One must use judo, karate, boxing or some form of armed or unarmed attack. Then the other, using aiki, simply evades. When the attacker lunges out of control past a target that's no longer there the aiki-ka takes him under control, lets him destroy himself by his own weight and momentum with the attacker's own strength or alternately pacifies him harmlessly.

It is judo, jujutsu, karate, boxing and all the rest combined reduced to the absolute quintessence ... mental strength. Then chief aiki instructor Tohei opposed over 700 pounds of huffing United States military policemen with only his upraised pinkie, simply, as he put it, "By thinking all my power into the finger." One needs no muscle in aiki. When muscle work is called for, the aiki-ka "borrows" the attacker's by causing him to use it against himself. A simple, static example was given in *Life* magazine:

"What Keeps Johnny On The Spot?"

Johnny Coulon, a gnomelike 67-year-old who was once (1909–14) world bantamweight boxing champion, has been defying anyone to lift his 109 pounds for nearly half a century. Some of the world's brawniest athletes, including a roster of heavyweight champions ... have struggled vainly to lift Coulon. The latest to try was an awesomely muscled wrestler named Dick (The Bruiser) Afflis. He lifted some of Coulon's weight but could not get his feet off the scale platform.

Coulon, who is starting on a world tour this month to exhibit his trick, maintains complete silence about how it works, but scientists say it is really no trick at all. By placing one hand lightly under the chin of the lifter, Coulon exerts a strong but subtle counterforce, putting the strong men in the impossible position of having to lift themselves by their bootstraps.

Thus *Life* magazine way back in spring of 1956.

The "scientists" are right, as far as they go, and *Life* readers may agree with the "scientists'" physics. But those thousands who undoubtedly tried it—unsuccessfully—will question *Life's* knowledge of anatomy and wonder just how they can explain a "109-pound gnome" holding the muscles of his wrist, elbow and shoulder stiff against the full muscle power of the champion Goliaths, and for an indefinite length of time without fatiguing.

210 LBS. OF M.P.
TRIES TO LIFT 86 LB.
TEENAGE AIKI-KA
—AND CAN'T BUDGE HER!

If Johnny Coulon on his world tour had stopped in Japan, it would not have been to demonstrate but to study, for Johnny's trick is no secret here. The Japanese call it aiki— strength from the unity of mind and spirit—and Johnny's trick can be taught anyone in a minute, as it was to me and my not too gnomelike 95-pound wife. Other somewhat more spectacular "tricks" take minutes, still others months and the most fantastic ones, well....

Applying aikido, I have done it myself. My tiny wife has done it with 200-pound judo third rank black belt Lindy Avakian (author of a most sensible judo book). The principle is the same as the baby uses. Relax completely and don't look at the subject, "fix your mind without fixing it anywhere," project your mind out through your arm to infinity. Use no muscle, no tension. Relax, clear your mind; think of nothing. You are not even conscious of the man who is trying to lift you. You are as the description of the yogi states "above the spatiotemporal plane." Perhaps only a millimeter or so above it, but if you're doing it right you should certainly feel above something. First thing you will become aware of is the look on the face of the man who cannot budge you.

This use of aikido sends its victims, recipients, into spasms of laughter. My pioneering karate article in *True* magazine in March, 1957 brought a mail avalanche, establishment of 17 dojos. The editors asked for more articles on Japanese martial arts. I did one on aikido, over 100 photos of burly yanks flying through ether. Everyone was laughing hysterically or grinning like an idiot. Editor said the photos were posed. ~~Rejected!~~ I asked the MPs why they laughed. "We felt so silly, helpless.... the situation seemed ridiculous, however real."

A physicist explained *Life's* photos in simple mechanics. But how do you explain this: extend an arm out straight from the shoulder. Crook it slightly at the elbow, ask anyone to try and bend it while you fix your mind out through your arm without fixing it anywhere. The would-be bender can rest your hand on his shoulder, put both hands across your elbow to wrench down with full force, with full benefit of maximum leverage. He may try until exhausted—until long after you should be exhausted were you opposing him with muscle.

What is Aiki

Man has long been aware of what tremendous feats of strength he is capable of under great emotional strain. My files tell of a Norwegian commando who leaps a wall so high he can't understand it later; a black truck driver lifts a transcontinental truck to save an underpinned fellow and is quoted in *Reader's Digest* as "A man don't know what he can do until he has to do it." Scrawny taxi driver tears a door off a burning cab, bends its steering column to free trapped driver, a small boy hauls a large adult to safety, and so on through the ages.

One clue that this strength is present in everyone is that ordinary people under hypnosis are capable of great feats of strength. Sensational is the suspension of a hypnotized person across two chairs, supported only at head and heels, while several persons stand on his midsection. Aiki-ka say anyone can do this, and I have suspended myself so, though I could not support over 100 pounds extra until I learned to 'let go.'

I tried it with my 9-year-old son and he repeatedly, even at school PTA demonstrations, held two adults, their feet off the floor. Then his classmates picked it up and all could do it, boys and girls. But while the hypnotic is in trance and under the suggestive control of an outsider, the aiki-ka is fully awake and in complete control of him- or herself.

This combination of complete control and complete physical relaxation is what really sets aiki apart. The two are interrelated so that the control is a result of the relaxation while the relaxation itself is controlled. One result is the near absence

TEACHING THE UNBENDABLE ARM

of injuries in aiki dojos, though there may be dozens of pairs of students flipping one another around simultaneously, one, two or three yards apart. Control prevents collisions; relaxation makes the occasional collision harmless, like a drunk falling downstairs. Most other martial arts bring injury in six months.

Even in combat against fantastic odds, the aiki adept has his attackers under such complete control that he can evade, throw or pin one or more without even ruffling them. He could just as easily tear them asunder, but that would be "un-aiki." As evasion is the basic technique of aiki, so is the proscription against harming another living being basic. The Old Master told me, "Your Golden Rule says turn the other cheek when someone would strike you. This is aiki except that we would turn it before being struck. Thus the attacked is saved hurt and the attacker is saved from committing sin."

So, too, the aiki-ka will not hurt another to save himself injury and the aiki 'throw' is a maneuver designed to redirect an assailant's force in a vector that leaves him helpless, but not in a position to hurt himself. And the entire defensive action is performed while smiling; the smile that the student first broaches at the foolishness of the whole situation, he soon realizes is the most potent of weapons. The ultimate follow-through of the aiki-ka is not only to make the assailant unwilling to resume the attack, but if possible, to win his friendship, the safest defense of all. The smile, with the noninjurious throw or pin will usually negate his aggressive attitude.

How? To the aiki-ka, strength is mental. The body is but a tool. "Mind moves body." If the body alone is trained, imbalance results and in old age the athlete suffers, must always "keep in trim" though his internal organs may not be able to support the necessary muscular exertion. But the body only follows the mind, thus the aiki man trains the mind, developing his nervous system to the utmost so that the muscles may be more efficiently used. The result is a body strength the aiki people call *ki,* or in English usually "life force," a name we shall have to use until western physiologists study this phenomenon and give it a more palatable "scientific" name.

The muscle athlete is strong through muscular contraction —the weight lifter, the wrestler being the best examples. The aiki man is strong through "force projection," a concept a modern dancer (who would call it "extension") or ballerina can understand and one which athletes, who realize their best performance is the product of relaxation and follow-through, should understand.

Tohei explained the unbendable arm and the unbendable pinkie—and the chair suspension above—in terms of flowing water. A fire hose is limp and easily bent when empty or even when full of still water. But turn on the flow of water and it becomes as rigid as an iron bar. So the human arm is limp and easily bent at the joints, but turn on the flow of "life force" and it also becomes like iron.

To suspend oneself across chairs, lie on floor near properly spaced chairs, arms by sides, stretch body, relax and project the "flow of water" simultaneously through toes and tip of head the way you projected through fingertips for unbendable arm. Have two companions lift you by feet and back of neck and place your heels or calves and head on chairs. Maintain extension. Maintain your cool. Ignore person who straddles you and sits on you. Think about him and you collapse.

To suspend a child, do as above. Then stroke the child's arms from top to bottom encouraging projection or flow of ki and total relaxation—key to "gentle" strength. Then straddle with extreme care and slowly shift weight from feet to seat. Repeat as people are added. We have commonly 'horsebacked' four adults on a seven- or eight-year-old for several minutes.

To suspend self alone, sit down between chairs, rest your head on one chair, your heels on the other, lay hands by sides, then stiffen body by heaving hips up till you are horizontal. Project ki through toes and scalp.

If this description of aiki sounds somewhat sexy, it may be that here is a hint. The male rigidity is a hydraulic action, with blood the fluid. The basic aiki drills are to improve the blood circulation in the extremities, as we shall see. Photos of an aiki ace, such as Tohei or Ueshiba's son, Kisshomaru, reveal expansions in the arm and leg that seem from their location not to come from muscle but from the blood vessels. A half hour or so of aiki drill leaves one with a peculiar, yet somehow familiar, afterglow. It is nothing like the pleasant fatigue which follows normal exercise, for there is no fatigue at all, but energy.

It is an elation, a mental alertness, a sensual awakening. The closest thing to it, indeed almost the identical feeling, is that of being in love, and satisfactorily so. The aiki techniques, which are those all oriental artists search out in various methods—Hemingway called it "getting the juice to flow"—also work most satisfactorily in bed. Oriental cults have been built upon this simple discovery. But overspecialization destroys. The aiki techniques teach the adept to be able to "project" his "life force" into any part of the body. (In Chinese, *aiki* means a great sexual liaison.) Then one develops the ability to spread it out over the body in a complete circle, then circle this circle into a sphere, which increases the strength in any particular part. The successful aiki-ka is an all-around man (or woman). Concentrating too heavily on one's tool, whether it be the artist's brush, the love-cultist's bed or the warrior's bushido insanity, is self-defeating, the very error I, as so many novices, was warned about at the very beginning.

Korin Turley of the 825th Military Police Company, United States Army Japan, learned just how concentrated Tohei could project his aiki strength. Tohei, completely relaxed and even laughing, held Turley back with his upraised little finger, though Turley pushed against it with both forearms with all his power. Then Jack Bogan backed up Arthur H. St. Cyr backing up Korin Turley as almost 700 pounds of trained fighting muscle of United States military policemen got nowhere against the upraised pinkie of aiki instructor Tohei.

Finally, they all rapidly advanced backwards to a sitting position at the flick of Tohei's pinkie. All the men tried this several times and vouch that Tohei touched them only with his little finger which was always vertical. Never once did he use another finger or even allow the base of the little finger to touch them.

Master Tohei sat on the padded rush mats, balanced on his rump, feet lifted from contact with the floor, and invited Jack Bogan to try and tip him over by pushing against his head or shoulders. Even when Jack got the knack of keeping his feet from slipping backward on the mats, he couldn't budge Tohei. "He's immovable," he admitted. So Korin Turley lent a hand pushing Jack who was pushing Tohei. The two got nowhere together until Tohei demonstrated his total control over the situation, and flicked them off. Tohei felt he had an unfair advantage over the Yanks, being used to sitting on the floor as old-style Japanese do in their homes. So he sat on a wobbly four-legged stool that had never seen but three legs at a time touch the floor, lifted his feet off the floor and invited all the MPs to push—again to no avail.

The aiki-ka says he is getting in tune with the universe. And being in tune with all, one is in tune with any part—bed, brush or bushido—at any time. The part and the whole are inseparable. To learn, or better said, to experience one's part in the order of creation is to learn that there is this universal order. You are a hologram of the universe.

Aiki differs from the other budo sports in going beyond them; the others are governed by rules, but aiki is governed only by a recognition of natural order in which there are no simple rules. Skip the philosophy except to say this parallels and substantiates our scientific ideas—Euclidean geometry we learned in school works in school and in the limited experience of most of us, but not in the great reaches of the cosmos. For the sportsman or the person concerned with self-defense, this recognizes that the arbitrary rules of sports don't hold in fighting, where there are no rules, where anything that gets results goes.

There may be no rules, but there are attitudes one must develop. In case of attack (or competition or living or loving), regardless of the number of opponents or size of the problem, one must have no fear. This we have said. But one must

TAKING O-SENSEI FROM BEHIND

equally avoid any feeling about, any concern for winning. Guard the mind and body from the opponent by maintaining complete and constant motion, or 'charge' as the Chinese prefer to call it. There is an aiki term, "*kyu-ten*"—the ever-changingness of the rolling ball. If you fear something, your mind freezes on that problem, motion is stopped and you are defeated. If you fix your mind on victory, your motion is equally stopped. Let it float, allow your mind to float, ignoring the problem of fear or confidence. Fear, a healthy fear, acts as a stimulant. But we are going beyond this. Actually, I have found that a healthy fear, or respect for the problem faced, stimulates this attitude of mental floating—not to be confused with the floating feeling of faintheartedness. We want detachment, not just resignation.

Fundamentals: Emptying the Head

In any sort of practical interpretation of the early Zen philosophies, all motion moves in circles. To the Taoist all motion is circular. The aiki principle is that "life force," ki, moves in circles—not in closed or limited circles but in circles strung toward infinity where only a fraction of a second of arc may be directly involved or in a circle so small as to be almost the circumference of a point. No motion is closed, no matter how small the circle. All motion strives toward infinity; all motion is a circle—sounds more like Einstein's curving

217

MIND MOVES BODY

finite infinity than an instruction for mayhem. The simplest way to approach the fact that energy moves in a circle: all lines of energy join at infinity.

Any combative or competitive contact can be charted in two circles or more—that of the attacker, or one for each attacker, and one for the defense. On contact, these should be led to become concentric circles, with your sphere of action the innermost circle. Once you control this, the opponent must be pulled into your pace, into your orbit. As he is moving in a larger circle, he must then be made to move faster than you, giving you the simple physical advantage of centrifugal force. If you work in a radius of one foot, make the opponent move in a three-foot radius.

It is impossible for him, even if he is another aiki man, to control his mind and body and sphere of action against such geometric odds. Any attack he attempts against your smaller circle, or sphere as it is in all dimensions, must throw him off balance. This presents you with an opening, the Japanese call it "*suki*."

When attacked then, you must instantaneously compute your attacker's directional arc—or to use an air force term you may better savvy, his pursuit curve. When an aiki-ka goes into a fight, it's very much like your western cowboy. Your hands hang as if ready to draw invisible six-guns; this is *shizen-tai*, natural pose. You are completely unarmed, but you are ready. As various Zen philosophers have admonished —ready, but never to attack. Romantic ideal in actuality, and

theory realized. You then move enough to evade, moving aside his projected collision point so that his pursuit curve meets your circle in a tangent. You then redirect his path—if you are inside his curve, by shortening his arc and flipping him. But better yet, if you have stepped outside his curve so that he meets you as in a backhand, you redirect him into your circle so that he describes a long "S." And in this motion, the results are to him most disastrous.

In either event, the attacker is in the position of a coin which has been flipped against the rim of a spinning platter. The aiki-ka in such a situation can then redirect the attacker's motion anywhere at will and I have seen a 200 pounder throw a punch point-blank at an aiki man half his weight, only to have the aiki-ka step aside, place his little finger on the attacker's wrist and proceed to spin and flip him like a human yo-yo.

The aiki-ka is forbidden to use lineal motion, as most Japanese karate-ka do. (Oyama in the first years I knew him rediscovered the ancient Chinese concepts and worked his karate drills in circles, which is why his school broke away from the Cat's Go-ju-ryu lineal school—but Mass seemed to abandon this with "full contact" matches.) Tremendous power can be generated by this linear "drive," but used against circular motion it is self-destroying. In bodybuilding, this linear development leads to muscle-boundedness, or in such as karate, scarification. But circular motion is almost always misunderstood even in the Orient: it leads to that indirectness and the evading of problems and responsibilities that is the illness of modern Asia.

In developing the mind's awareness of its own body, the aiki man concurrently develops almost superhuman senses of observation. Prominent among these are full 165–180 degree vision and subliminal hearing. This ability to hear sounds below the audible range of sensitivity is frequently observed in hypnotic subjects and is, of course, the "secret" in most mathematical horse and dog acts.

The Old Master bare-handed fended arrows fired at him point-blank. In an early episode of the TV series *Kung Fu*, hero David Carradine was attacked by American Indians and emulated O-Sensei to perform this feat. Steven Seagal, when teaching aikido at my son's high school in Kobe, Japan, in his pre-Hollywood days, put on a demonstration of this for the PTA with me as archer at 15 yards on a Japanese longbow. Steve was worried about the speed of the arrow, so had me use a lighter bow—a physicist Steve is not.

Old Master demonstrated his ability to evade bullets fired point-blank at him by a marksman. He could disarm a pistol toter from fifty yards away though the pistol be aimed directly at him from the beginning. I have seen Tohei repeatedly disarm Frank Goody, second degree black belt in judo and yawara (warrior jujutsu), ex-Marine hand-to-hand instructor and crack shot Denver policeman from 18 feet, three mat-lengths. Goody claims he tried several hundred times over a period of a few weeks to get Tohei, and admits he could rarely even get a shot off before Tohei painlessly pinned him with his own pistol … and that shot always went where Tohei wasn't any longer.

A knife held against Tohei's throat will be across the assailant's throat before he can scream "aiki!" "Of course," said Tohei, "it is unnecessary, really, to demonstrate this as no one with a knife could ever get this close to an aiki adept.".

During World War II Ueshiba O-Sensei demonstrated evading bullets fired by riflemen. The generals were elated. "Teach this to all our soldiers and we will be invincible." Ueshiba shrugged them off. "I could see the gunner's eyes. But there is no defense against the random." And he disappeared into the mountains for the duration.

Military policeman St. Cyr claimed that no human being could possibly get out of his armlock. Jack Bogan and Korin Turley couldn't do anything against it, despite their military police judo training. But for Tohei it was "as simple as slipping out of my kimono."

Police throughout the world consider a foolproof frisk is to have the suspect lean against the wall as close to a 45-degree angle as possible, balanced on his fingertips, feet spread apart. The frisking policeman stands with one foot inside the suspect's in order to trip him up should he try to move. If there are two officers, one stands the other side and to the rear covering the suspect with his gun. Denver police officer Frank Goody tried this frisk on Tohei many times, always unsuccessfully. I had two United States military police try it, photographed their fourth attempt. The frisking officer held his left hand on Tohei's spine to feel for any telegraphing muscle movements, which he said he never felt. On every attempt, Tohei moved inside using the frisker for a shield against the covering officer before either knew what was happening. Both men said they could have done absolutely nothing except possibly shoot one another.

This move has been taught in aikido classes for the past 30-odd years, as introduced in the original edition of this book. Alas, in the TV police series *Hooker,* it is shown being taught, successfully, to convicts in jail. Practicing aikido forms alone is not an automatic formula for making a good guy.

The MPs exhausted their full repertoire of "foolproof" police grips, restraints and arrests.

The Westerner who starts aiki instruction—and many have —usually realizes these latent powers and abilities within the first half hour of practice. I recall my own first lesson. I stood there completely relaxed, gazing outward, while Tohei heaved and pushed against my hand or body to try, unsuccessfully, to budge me. I think I spent the next half hour on the floor in hysterics, laughing at how easy it all is and at myself for not having caught on to it all long, long ago.

Here is the saving grace of aiki, the thing that keeps it from degenerating to a mumbo jumbo. The ultraserious pseudomystic rarely has any way of differentiating his real advancement from pure hallucination. His body meanwhile degenerates. The Buddha warned against this.

The aiki man has checks: if his mental development is off balance even the slightest, he ends up on the mat. As he develops, he can see it in the parallel development of physical impregnability and personality improvement, visible tricks he can perform become more amazing. He does not dissolve into an antisocial freak, but enjoys both an above average social and physical health.

And somewhere along the line, he discovers what the Western psychologist calls the unconscious, and beyond, what Jung called "living spirit." Tohei calls it in his simple but efficient English, "the world spirit, the life spirit." And when one can begin to bring this into rapport with his now blended conscious-subconscious, his strength approaches the infinite.

These discoveries are not exclusively Ueshiba's, as their parallels to western discoveries indicate they are not exclusively the Orient's. There have been many masters like Ueshiba in the history of Japan, Korea and China. But past masters have kept their discoveries secret either passing them on to one or two disciples with their resultant subsequent degeneration into magic cult, or taking them to the grave with them. Any science, any knowledge, must degenerate under a restrictive, exclusive security system, and so has aiki, under whatever name its past masters may have called it.

Ueshiba differed from the ancient venerables in that he realized this, as he realized that he had only scratched the surface in his researches. What he learned may help the biblical scholar understand such things as the physical miracles of Jesus as in the previously mentioned Luke and John selections. They may help the dancer understand the enigmatic pronouncement of Nijinsky when he tried to explain his marvelous leaping ability, "I just leap up there and pause a while," and lead to the development of more, modern Nijinskys.

What could athletes do with concurrent aiki training? Not only might more records fall but the general level of athletic performance could be raised (as we will see home run king Oh Sadaharu and sumo great Takamiyama did, on page 263) and, most important, the degenerative diseases of athletes might be conquered.

Psychologists have discovered that hypnotic subjects evince no fatigue when put to physical tests: and aiki has shown that this condition can be fully duplicated in the conscious state. Aiki is so ridiculously simple that the bugaboo which physical exercise—even setting-up exercises or golf—hold out to the common deskbound modern should be easily sidestepped.

And it should open up as much a new vista to the mystic who has run out of yoga postures as to the dynamic tension addict who has had enough tension and wants more dynamism. Just as it should present a new road of research for the psychologist or the Jungian soul searcher.

Aiki is not only effective, it is easy, fun and mentally stimulating. At 85, Ueshiba still had the verve of a teenager, the active mind of a devoted scholar. He was always laughing too, but probably at mankind in general for not having caught on long ago.

In the Dojo

My favorite Japanese sport cartoon (mentioned earlier) shows a judo white belt novice being flipped about by a suave black belter. In the second frame he bows and asks the black belter to swap belts for a few minutes. Then the white belter in the borrowed black belt flips the real black belter around.

The advantage of the aiki costume is that you can't easily tell just who has a black belt and who hasn't. The blouse is the standard judo or karate blouse, the bottom is the usual judo-karate pajamalike pants with over this the traditional floor-length divided skirt as worn by kendo-kas and some archers. I brought my kendo/kyudo outfit, wearing the skirt in the same way over the blouse to cover the belt. Most of the students in the main aiki dojo in Tokyo hold black belts in at least one other sport—and are permitted to wear them if they wish, though many other gyms prefer, even insist, you do not. My partner one day might be a novice like myself; the next day I'd draw a Kodokan fourth ranker. It didn't make any difference. Aiki works for or against anyone.

For non-Japanese, the Tokyo main, *hon*-dojo was then especially ideal as two of the best teachers spoke English, Tohei and Tamura, a junior instructor who it was obvious might someday be another Tohei, or even a Ueshiba (he subsequently moved to France). The advantage of this was more than merely linguistic. Tohei is a man of this age, of modern westernized culture. Old master Ueshiba was of the ancient oriental tradition who had done a good job of coming to terms with the new world, but he was old style and communication was difficult between such as Ueshiba and fully western Americans with little knowledge of the different way of thinking of the Orient. Tohei bridges the language gap. More important, he bridges the gap between old East and new East-West. Tohei has since opened his own school.

The first thing the new student in the dojo is taught is the unbendable arm trick. Often, it is taught to the casual visitor who soon thereafter becomes a student.

The second thing we were shown—I say we, for first I was pinned by this method, then my minuscule 145 cm/4'10" wife held policeman Frank Goody glued to the mats. Frank lay down flat on his back. My wife then kneeled down, her knees just about at his waist and lower part of his rib cage.

Then she looked straight ahead, focusing no place in particular. "Look off to infinity," Tohei told her. Relaxed, she assumed the unbendable arm with both arms, gently placing the knife edge of her hands on Frank Goody's midriff and chest. Frank was then invited to get up. He couldn't, no matter what he did. Oddly, he could move either of my wife's restraining hands with only a light push, but doing so seemed to send all that hand's former power into the other, so that he was still pinned. He heaved, tried to arch his back, roll over, snake out—but it was futile. As absurd as the whole affair sounds, so absurd does it look. Even more absurd does it feel to the man on the bottom. And equally mystifying to the one on top.

Then the student is started on basic drills. These are outlined below, based on private instruction from Tohei, diagrams he drew for me in my sketchbook, and diagrams of my own. You can try the drills for yourself.

The illustrations are based on several hundred still photos taken of Tohei (who subsequently started his own school) and the old master's son, Ueshiba Kisshomaru (who now heads the *honbu*) as well as junior instructors and fellow students. Over 100 feet of 16 mm movie was shot at 64 frames per second (slow-motion speed) of the old master evading attackers. Prizewinning cameraman Kawai Takeshi shot from atop the roof door with a 16 mm newsreel camera,

OLD MASTER UESHIBA BOWS TO HIS ATTACKER
Nine successive 16 mm frames shot at 64 fps
Elapsed time under 1/7th of one second

while I got close in on foot with a handheld Keystone-16. This may not sound like much, but none of these maneuvers took more than a few seconds each. Copies of this film have been generously distributed among aiki-ka, and I am pleased that a scene of O-Sensei with the APs appears in Pranin's Aiki News video series on O-Sensei vol 2, *Takemusu Aiki*.

Without the wholehearted cooperation of the dojo, this section would have been impossible. I hope I manage to communicate a difficult concept—difficult because so simple. I describe the physical, leave esoterica to John Stevens' books.

Let's Dance

As in all forms of zen combat, the basic training in aiki consists of a series of dance routines. As in judo or karate, these basic dance steps are all utilized later as basic defense maneuvers. Keep in mind the old admonition "… when drilling by rote, *allow* the mind to wander (to *force* it to do so results not in passive inaction, but active exile), to think elsewhere."

The student is shown which dance routines to react with to various basic situations. We drill in them until they become second nature, so that reaction in an actual defense situation will be spontaneous and instantaneous. But in aiki these are more than mere formula responses-cum-calisthenics. Each aiki form is a technique for training us in the control of the ki, that illusive, elusive, indefinable fluid force.

They are graduated in intensity and should be done in fixed order as warm-up. When done under direction in the dojo, the entire series takes between 20 and 30 minutes. More experienced adepts are assumed to have their ki in tune, "turned on," most or all of the time and so do not need much warm-up. This does not concern such as you or myself.

In all exercises two attitudes must be scrupulously maintained. First is the unbendable arm. Second is the point of reference, the axis which in meditation we projected our concentration upon and which in movement we must at all times revolve upon. This is called in Japanese "*seika no itten,*" which Tohei translates as "one point." I prefer "inner point." If either of these attitudes is interfered with or allowed to stray while doing an aiki exercise, or when using aiki in life, the result will be negative.

226

The Limbered Wrist

The first three drills are basically for wrist toning. They are the only ones which can be done anywhere, even while sitting in the subway. The first two must be mastered both for defensive and counteroffensive use. They are pain holds which no one can withstand, yet which will do no lasting harm. Though they can be done seated, or even flat on the back, let's begin them as in the dojo. Assume a comfortable stance, the fudo or immovable stance of karate, feet comfortably apart in a parade rest. Relax thoroughly, shoulders back and down. Take a breath drill.

Raise both hands, bent at the elbow, in front of you as if in prayer or as if to clasp hands. Before your palms touch, droop your left hand at the wrist, grasp it by its back with the right hand; right palm on left backhand, right middle finger and thumb loosely around base just above wrist. The forefinger is not important for grasping—but main contact being right heel against left forefinger knuckle. Now, on steady exhale, press right hand against left, main pressure right heel against left forefinger knuckle, pushing left fingers toward left elbow. At same time both elbows should be drawn in toward each other. This will be very painful at first; good. Do it five times to left hand, then reverse and do five times to right hand, each single bend should be accompanied by an exhale huff, followed by relaxation with an inhale.

When you properly balance the flow of ki through the hose that is your attacked arm, the pain will be brought under control. But even at best, this takes weeks as the muscles in the back of the forearm, which tighten under modern age laziness, must first be reconditioned, relaxed. You will tend to flinch against the pain. Try to control the flinch by directing it back inward at your inner point. Don't look at the exercise, but gaze or stare blankly, detachedly ahead toward an imagined or imaginary-projected infinity. Do left hand five times, then right, then left and right again and perhaps a third set—but no more. This develops typical aiki-ka 'Popeye' forearm.

In defense, use this grasp against an attacker grabbing your lapel or collar.

Place hands toward prayer position again, but twist left wrist inward so that it is upright but reversed, with back of hand facing right palm. Place right thumb butt against back of left hand at point just below knuckle and between middle and ring finger knuckles. Four fingers of right hand circle left palm below the thumb, grasping left palm on thumb mount, the palmist's Mount of Venus. Now press with right thumb to pressure left fingers toward left elbow, again as before bringing both elbows down and slightly toward each other to counter their tendency to rise apart. Actual movement must see the left hand remaining vertical, while moving straight downward describing a dissection of the torso; the angle between left palm and left forearm being painfully reduced by a lowering of the left forearm. Stop when left wrist approaches navel. Inhale and return to first position and do it again on a huff exhale. As with first exercise, do five times to each hand for two or three sets. Watch your shoulders, which must remain neutral and relaxed; don't allow them to hunch up. Don't allow yourself to switch breathing over to

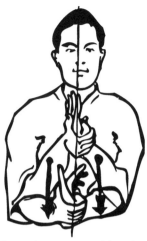

an inhale on the action, a natural but incorrect painkilling reaction. When your muscles are toned and you have learned to keep the ki flowing through the hoselike forearm, pain will fade. This grip is the basic aiki throw.

Now drop your arms. Concentrate your ki through your fingertips and shake the hands and loose fingers from the wrists—being careful to keep looking detachedly ahead. Shake violently as if you have gum stuck to your fingerprints and want to shake it off. Don't allow the hands to give in to tendency to ride up, to rise toward your shoulders. If this happens, it means your ki is not flowing and you are just flopping your hands like grounded, dying fish. For the first few times you will feel strain behind your shoulder blade; good. Do this for thirty seconds or so, with regular but deep breathing during the process. Do anything you wish, or may be used to doing now, to limber your fingers or wrists.

You will feel an afterglow in your hands. They will be invigoratingly warm, radiating an inner heat. They will feel alive as never before. Try this in dead of winter and then handle snow or ice bare-handed. You have successfully learned the technique Tibetan ascetics use for surviving in the Himalayas in the winter, unclothed. This is the first step in learning to generate this "inner heat." At the aiki dojo in Tokyo, students during *kan-geiko*, midwinter drill, quite literally warm up with aiki drills and then go out half-naked to squat in the snow; take ice-cold showers with the windows wide open in below freezing temperatures and are not even aware of the cold. I have done it, in my first week of drill. I am no comic book back-cover he-man (I confess to looking far more like the "before" of those famed advertisements). Most of my fellow students were collegians, doctors, artists, professional folks—no strength faddists.

When your wrists are properly toned by these exercises, you can show up your muscle-bound he-man pals at parties when they start doing competition push-ups. Hand your glass to your girlfriend. Assume a push-up position flat on the floor. But don't place your palms down, place the backs of your hands down, palms up, fingers pointing outward. Now do push-ups, easily as many this way as you can do from the normal position. Ask a fullback friend who can normally do a hundred push-ups to try five this way. Bet him the use of his convertible that he can't even do one—no, don't bet him, for betting on sure things is "un-aiki," unsportsmanlike.

The following aiki exercises should be done only in an unencumbered area, preferably a gym or dojo.

Mowing the Lawn

To develop the ability to keep one's ki "turned on" while moving, Master Ueshiba developed the rowing exercise. This one is easily understood by Japanese as it mimics the peculiar sculling used by Japanese fishermen. I can't think of any occidental work motion to match it exactly, the closest is mowing the lawn, but then we walk forward.

The reference to rowing does fit the wrist action of a western shell oarsman in his 90-degree twirling of his oar blade so that it is vertical to the water plane on the pull, and streamlined horizontal to cut through the air on the return except that in aiki there is no pullback just a neutral return. The idea that one is rowing a long oar also simulates the projection of your effort (the flow of ki) to a working point well beyond your physical body, lowering center of gravity. The hip and leg action is that of a western fencer as used in the short lunge, in which the feet remain planted.

ROWING THE BOAT, OR MOWING THE LAWN

Stance is as western boxer or fencer, except that the exercise is done in two ways, a left-foot-forward lead, and a right-foot-forward lead. The left-foot-forward is basic as it is used more in defense in working against a right-hand attack. We describe it, though exercise should be duplicated with right-foot lead.

Take short step forward with left foot, turning right foot to comfortable 90-degree angle. Weight is on right leg which is naturally bent at knee. Hands are loose fists (as if holding an egg in each) at your hip points, thumbs in, elbows back.

Your ki is centered in your inner point, charged but not flowing, like a faucet with the water straining against its sealing washers waiting to be allowed to flow out the limp hoses which are your arms and legs and around the now limp but closed-hose circuit within your hips. Now turn on the ki by thrusting your hips forward so as to move axis of body over the left leg, which now bends. The trunk remains vertical (do not let it tip forward), the right or rear leg straightens naturally, the arms, no longer limp, come forward. The wrists are bent, knuckles down, having revolved 90 degrees as in rowing. They are now as if choking off the ends of the arm hoses so that the pressure of the flow of ki maintains them as illustrated.

Next count in this one-two, one-two drill is a swing back to the original position on inhale. This time fists bending back against their wrists. Action is centered in the hip swinging back, not the shoulders or arms, which merely follow hips. Surge forward again on exhale then back in "one-two, one-two."

Have partner test your ki extension. At out position have him pause, then push against back of your hands, his force exerted up your arm against your shoulder (illustrated as black hand). You should be immovable, and unconscious of his effort. He should be able to push against your hips from behind (black figure) with similar futility. In return position he should be able to push against your shoulders. This does not take weeks of training, but should be attained on the first day if you understand the idea of projection.

When you have the rhythm and can do it leading with either foot, on every tenth count (fifth return) skip shift so that your feet reverse their positions and leads.

The High Parry

Take fencing stance on a left-foot lead. Again this exercise is done with alternate leads, but as it is important as a parry against high or overhead blows and most attacks will be right-handed, the left-foot lead is basic. Inhale, deep. Hands are loosely open, fingers relaxed and extended, at hips. On count, hips surge forward as in previous exercise. Arms, with ki flowing through them, surge forward and up, fingers surging straight. As in karate hand-sword the main line of power is up the little finger edge of the palm. This power surge will run up the underside, which here is the outer edge, of the arm to the pinkie. Hands raise to eye level, elbows naturally slightly bent in the natural circular surge of force. Your eyes are gazing detachedly off to infinity, your breathing is with pit of the stomach, but lightly, as a baby's.

In the dojo in Tokyo I was only dimly aware of Tohei or young Tamura standing in front of me, exerting their full muscular weight against my wrists, leaning their full weight upon me. There was no feeling of their doing so, just this strange, unreal vision of their presence. I fell prey to the common reaction of the novitiate in this situation, and smiled, inwardly as well as facially. One time I lost composure (not that I was required to maintain any) and started to laugh heavily, heartily, suddenly aware that I was literally doing a belly laugh, my lower abdomen, even my groin, vibrating. I became self-conscious of it and reacted. My belly-centrism was lost, my ki dissipated, and Tamura's head, until then

HIGH PARRY

leaning against the base of my palm edges, came crashing forward at my face.

Do this act with either leg, then skip change on the return of the hands to the neutral hip position every fifth set.

When you have the balance of the one-two rhythm, reverse direction, as preparing to meet a second attacker coming from the rear. The two count, the return, becomes a complex maneuver, but one which must be done spontaneously as one smooth action. As you return to the ready position, pivot your hip 180 degrees right, on the balls of both feet which pivot only 90 degrees. This places you facing rear, leading with the right foot. On count three surge forward as on one, with return on count four a simultaneous pivot left to return you to original position, on a left-foot lead. On the pivot you will also have to switch the bend of the legs so that the rear leg is always bent on the ready position, and the trunk is always positioned above it.

Against overhead club, hips surge forward as in above. Arms, or single arm, with ki flowing, surge forward and up, fingers surging straight. As in karate hand-sword the main line of power is up little finger edge of the palm. This power surge will run up the underside, which here is the outer edge of the arm to the pinkie. Hands raise to eye level, elbows naturally slightly bent in the natural circular surge of force.

233

Skip Advance

The skipping one step advance to develop footwork and mobility is common to western fencing and kendo as well. Work the reverse as above, but on the extension take a skipping step forward with the lead foot, following with the rear. The timing of the advance must be to start the forward foot advancing as the hands rise from the hips, and to have completed bringing the rear foot in by the time the hands reach eye level. A natural advance timing, as in a fencing lunge. On the return, as hands drop, skip back with rear foot and follow.

Dance of Eight Directions

The Dance of the Eight Directions can be started when this advance and reverse are coupled smoothly. Here again is the old mystic octagon—the semantics of these arts in ancient times was mystic. It may be today as well but, to the pragmatic Yankee, eight directions is just a good all-around coverage and, in a practical test of the art, that definition will suffice. If you can handle the eight angles, you can handle any. In terms of defense, five or six is the optimum number of attackers that can move in at any one time. If there are more, the advantage is yours because they will get in each others' way, as the dozen MPs and judoists we sicked on old master Ueshiba found out.

The dance is the advance and recover described above and a 180-degree reverse (footwork is a 90-degree pivot) onto a right-foot lead. Advance and recover. Now, weight on left foot (rear foot), gently shift weight to forward foot, simultaneously pivoting body on right knee 90 degrees left and sliding left foot, without changing its direction, forward at a 45-degree angle so that you are now facing 90 degrees left in a left-foot lead. Advance and recover, do a 180-degree reverse onto a right-foot lead, advance and recover. Now again from the right-foot lead, change direction by 45 degrees to the left onto a left foot lead, which requires a slight pivot on the right foot. Advance and recover and reverse 180 degrees, advance and recover and from right-foot lead again work a

234

DANCE OF THE EIGHT DIRECTIONS

90-degree left changeover onto a left-foot lead. Advance, recover, reverse and you have moved into your eighth direction for final advance and recover. You are not facing the original direction, but are 135 degrees off to the right, at an hour hand position of 4:30, if position one were noon. You would have to go through this entire routine eight times, or 64 positions, to return to noon. You can vary it by practicing half and full right faces from a left-foot lead and quick lead foot reverses to turn against the lead foot.

This is not an easy set of maneuvers and must be done slowly at first. Steadily increase your rate, pausing to be tested. It is pleasant to watch a good aiki-ka do it, a pleasure to watch a good instructor like Tamura. And if Kisshomaru or Tohei run through it, it is a dizzying dance. But old master Ueshiba seemed almost transparent, churning himself into butter—or perhaps into chi's.

The Wrist Break

The wrist break is a reverse, used in defense when a person grabs your right wrist with his left hand, or your left with his right. Start with the left, which is most natural, most attackers being right-handed. Hold left arm out forward, raised at 45-

235

THE WRIST BREAK

degree angle, turn palm down and bend wrist, turning on the ki to flow down the arm, stepping forward to place left foot under left wrist, right foot at 90-degree angle and bearing the weight. At this position, testing pressure exerted against bent wrist up arm should find you immovable. Now move, surging hips forward toward left hand. Weight moves forward to left foot on which you now wheel clockwise bringing right foot around back so that you face in opposite direction with left arm forward but bent wrist pointing fingers skyward.

Your ki should surge through your arm. In a defensive application you would continue to raise your left arm, allowing fingers to follow the line projected in a curve from them up and back in a curve at arm's length across your face just above eye level and on down, pivoting your body to follow the arm so that your weight again shifts to the right foot and you have again turned 180 degrees and are now facing your original direction but two steps advanced. You can continue the smooth flow of motion by stepping out with your left foot and walking away from a thoroughly confused attacker, or take another right wheel and be right behind him, continuing your flow of ki to use it in a counterattack.

In drill, however, you will pause in the finger-up position. Have companion grasp wrist from rear and attempt to tug it back; it is immovable. Point fingers down again and have him grab your wrist as an attacker, repeating the procedure

 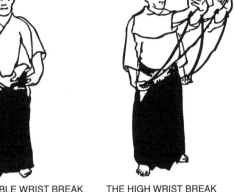

THE DOUBLE WRIST BREAK   THE HIGH WRIST BREAK

of above. Do five times or so till footwork is light, then try with right hand. Regardless of how strong your opponent is, if your ki is flowing, he cannot hold you. When I was at the aiki dojo my partner was often Lindy Avakian, who had about 6 inches in height and at least 50 pounds weight on me, as well as a judo black belt of good rank and a background as a football player and college coach. None of it helped him any.

Double Wrist Break

This double wrist break is used when an opponent seizes both your wrists. Drill it out, and when your companion has tested you out, have him grab your wrists and go through it. Stand in immovable stance, hands hanging in front of your hips.

Turn the wrists so that fingers are pointed at each other. Turn on the ki. On huff exhale swing hands, allowing them to move from shoulders, so that they pass each other, one forward of the other, and cease action with wrists crossed. Repeat this the usual five times, each cross on a huff, return on inhale, first with one hand forward, then with the other. Test is to have companion place his hands, palms up, under your knuckles and attempt to heave up against your arms. You must be immovable.

High Wrist Break

This wrist break is a high variation on the previous maneuver, your fingers are pointed 45 degrees forward. When your hands swing, they will follow the line of projection forward and up, wrists crossing at shoulder level, directly in front of you, arms almost fully extended from shoulder to wrists except for a natural bending at the elbow. Again repeat five times leading with each hand. Your companion can test you by pushing directly at your wrists in the direction of your forehead, as illustrated.

In both of the previous movements, your trunk should not react in any way, should not move in the slightest when your hands bring your arms forward. The hands should operate completely independent of the torso, as two flexible hoses hanging out of a cast-iron hydrant.

THE
LATERAL
SWING

Lateral Swing

The lateral swing is one of the most unnatural movements, requiring as it does a bodily lean yet with an erect trunk. Take the position illustrated, hands out to left, palms up. Bend left knee, keeping right straight. Your hip must swing left, and the trunk remain vertical. If it leans, you are lost. Have a companion push from side against your hips in the

238

direction your hands are pointing. You feel a strain on the underside of the arms, especially midway between shoulder and elbow, your mind is drawn to this area. Your companion cannot raise your arms. Return to start position, test arms again by attempting to lift. Shift arms to point to other side and swing over bending right leg, as above.

Forearm Swing

The forearm swing is the beginning of the whirling dervish dance of evasion which more than anything else sets aiki off from the other defense forms. As the rolling stone gathers no moss, the rolling defense allows no attackers to gather. Assume the immovable stance. Hold hands relaxed, open flat, palms down at navel level. Swing them flat out in a full arc, at same level, first to left, then to right. Ki will flow out the fingers, as if you were sprinkling the lawn with it. One arm will curve

THE
FOREARM
SWING

well to the back, straightening the elbow. The other arm will cross the body, its thumb stopping against the opposite side, between the ribs and hip. In reaction the hip will recoil—right when hands swing left, left when hands swing right. This is important as a defense maneuver, as Tohei showed when the MPs charged him with bayonet, or held a knife against his belly. The hip reaction will be such that the torso will revolve around an imaginary pivot point just forward of the navel.

239

Thus a weapon held against the navel will be found to be pointed at empty air across the front of the now turned-aside stomach. Were the attacker to lunge as you perform this maneuver, he would lunge through empty air and destroy himself.

If, say, he were holding a gun at contact range in his right hand, you would swing your arms right, your hip would recoil to your left, outside his gun angle (never work within his attack angle as you move into range of his other hand and within his sphere of action). Your left hand in swinging at your right hip could then slap his weapon aside or grab it, getting the basic pain hold, fingers over the mount of his thumb, thumb against the back of his hand.

Then lead him forward along his own line of projection, redirecting it up and back to bend his weapon hand back on him. Or merely slap it aside and continue your own projection of ki in the full dance maneuver described below. In the dojo we practiced this standing slap aside having a companion throw successive left and right jabs at our solar plexus.

But first, to test this action in the dojo, have companion try to push you toward the side to which your hands have swung. As you swing hands from right side position to left, step forward with right foot, but allow it to follow the arc of the arms left, planting it down directly in front of your navel. In one smooth, flowing action, shift weight to right foot and pivot counterclockwise on it, swinging left foot around in same arc. You end up facing opposite direction and hands have described 359 degrees of arc. Repeat action, swinging arms right, left foot forward, pivot on left, right foot back.

This whole movement should flow as a single count. Repeat it, speeding the tempo, leaping forward, backward or at angles. You should make no foot slap, but move in total silence. Forget the sense of vision, of sight, your sole sense is the pouring forth of ki from your fingertips, spraying the whole room. A fullback could throw a flying tackle at you and he would bounce off like a drop of rainwater falling against a flywheel. I have seen two aiki students, indeed I have been one of them, both working at this exercise, collide with no effect but to deflect each other aside.

The Curtsy Flip

The curtsy, as the American students at the aiki dojo used to call this one, is the basic defense against an attacker from the rear who pins your arms, above the elbow, to your side in a bear hug. I stress the "above the elbow," for a lower arm pin is easier dealt with by the salaam, which follows. The curtsy can be used, but not always as readily. As a party trick, the first half of the maneuver never fails to startle. But do only the first half—no sense in breaking furniture or necks.

Stand at attention. Now, imagining you have been pinned from behind in a bear hug, step forward with left foot and cause the ki to surge out your arms and out your open, spread fingers. Your elbows will rotate forward as in the archer's draw. If you've gotten your ki turned on, your arms cannot be pinned down; you can walk about dragging your attacker, who is now only a passenger, as if he were an old Inverness cape.

To throw your passenger (not at party please), thrust your trunk forward, your left fingers surging down their projected line of force to a point a foot or so in front of your left toes, your right arm going back and up naturally in counterreaction. In this position freeze and have companion test you, pushing your hips forward; you will be immovable.

FOR THIS SITUATION—SALAAM

No matter how heavy or strong an attacker, he can't possibly retain hold or avoid being thrown if you remain calm, keep your ki flowing. Beginner students even throw Tohei. There is no "counterdefense" against an aiki defense, not even aiki.

The Salaam – or Dive Flip

The salaam, or dive as some of us called it, is for use against an attacker from the rear who grabs your wrists or forearms, or tries a neck-lock or shoulder grab with knee in back. The name dive describes it well, except that it has a variant which looks very much like an old-style Hollywood burlesque of the grand salaam.

Take your stance at ease, and twist hands so that palms are up, fingers forward. If tested, you are immovable. Move one foot forward, preferably the left, as a right-handed attacker has poor leftward balance. Bring hands up in an arc, the radius of the arm length. As they reach eye level, twist the forearm so that fingers are pointing forward just before they reach the apex of the arc, whence spiral of hands projects forward and down and body bows forward and down in their wake, left (leading) leg bending, till chin approaches the

242

left knee and hands approach floor. At the full salaam, your wrists are bent in, the head is tucked well down between the arms, the right leg (you can work it with either leg), is straight out behind.

Grand Salaam

The grand salaam variation is a little harder to coordinate, but even more effective. As the hands move up, take half step backward with either foot and shift weight to it; when arms reach apex and start forward and down, take full step back with the other foot. You will end up in same final position as with salaam.

Tumbling

Tumbling is an essential point of defense. You may get thrown, or hit by a sudden tackle, or just fall off a horse or bicycle. Even an egg will survive a fall against pavement, if it hits so as to roll. I have gone off horses at full gallop and landed after a roll, on my feet and running, unhurt. An aiki-ka friend in Japan barreled over the top of his bicycle when only the

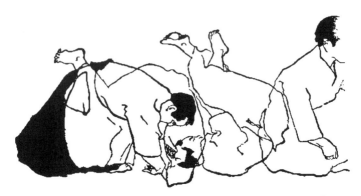

front brake held in a downhill emergency speed stop, and walked away from it with only a scratch.

Kneel on one leg, the other foot planted in front of you, foreleg vertical. Roll onto your back, as high up on your shoulder as possible, immediately yo-yo-ing to return onto your feet. As an aid, on the return way forward point forward with one finger to help direct your ki. You should roll to your kneeling position, and be immovable.

Stand. Drop like a discarded *dogi* to the floor, pelvis angling under-and-forward under you so that you fall into a position similar to above, through which you move smoothly, as preceding, through a tumble back onto your shoulders. Then from the apogee of your roll-back pendulum forward, using the finger point as an aid, onto your feet, into what should be a casual but immovable stance.

Variations on these are many. Sit flat on the floor, legs forward. Roll back, legs into air, again rolling down into first sitting posture and continuing on up smoothly into standing position.

Start from position flat on back. Bring knees up and roll back on shoulders as above, swinging forward into a standing position. Flat on back, just point fingers forward, follow projection with your eyes and roll up into a fudo, immovable standing position. Have someone test your stability.

In a full tumble you must roll yourself up into a ball so that, as Tohei puts it, "you leave no corners, make yourself round." The judo tumble is to slap the ground with the flat

arm to break the fall. But try this on a cement pavement or worse yet, a gravel road.

The trick of the fully round tumble is to reduce the radius of the ball as it rolls. Do this by directing your ki out your arm, but in a diagonal or spiral directed just within the point of the opposite foot. In rolling forward, keep the head tucked well inside your ki orb, an imaginary circle projected from your inner point, up through your arm and out your finger to run parallel to but within the arc formed by the opposite leg and hip back to a point within the arc, or forward of the original inner point. In rolling forward, the inner point will have reached a new position forward, coinciding with the center of this smaller circle. When you get to your feet, expand the radius of your projected arc of ki. Maintain its flow. You should land in an immovable stance. But for practice, continue rolling around the gym, changing direction to perfect the tumble for all eventualities.

Working with the ultimate 'Zen combat' form we find we are beyond Zen to the non-Zen's (nonsense) combat. O-Sensei denied aiki had links to Zen: "Zen is *mu*, emptiness, whereas aiki is *yu*, fullness." We have at this point successfully emptied ourselves of falseness, of aggressiveness. Now we are ready to become Don Juan's warrior in the mold of O-Sensei. Being empty we must now fill ourselves with ki. Like Rube Goldberg's Ikey & Mikey—aiki & mu-aiki—they look alikey.

Fill up and tumble. . .

KNEELING POSITION BACK ROLL

The aiki dojo at tumble-time looked like some surrealist pinball parlor. Human pinballs spinning around, on occasion stopping and standing upright to transform themselves temporarily into the bumpers, balls bouncing off them and bouncing them back into the rolling role of pinball. If anyone's aiki failed, he rang a tilt with the colored lights flashing and bells ringing in his head; while the other pinballs continued in their apparent disorder; unaware, unconcerned, thoroughly . . . detached.

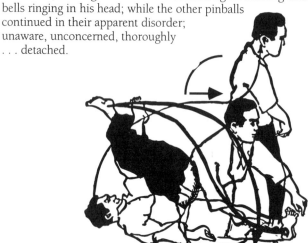

BACK ROLL FROM STANDING POSITION

MODERN ZEN FOOLS

Zen literary tradition is full of antique tales of wise old fools: swordsman Miyamoto Musashi, discussed earlier, was a student of one of the greatest and zaniest; then there are Kanzan and Jittoku (Chinese Hanshan and Shitte). Typical of them could be the Yiddish hero Gimple the Fool, who might be called a Jewish Zenist (Zen Juddhist?), or Persia's Mullah Nasreddin. An anthology of their stories would be hilarious. Alas, where now are such as these marvelous goofs of yore?

Tales of O-Sensei

O-Sensei was a devoted follower of the Ohmoto sect of Shintoism. It is based in pacifist folk tradition, not Imperial or State Shinto with its prewar militarism. Several new Shinto sects appeared in the late part of the Tokugawa Shogunate, when Japan was cut off from the world and the common people were as miserable as in imperial Russia, without the safety valve Europe had of an expanding industrial economy. The new Japan of the twentieth century saw explosive growth of these simple sects. By the 1930s, Ohmoto was largest, perhaps 5,000,000 followers in a population of 70,000,000. Prewar persecutions cut into enrollment drastically, as did break-offs like P.L., M.O.A., Shinji Shumeikai and others. Still other major "new religions," not related but still active, include Tenrikyo. Like primeval Shinto with its dominant Sun Goddess Amaterasu and Rice Goddess, all were founded and led by women. They stressed channeling by, or spirit possession of, an illiterate leader who suddenly spouted forth religious tracts to be recorded by scribes. Healing was a basic tenet, as it is yet—often some form of 'laying on of hands.'

Ohmoto was headquartered in an ancient castle just north of the ex-imperial capital, Kyoto. Their founding matriarch married a charismatic peasant-seer Deguchi Onisaburo. He adopted the risky ritual of parading around on a white horse like emperor Hirohito and was soon prosecuted for *lèse-majesté* —insulting the throne. They practiced kyudo and aikido as sect calisthenics. O-Sensei was aikido master and Onisaburo's personal bodyguard. Unlike State Shinto, with its eight million *kami*—gods, or literally higher spirits—Ohmoto is monotheistic recognizing a single Creator. The other 7,999,999 were demoted to lesser ranks. They claim their teachings derive from old tradition going back to a great sage far in the West, in Assalem, a holy city with a sea to its east.[1] From reading our Old Testament they took this sea to be the Mediterranean and so the city to be Jerusalem. Except that locations relative to the sea and mountain are reversed.

Anyway, in 1924 Onisaburo decided to mount his white charger and lead a mass pilgrimage, or a migration, to Jerusalem. They obviously were not aware of the scale of the map they were using. He and a crowd of followers crossed over to Korea by ferryboat, marched up the peninsula, then a colony of Japan, and into bandit-torn Manchuria. There the sea of opposition failed to part and they were captured by a local warlord and held for ransom. The Imperial Japanese Government might well have welcomed this chance to get rid of them, but if bandits could dispose of its subjects so casually, national face would be lost. Tokyo paid up. Onisaburo and O-Sensei returned to Japan in chains.

After several run ins with Tokyo, Japan's only modern pogrom took place. Sect headquarters were bombarded by army field artillery, members machine-gunned, new buildings built to last forever were dynamited, leaders were imprisoned in solitary for years until released in 1945 by MacArthur.

Somewhere along the line O-Sensei left Ohmoto, avoiding jail. His aikido was becoming widely recognized and the General Staff asked for a demonstration. He agreed to face a firing squad of sharpshooters, without of course the blindfold. He stood in a field before the marksmen and an audience of top military brass. Guns popped away as O-Sensei weaved and bobbed, laughing. The brass were ecstatic. This 60-odd-year-old man showed the "innate superiority of the Japanese spirit," Yamato-damashi. He would teach it to all their soldiers and Japan with its impregnable magic army would conquer the world—from China westward.

[1] Southwest of the Caspian Sea in Iran is a small city of Assalem, of great antiquity, properly set in relation to mountain and sea—the Caspian. It is reputed home of the teacher of the first Biblical prophet, Abraham. I went in 1977. There is a hoary shrine, little tended but for candles stubs, and in a style predating Islam. No one would talk about it. I intended to return with Persian-speaking help, but the Islamic Revolution intervened.

O-Sensei laughed in their mustachioed faces. "*Damé!* No good! It won't work. I was watching the shooters' eyes. There is no defense against the random!" He roared in laughter and stomped off the field, head shaking, heading for the mountains, never to be seen again until well after the war.

Several months after the Bomb he came down out of his seclusion in the mountains of Wakayama and was walking along the road "back to civilization." Coming the other way was a group of drunken US Army of Occupation hotshots. (Probably of the second wave of troops—the first wave were veterans of some of the war's most vicious close range combat and were conspicuously well-behaved—they'd seen enough fighting: "You can't hate a man you've been to hell with." The next wave had never heard a shot fired in anger and included a lot of would-be heroes.) The GIs reckoned the road too narrow for them and the tiny little man and shooed him aside. He didn't shoo. So they grabbed at him to chuck him into the rice paddy. Several seconds later they were in the paddy mud and he was sauntering down the road.

America had encountered aikido.

Rube Goldberg Zen

It was my privilege to be party to a bit of twentieth-century epitomic 'zeniness',' Zen zaniness. Rube Goldberg, whacky cartoonist of the first half of this century-cum-master mechanical engineer in the Zen tradition whose ridiculous inventions that go to the extremes of barely functional complications, earned himself a place in American dictionaries:

> rube goldberg, *adj, usu cap R&G*: accomplishing by extremely complicated means what actually or seemingly could be done simply…phantasmagoria.

Rube was visiting Japan and wanted to see the "Real Thing" not in travel books, and preferably Human. I couldn't take him myself, but I sent him with an introduction to the dojo.

Rube wore a porkpie hat like a 1930s' Hollywood-movie police reporter, and spent his waking hours with an immense cigar protruding from his maw like a naval cannon. His translator was his Hearst papers' Tokyo rep (he was then editorial cartoonist for Hearst, and as his son said, "He's a Republican because he thinks Teddy Roosevelt is still President"). Rube entered the rickety dojo building and stepped up onto the elevated floor platform—with his shoes on, of course.

It happened to be one of those rare days when O-Sensei was there. Just then he came out of the back room to see what the shoe ruckus was about. His eyes met Rube's—who was not all that much taller. O-Sensei's eyebrows rose, his eyes lit up, his straggly beard vibrated. "Haw!" he hawed, and as students rushed to get Rube's shoes off, he took his fuddle-faced guest by the arm and urged him into the matted dojo. Few of the students had ever seen O-Sensei do more than walk into the dojo and stare at them. A few of the older ones had seen in him in action, and some teachers had worked out with him. Now they saw him lead this small human puffing-steam locomotive onto the mats, push him onto the elevated *tokonoma* alcove and set him down in the sacred area in front of the ink painting of their talismanic dragon.

O-Sensei snapped orders. Students went into shock and ran about taking dummy weapons off the walls—wooden naginata, spears, swords, rifles. They were all about to be awarded the honor of their lives, to do actual battle with O-Sensei himself. To be thrown by the old man was like getting the Congressional Medal or the V.C.—and living to tell one's grandchildren.

Spearmen in twos and threes, then fours advanced in ranks and charged, swordsmen screamed *kiai*s and attacked, squads of riflemen feigned bayonet sallies. They picked themselves up and attacked again, from all directions. There was bedlam, bodies flying all over the place, over each other's heads. And in the center of the vortex was O-Sensei, arms whirling like a juggler, slipping aside, ducking, spinning. No witness recalls how long it went on. Then as suddenly as it had begun, it stopped. Exhausted warriors splayed over the mats, panting in ecstasy of having gone it with the grand master.

O-Sensei, calm and unruffled, smiled at Rube. Rube waddled out of the alcove, his cigar smoke streaming like dragon spoor. The two old fools met eye to eye. Rube laughed and tugged the wispy white beard. O-Sensei reached up with one hand and raised Rube's hat, and with the other pulled the immense stogie out of his mouth and bopped him on the head with it, jammed it back into his mouth and laughed. Rube guffawed. They both laughed like the ancient fools. Then both turned and left.

Not a word had been uttered.

Sistine Chapel

気

ki - spirit

XIII. SECRET ENERGY

I WAS SITTING on a stool in the narrow hall-foyer, waiting.
An adorable little kindergarten girl ran in, kicked off her
shoes and called out, "Papa, I'm home ... I found an old
battery on the road ... fix it for my toys, please." He came
out of the back room, "*tch*-ing" for her to be quiet, and took
the battery. "Not now, later ... I'll take care of it," tucking it
into the foldover of the black-belted indigo judo-gi he wore.
He waved her into the kitchen and smiled for me to enter the
small, tatami-matted room furnished with a simple massage
table, wall clock, VTR, family altar with a grimacing image of
Fudo the Immovable–the healer—and nothing else. With us
both in, there was no room for anything else. In his coarse
pajamalike outfit, scraggly beard and shaven conical head he
looked like something out of a medieval Zen ink painting.

I had been ill for some time—neurological. Hell, I have
Parkinson's (whatever that is, and Mr. Parkinson can have it
back anytime). So my pilgrimage had taken on a new slant
—a search for healers, bringing me now to Ugajin Yasuo.

"I hope I'm not late," I said.

"It's time, I think," he said, "... *eh*, what time is it?"

A quick glance at the wall clock told me it wasn't going.
"I don't wear a watch," I apologized.

His young wife poked her head in. "It *is* time....Can't you
fix the clock? I'm taking daughter out, so take the phone
calls, you have full appointments every half hour until seven—
and *f i x* ..." she strained at each syllable, "... *t h e* ... *c l o c k* !"

251

He glanced up at the offending clock, cocked his head quizzically as if this might urge it on, "*Tch*-ed" again and took it down. He opened its back, took out its penlite battery heart and pinching it end-on between his thumb and forefinger, frowned, sighed, paused. "It's dead." In one continuing motion he began to wave it in figure eights, or infinities? Then holding it at arm's length he shouted a *ki-ai*. He patted it back into the clock. The minute hand jerked into its orbital course.

A sheepish grin wiggled his beard. "The clock will only go for a few days. I can't bring batteries back fully."

(He claims his electric output has been measured at 250 microvolts, which seems far too low to charge a 1.4-volt dry cell. But the ticking was audible and the second hand clicked onward and was still doing so a week later. The Menninger Foundation has recorded 1–2 second 80-volt surges in healers. Other 'mainstream' researchers record up to 200 volts, one qi-gung master can "turn on a light . . . wasn't plugged in".)

We spoke of martial arts, definitions and kinds of strengths and ki. He brought up karate brick-splitting, that it could be done by sheer brawn as well as by that mysterious ki-strength. "But not this, not muscle for this. . ." He took out a black riverbed rock the size of an open hand, 3–4 cm (1–1.5 in.) thick. He knelt down, open left hand on the floor. Shades of my first meeting four decades earlier with Oyama. Cradling the stone, its free end not quite touching ground, he chatted amiably. There was none of Oyama's tiger tension. He raised his open right hand, knuckles up, level with his chin, elbow jutting out. This stone was smaller, but so was his stroke.

Brick-splitting is old hat. I'd never accomplished it studying karate, almost broke my hand trying. But after a few days of aikido under Tohei, weighing 55 kg (122 lbs), I halved my first brick resting it on my left palm atop a rock. I can never forget the absence of feeling, any awareness of contact other than the eerie crack I heard in my shoulder, the sound of the brick breaking in my left hand telegraphed up my bone.

But a riverbed stone? Overhead slams with a sledgehammer bounce off these stones amidst sparks. His right hand "beamed down" with the instantaneous speed of a Startrek transporter. There were no sparks, no bounce as the heel of his hand hit. Not even a crack. The free half of the rock dissolved into minuscule fragments and black dust.

MASTER UGAJIN YASUO

His beard parted with a ghost of a smile. "Muscle cannot do that."

Just what are we dealing with if not muscular power? There is no English terminology for it, nor even any dream of it in our philosophy. The fact that you are not aware of the presence of a natural phenomenon does not make it any less real. People were killed by lightning before Ben Franklin flew his kite. Stick your finger in a socket anywhere on earth, whatever name you call the juice—whether European variants of 'electricity' (Greek *elektron* meaning 'amber' or source of static charge) or Japanese *denki* (written with ancient Chinese ideograms meaning 'dragon energy')—it knocks you on your arse. If we are unaware of it, it is no less real. What a blind man cannot see is still there to bump into. Some folks can't smell odors, even flowers. My mother couldn't. I've been losing my sense of smell recently, and I used to be able to smell a cockroach in a room. I could smell people's ethnicity —probably diet-based. Sometimes even their extreme moods. A dangerously distrustful mood in a person smelled much like a cockroach.

All the zen combat forms evidence some mysterious energy attainable after long, sincere practice. Oyama first demonstrated that to me in Tokyo decades back, in front of the temple guardian statues. Tohei showed it with his resisting several people pushing him. And Ueshiba O-Sensei did not use his near-80-year-old muscles in his *randori* free-for-all against the dozen US Air Police and Kodokan judo-ka.

Ugajin trained in Sendai in north Japan in an esoteric jujutsu style called Yagyu-Daito Aikijutsu. This school is related to Daito Aikijutsu, in which Ueshiba O-Sensei started his martial arts study under Takeda Sokaku. It is still continued in Tanabe town, south of Osaka in Wakayama, as Takeda-ryu Aikijutsu. Both masters could reportedly knock a man down from beyond arm's reach by projection. Many older practitioners of Ueshiba Aikido tell of the old master's annoyance at Tohei's youthful rambunctiousness bringing on a zap from O-Sensei from across the room to knock Tohei on his ear.

Ugajin says he can do this, and has. "But what good does it accomplish? Then I figured, if I could do that much harm with this energy, then I can find some good use for it just as well. So on my own I studied traditional oriental medicine, learned the meridians and principles of acupuncture, and read widely in western allopathic medicine. I now give seminars and lecture at conventional medical colleges."

Acupuncture without Needles

He considers he is doing acupuncture without needles—which he believes are but antennae to catch and direct radiant energy. Different rationales behind the effectiveness of acupuncture consider it an effect caused by the placing of needles in points of a nervous system parallel to and independent of that recognized in western medicine. Another theory views the needles merely as a conduit for ki from the practitioner directing it into the target points. Thus the needles are a convenience, a supplement and not a necessity. The main effect of the needling process comes from the fingering of the needles by the practitioner which reputedly transfers ki from himself to the patient's target points. Under Kirlian photography the fingertips of a healer are seen to emit 'rays' of electromagnetism. However simply sticking the needles in relevant *tsubo,* target points, and leaving them for various periods, has its benefit, too.

254

I have myself seen some remarkable effects from acupuncture, or *hari*, "needles" in Japan. The best acupuncturists, Chinese or Japanese, place the needles in specific points found empirically over the millennia to effect specific functions and organs over a separate nervous system. But they do not just insert them. They 'finger' them to 'inject their ki' into them. One of the best is Dr. Mii of Osaka, who says he is merely a medium for the transmission of universal ki which he draws in through the chakra, or master point, at the crown of his head into his 'one point' below his navel, from which he then controls its injection through his fingertips into the patient's ki-poor target. "I act like a valve and control the flow, only."

Western acupuncturists have less understanding of ki and often use a light electric charge on the needles, both AC and DC. This also seems to have beneficial results—which may indicate, like the slight but measurable charge in Ugajin, an electromagnetic quality to ki—what Russian scientists call 'electrical-type empirical energy' and 'bio-plasmic energy.' Some occidental scientists are working with electric or magnetic charges. One doctor in England varies both the intensity and frequency of his magnetism on the theory that each illness has its own critical frequency—much like the selectivity of touch practiced by the acupuncturist. One New York homeopath-acupuncturist uses BB-sized magnets of gauss strength 1, equal to the background magnetism of the earth. In Japan similar BBs, sold over the counter, are used with an immense charge of thousands of gauss. Canadian researchers use hefty high-gauss bar magnets: S pole kills pain, N heals.

Magnetism as a possible medical tool has been an object of study since the early days of mysterious electricity. Most anything unexplainable was attributed to it—even hypnotism. The scientific establishment refused to look carefully at results, no matter how well documented. Now with accurate, controllable generators and measuring instruments, the time has come for proper, scientific investigation.

The powdered stone at Ugajin's was no evidence of transmission of any energy other than an inconceivable strength. But what happened next was something else. We walked for twenty minutes to a ryokan, a Japanese-style inn, where he was to lecture a women's club in the tatami mat-floored dining room. He explained his treatment to the ladies in esoteric

Tantric Buddhist terms, which made no more sense to me than the medieval Christian arguments over the threefold nature of Christ versus the single. Then he demonstrated his transmission of vital energy.

He asked four kimonoed matrons to stand in a line with their backs to the large sliding-panel wall to the next room. He went into that room and shut himself in, standing five or six meters (yards) from the ladies with the paper and wood panel intervening. I stood with a video cameraman in another side doorway where we could see into both rooms.

He called out to the ladies to bend over and touch their toes. Hands dangling between knees and ankles well short of target, they broke into embarrassed giggles. He stood them back up. Then he assumed the classic vaudeville 'Svengali pose,' hands outstretched, fingers waving at the wall.

"Now, touch your toes!" he shouted.

And they did, to a chorus of incredulous hilarity.

He went back into their room. Standing unseen behind them with his hand at a distance of about a meter, he pointed at them one by one, not touching. As he did, each one leaned forward as if gently pushed.

I decided to submit myself to his treatment. I had nothing to lose but a few half-hour sessions and a very reasonable fee. I took with me my associate "C" who had worked with me years earlier in Iran and who'd come to Japan to help me. I had months earlier seen news on CNN from Yemen (ally of Iraq in the Gulf War) in which a mob burned a jeep wagon driven by an American civilian—but they did not show much of the brutal kicking attack on the driver who, it turns out, was C. One spinal disk had slipped out of place, the adjoining vertebra had three vertical fractures. C was evacuated to Saudi Arabia, where American doctors said he was lucky he could walk. He was in constant pain, could not sleep for it, had to get up at night for toilet, and couldn't handle heavy things. Doctors said he needed surgery. He declined, "I can always get surgery if there is no alternative: I can't get un-surgery."

Ugajin gave him three daily sessions of light massage and zapping for 20–30 minutes, a fourth a week later. Then dismissed him, "I have others in need." C is still in disbelief at the result: back pain disappeared, need to urinate during night was relieved. He returned to his US doctor for X-ray examination to be compared with the old X-ray, and was told: "Your displaced disc has returned to its place, that sort of spontaneous healing sometimes happens. But the adjoining vertebra with vertical fractures has healed—fractures in vertebrae simply do not heal. It is a medical impossibility. What did you do?"

C replied, "Well, I went to this Oriental doctor...."

The 'scientific-minded' US doctor frowned, "Oh?" dropped both 'before-and-after' X-ray films into the open folder, handed it back to C without further word, and saw him to the door.

As for my Parkinson's, it is more complex than a physical dislocation or fracture. But there is obvious improvement in my condition. Treatment continues. I have seen Ugajin correct whiplash, minor joint dislocations of the kind that often respond to chiropractic manipulation. His wife was a masseuse, a profession traditionally reserved to the legally blind. He treated her. She now uses a telephone directory without glasses. I have watched him work on kindergarten kids who have just had a first eye test and scored as low as 0.2. In three to five sessions they are 0.9—with 1.0 equal to US 20/20. And more spectacular corrections I won't discuss here equate to research at the Menninger Foundation.

Soviet researchers in the esoteric bridge the gap to 'legitimacy' by christening with new names. Thus 'ki' is 'bio-plasmic energy' or 'electrical-type empirical energy.' Somehow, a jaw-breaking Greco-Latin label is more scientifically palatable than a concise oriental tag. As the Crowleys note in *Moving with the Wind* even the Russians "hesitate to call [ki] energy 'psychic,' referring to it as 'electrical-type empirical energy' [or Wilhelm Reich's 'orgone']. Perhaps one day science will come to recognize that the so-called supernatural is merely an extension of natural forces." Shades of Lyall Watson's *Supernature*.

My first encounter with this healing power was in the Ueshiba dojo where Tohei-sensei was instructing in *ki-atsu*, ki-injection. Healing arts have long been a part of martial arts instruction due to the necessity of treating in-dojo injuries. Prior to World War II the Kodokan required proficiency in *honétsugi,* bone setting, for the 4th dan black belt. A result was the development of a native system of chiropractic. Practitioners wear judo-gi. Most Japanese neighborhoods have a honétsugi clinic. Raising two active sons, we found honétsugi more efficient than hospital emergency rooms.

This is not exclusive to Japanese martial arts. Shorinji Kempo has its "no-needle acupuncture," (*seiho*). Persian zur khané invokes a chiropractic technique in which the wrestler-practitioner wraps his arms around his subject from behind, lifting him by bending back, then snapping him like snapping a beach towel to jolt the sand out, thus pop all joints back into place. Other Asian fighting arts have similar therapies.

Aikido took a long step farther with *kiatsu* (ki injection), to relieve sprains and strains and sore muscles. I found it a wonder for relieving headaches, especially Tokyo (and New York) humid hot weather eye-pounders. I haven't taken aspirin, by any name, since—that's 40 years. Usually works well on hangovers, common in dojos in Japan. Great for female-complaint headaches. And I enjoy being called upon at parties to fondle and press lovely ladies' necks and feet. (What samurai can refuse a call to duty?) More later.

In China, such things as martial arts and healing have always been organized. The Occident would call it more 'scientific,' as it is empirically observed, standardized, recorded and repeated. Healing by radiation of life energy is called *qi-gung*, variously latinized as *chi-gung*, or in Japanese pronunciation *ki-ko*. I first learned of it on a Japanese TV report in 1988 on a Chinese army hospital in Shanghai where, as in all main Chinese hospitals, patients may choose either traditional Han (Chinese) medical practice or occidental allopathic, or even a mixture. The program dealt with a Chinese lady surgeon who was to have an immense benign tumor on the back of her neck surgically removed. She elected for occidental surgery, but for anesthesia chose qi-gung. The camera came into the surgical theater and showed her propped up seated on the operating table, a curtain aside her head to avert her viewing her own bleeding—which could be a cause of shock. My screen showed a high view of her almost head-sized tumor being removed while she conversed with the interviewer, with no evidence of pain, while in the foreground the qi-gung man, sweat pouring off his forehead, held his palms up close to the tumor into which he projected his anesthetizing ki.

I decided to find a qi-gung practitioner, even go to Shanghai, a 90-minute flight. Then Dr. Yuan, head of outpatient qi-gung at Shanghai University Hospital of Traditional Medicine, came to lecture in Osaka. I had an examination, two brief treatments.

The National Parkinson Foundation states, "Parkinson's disease is a degenerative disorder that primarily effects nerve cells in a region of the brain called the substantia nigra,... disease occurs when there is a 60 to 80 percent loss in nigral neurons." My US Parkinson MD said neuron sources die. With 'death' there thus can be no 'cure' or even improvement.

Dr. Yuan did acupuncture to my head, including a needle deep in my crown chakra—*not* painless, as most were. After fingering, he hovered over me, transmitted qi into the antenna-like needles. After a half hour he withdrew the needles, asked how I felt. I am a cartoonist, but hadn't been able to draw for five years. Now I picked up a sheet of paper and a felt-tip pen and drew a good caricature of the doctor. Obviously neurons were not dead, just turned off. They had been turned back on. The good effects tapered off in a few days.

Weeks later Dr. Yuan visited Tokyo on research. December 13th 1991, NHK TV *Today's Japan* made to air in US showed this Tokyo research: cancerous patients doing qi-gung exercises and receiving energy from a practitioner raised their serotin levels. A practitioner 'zapped' a beaker of water and it passed electricity better. They called it the "energy of the 21st century." At NYU, healer-zapped water on plants increases chlorophyll. So, too, Dr. Becker, "This will be judged to be the primary scientific discovery of the twentieth century ... that living organisms are sensitive to ... [and] produce electrical fields."

I made two visits to Shanghai of a fortnight each for daily treatments to much benefit, alleviating different symptoms to different degrees. I can draw again. It's holding.

Healers in antiquity were usually known as holy men, whether minor prophets or Jesus or Buddha. Absence of clear reportage and plain expository writing on "miracle cures" by saints makes modern judgment impossible. (Chinese qi-gung doctors are considered by their patients, and themselves, as strictly lay medical scientists.) But firsthand scientific study is possible because modern faiths involve performing of healing. Several 20th-century Japanese so-called "new religions," Shinto sects of folk tradition, promote hands-on healing. Names like *reiki* or *jorei* indicate sacred energies (*rei*). These are not restricted to holy men (or women). They are systems taught to lay followers. Anyone can do it. But the knowledge is not free, any more than is Harvard medical school.

Laying on of Hands

My first experience with a working healing faith was no such exotic oriental cult—or even oriental. It was a group led and taught by midwestern American Christian missionary, Marvin Yoder, who practiced and taught the hoary Christian art of "laying on of the hands" to his Japanese followers. They are Mennonites, a sect originating in medieval Germany, whose extolling of education assured their success in illiterate Europe. But nonviolence with refusal to enter the military forced them to migrate to Russia where their education stood them well until Russia needed more troops. Many emigrated to America, where in wartime they have frequently served with distinction on the front lines as unarmed medics.

In Tokyo Yoder runs a special chiropractic clinic—special in that in adjusting he never touches a patient. A Japanese friend went with his plaint of painful piles. A single two-minute session of outward examination of his spinal column and a lay of the hand a quarter inch above his tailbone and piles never bothered him again. The healer adjusted his coccyx, tailbone. Chiropractors maintain displacement of this bone is the main cause of piles—in dancers, athletes, comedians from pratfalls, desk workers by sitting incorrectly. The condition is often relieved if not cured in two adjustments by inserting a prophylactic-gloved finger into the anus and jerking back on the coccyx against counterpressure to the small of the back. But these Japan Mennonites never even touch the body or even remove the underpants! They project ki, equating 'ki' as 'Holy Spirit' or 'Christian Love.' This two-minute non-invasive treatment costs little more than a tube of Preparation H. Other Christian churches use similar healing techniques to 'purge the soul of possessing demons'—but in the Orient such a concept is considered witchcraft, medieval superstition.

Most important part about this healing mission is that it is not performed by a charismatic soloist. The leader, Yoder, has developed a system (originally veterinary) to teach it and expand his corps of healers, and has done so. So also, Tohei with kiatsu. And Ugajin lectures to allopathic medical schools and has numerous practicing MD-disciples. In America now many hospital nurses relieve physical discomfort by administering one of several hands-on ki-projection systems like Touch for Health and Therapeutic Touch developed empirically in a "wedding" of Oriental and Occidental therapies.

Touch for Health is essentially stroking the meridians, or nerve channels recognized in Oriental medicine in parallel with the lymphatic system known to western medicine.[1] This is used with kinesiology, or MRT (muscle reaction test) for diagnosing weaknesses and checking results. I combine kiatsu with foot reflexology, mentally projecting as I apply finger pressure, the way aikido teaches us to do foot massage on ourselves during warm-up. Using *Foot Massage* pressure point chart cards available in US health food stores, or in books on foot reflexology, you can get a lead on which organs may be weak, by which sole points are painful. This self-diagnosis can give helpful leads if you go to a doctor.

Therapeutic Touch is the projecting of ki over a short distance, without touching the patient. (Partly a legal ploy in the "Sue.S.A." for a potential medical malpractice suit defense of "But Judge, I never laid a hand on him.") Dr. Dolores Krieger, professor emeritus at NYU graduate school of nursing, is quoted by Maxine Lipner in *New Age Journal* as maintaining that "therapeutic touch is based on the belief that our bodies project a field of energy flow that when blocked causes pain or disease." This is fully in keeping with most oriental theories. In fact 'Touch' developed out of *Reiki*, prewar Japanese system early introduced into the USA, only to die out in Japan and be successfully reintroduced postwar. In postdoctoral research from 1964 on Hungarian hands-on healer, Oskar Estebany, she scientifically documented his "ability to raise a patient's hemoglobin level, a key to the healing that can result." They recognize it is ki, and call it 'ki', also "vital energy" or BIOenergy, part of a "universal energy" that "wasn't originating with us."

The healing targets are organ- or function-specific points used in acupuncture as well as Oriental hand technique from shiatsu-massage to Ugajin's powers and Chinese qi-gung. But even without a knowledge of these points, they can be located by feel, as described by Krieger in *New Age Journal*: "...our bodies project a field of energy flow....I placed my hand over the boy's back and subtly began to assess his energy field. *I*

---

[1] An excellent instruction book, superbly illustrated and almost as good as having a teacher: *Touch for Health* by Dr. John Thie, DC, T.H. Enterprises, PO Box 5547, Sherman Oaks, CA 91413. Also training seminar on tour.

could feel my hand being drawn to his lower back where without actually touching the boy's body, I began *to imagine a stream of energy flowing out of my palm and into the area* ... my hand hovering a few inches over his back."[2] Say this in Japanese and it could be Tohei or Ugajin speaking. The video *BIOenergy* says "Healer and patient, when measured by electroencephalograms, were 'in synch' electrically." Columbia University Complementary Medical studies, and Dr Mehmet Oz, Presbyterian Medical Center, are evaluating various hands-on systems.

No serious proponent or practitioner of this or any form of complementary medicine—a more accurate term than 'alternative medicine' and the officially preferred term in the UK—suggests abandoning allopathic treatments. This includes all the healers I refer to, most of whom maintain that treatment by ki enhances the effectiveness of standard chemical medicines, assuming they are valid in themselves and not net poisons. Most, and many conventional allopathic MDs I know who are acquainted, or experienced, with these systems, consider them valid as physical therapy. *Holographic Universe* recounts that many AMA-member MDs are working hands-on healers, but prefer not to go public with the fact. I am sure my childhood doctor-cousin, Lou Amsterdam, was one such.

It is time for mankind to become aware of teachings common to various ki-base zen combat forms. Similarly systems like Silva Mind Control and its various spin-offs, which work on functioning in the *alpha* brain wave state. Ki-attuning exercises are *alpha*-generating centerings, from martial arts warm-ups to mixing a bowl of *matcha*-tea. The end aim is to make the ki-*alpha* state one's normal state. In the book *Yagyu Family Traditions in the Art of War*, by Yagyu Munenori, Yagyu, the great swordsman, quotes his master Takuan:

A mendicant asks a saint, "What is the Way?"

The saint replies, "The normal mind is the Way."

How to Teach How-to-Teach

After my return to Japan in 1970 from some years in Iran, my friend, philosopher-philanthropist prince Shahram Pahlavi visited us. He had the original edition of this book and asked to see demonstrations by Oyama and Tohei—he had seen

[2] For help finding a practitioner contact: Nurse Healers Professional Association, 175 Fifth Ave, Suite 2755, New York, NY 10010

Onuma do kyudo in Tehran, where the normally unreceptive Iranian student audience was mesmerized. I left it to the Japanese foreign office to contact Oyama—teach them some humility in having to ask a favor of a Korean, which they did, and Oyama put on a brilliant demonstration. I phoned the Tokyo aiki dojo and was referred to Tohei's retreat in the north. I rang him up and was pleased that he remembered me immediately after several years. Without any oriental folderol, he gushed forth excitedly: "Jay... just the person I want to share my good news with. Real news. Revolutionary!"

I was flabbergasted, "What:...?"

"You can truly appreciate the importance!"

"... of what?"

"I have developed a system of how to teach how-to-teach aikido,...about ki energy in a way usable in any sport or art."

It seems that since we had met last he had trained Japanese baseball star (actually Taiwanese) Oh Sadaharu to apply ki to swing the oak. He subsequently surpassed home run records of Babe Ruth and Hank Aaron. Oh was physically much smaller than the American stars but ki boosted his batting power. The first non-Japanese sumo rikishi to win a basho, grand tournament, was Hawaiian giant, Takamiyama. He was one of the two heaviest wrestlers then contending, and one of the biggest and heaviest ever, so didn't have Oh's power vacuum. As we have seen, sumo is not a simple matter of "Where's the Beef." The smaller rikishi who can muster the special power can topple a giant, as many did to Takamiyama.

That special power is ki, but rarely mentioned by name in sumo circles. In the aikido dojo Takamiyama and Tohei faced down, open palms against each other, and pushed. Relatively minuscule Tohei, half the Hawaiian's weight, pushed him around like a lawnmower. But Takamiyama learned fast. He won the next sumo grand tournament. Then the sumo dons heard of his studying another martial art and ordered him to desist. He never won another tournament grand championship.

Many martial arts teachers today show the same baseless prejudice and forbid studying at another dojo, or other style of budo. This is valid only for beginners—to avoid confusion. But crossover is perfectly proper for advanced students to enhance their technical vocabulary and test themselves. All past masters did it, O-Sensei studied 30 styles. All do it.

What is "Ki"

Any American football lineman who has ridden a Japanese commuter train and gotten in front of a tiny 4'10" old lady bent over to kindergartner height and had her hit him in the small of the back to beat him to the last empty seat, has experienced the power of ki. It's one thing for a whole football line being pushed back by a 400-pound sumo wrestler—but a hundred-pound grandma!?

My kendo sensei Nakamura Sohei, 75 years old, was not much over five feet tall. He had an impish sense of humor befitting his resemblance to Disney's dwarf Happy. His glasses were like bottoms of 7-Up bottles, but his eyes missed nothing. He waddled like a duck, but moved like a wraith. He sometimes cackled like a hen, and when he did it meant trouble.

We were walking home from the dojo in the rain. I walked respectfully behind him with an open umbrella. We came up to the tiny alley barely 2 ft/60 cm wide that led to our old farmhouse. I reached up inside the bumbershoot with my right hand to half collapse the dome so it could pass between the narrow alley walls—and continued the downward motion rapidly to fully collapse the umbrella into a stave and bring it down in a single slash on sensei's head … cool, creamy rush across my face, cold wet on my chest, a sharp weight against my back pushed me hard against the ground. Then that cackle from way above. He had sensed my treason behind him, moved aside and swept me past him up the narrow alley. Then he used me as a footbridge across the mud puddles, cackling as he waddled on into our small garden.

A year later, training with sensei and drilling daily in aiki-do and kyudo as well as practicing calligraphy, my wife and I had ridden in from a movie in Hiroshima on the last trolley. The afternoon rain had stopped and my umbrella was rolled. The street was dark and muddy, the sliver of a new moon shimmered off the puddles, between which we sloshed. A suppressed giggling behind me informed that three toughs who had been on the tram had gotten off and were following us, though they didn't live at our end of the small village.

Another giggle, still closer. I spun and stepped out while windmilling the umbrella overhead in the dark, sliding into a

264

two-hand grip, brought it down on the lead man's crown, regained my 'sword' then still moving in the dark literally by my body's radar, jabbed it forward in kendo *tsuki* jab at each of the flanking men catching them midchest, then quickly at the lead man's Adam's apple, pulling it short of a fatal hit and at rest against the little crevice in the now stationary throat as he froze in his tracks. That instant I realized that what sensei had done to me in the muddy alley I had learned to do. The three toughs took off back toward the station.

KIAI SHOUT
Eighth Century Sculpture

At last I understood why Nakamura-sensei had often quoted Master Yagyu: "It is only when you see from the heart and mind that your eyes catch on....after that you should see with the body, hands and feet."

When we lived in the village I roamed the back country photographing traditional festivals by available light. I took my high ASA monochrome films to a small photo shop in the village. The darkroom was run by a teenage whiz whose skill at black-and-white photography was probably due to his love for sumi-ink painting and the powerful brush strokes of calligraphy. One day he was in the back room kneeling on tatami over a yard-long piece of rice paper[2] on which he was writing, or drawing, large Japanese characters. I came in at an angle behind him just as he began a long, top-down stroke. I surrendered to an urge—and sprang across the room to throw a body block at his back. I ricocheted off him and bounced on the floor. He continued with the long brush stroke, sat back on his heels, turning to where I had come in, then to where I lay sprawled. "Why did you tap me on the shoulder?"

[2] Not made from rice, called *washi* in Japanese, it may be made from any of several vegetable fibers, is acidfree and will last for centuries. Rembrandt used for sketches a type called kozu, imported to Europe as "Japan Vellum."

I got up and looked: a black stroke ran halfway down the paper straight as a sword slash, not a wiggle in it. Fudo.

Little wonder the kid always licked me at kendo.

Clear then, why martial arts masters are usually noted for their calligraphy, and why a scroll hangs in most dojos as a focus for contemplation, for meditation (=sword=brush).

There is an old 'Tea' saying, "A tea man can never be cut." I spent my first six months in Japan as a houseguest of the leading tea master (Zen priest and ex-kamikaze pilot who had been spared his final flight), and practiced this performance art regularly. I heard this adage almost daily but could never find anyone who would, or could, explain it to me.

'Way of Tea'—*cha-do* or *sa-do,* often Anglicized by the misnomer 'tea ceremony'—is usually associated with dumpling-faced matrons or giggling girls in lovely kimono. It was, however, a major tool in the education of a samurai. Aside from being an obvious polishing it was a honing in humility— the only time a samurai had to surrender his swords was to creep in through a crawl door to enter the ten-foot-square tearoom. It is the best instrument of instructing ki.

My Ethiopian friend Girma Belachew was a painter in his country's ancient Coptic Christian style, living in Kyoto and studying Japanese art and sado. I was conducting an American writer around the tea school international division and we entered Girma's tearoom. He was seated with his back to us in formal *seiza* position—tush on heels, knees forward and two fists apart (for men, together for women), spine straight, shoulders down and breathing deep. We squatted down behind him. I shuffled up to him and placed my hands on his shoulders and pushed him. Might as well be pushing the wall. I pushed harder, stood up leaning forward against his shoulders. No give, till he began to lean forward toward the tea bowl on the tatami in front of his knees. He picked it up with his right hand by its lip, thumb inside, placed it on his left palm. Then, cradling it caressingly, he leaned back to drink the thick green frothy brew. As he moved back, I fell back with him and collapsed on the floor while he finished his tea.

The strongest budo is sado.[3]

[3] Participate in a demonstration for a moderate charge at Urasenke tea schools in New York, Boston, Los Angeles, San Francisco, Seattle, Vancouver, London, and Eindhoven, Netherlands—in phone directory under "Urasenke."

A Little Child Led Him

As noted in the previous chapter (p. 208) "as if out of the Bible, 'a little child led him'. A good budo-ka can hold his fist closed so tightly that none can open it. This trick can take years to learn. Yet, Ueshiba saw, so can any baby do it. Who can open a baby's fist? It was evidently not a matter of learning, but of unlearning. Ueshiba had discovered the subconscious.

To an amazing degree, the development of aiki theory parallels the development of western, particularly Jungian, psychology, but while the psychiatrist attempts to push the conscious aside to reach or release the subconscious, the aiki-ka, in effect, brings his conscious and subconscious into rapport—calling them the mental and spiritual. He does so to a degree that seems mystical yet he completely avoids the superseriousness of other worldly mysticism, always laughs when in action. He does not retreat from the world but uses his knowledge to make life more palatable and compatible.

I contributed to aikido teaching applications in the 1950s by introducing the *Life* magazine article "What Keeps Johnny on the Spot?" (see p. 210). Tohei easily emulated it as an extension of 'the unbendable arm' and had the tiniest aiki-ka perform her 'unliftability' against the burliest, with ease. Next I brought the hypnotist's trick of the rigid human bench to his attention. This, too, became part of teaching curriculum. At a PTA meeting at my sons' school the aikido club gave a demonstration wherein an eight-year-old kid suspended himself head and heels on chairs and, fully conscious, supported five adults seated astride his midriff. Theatrics, yes, but useful as a good means for students to check their personal progress—the strongest aspect of aikido is this ready self-testing. Another fun test is applying the unbendable arm in tabletop or barroom arm wrestling.

Then after playing around with ki in tea, I added it to our regular menu. A Japanese World War II veteran friend of mine was visiting. He had taken judo at Kodokan and risen to 4th degree black belt—prewar. We talked of ki, and he said older instructors, Kano contemporaries, had often spoken of it. To them it was a mystery power that devolved upon some like a mystic visitation, not to be understood by mere mortals. I pooh-poohed this. As he was leaving, my second son, then ten years old and small for his age, came home. Knowing the guest was a budo-ka, aiki-ka son Garet greeted him at the door with a formal bow. I was pleased. Then I said to my friend, Garet would demonstrate ki.

Garet dropped to his knees into seiza position, as if to 'drink tea' right by the door. My friend placed his palms on Garet's back and pushed ... and pushed harder. He put his foot up against the door frame and pushed with all his might. At my command Garet leaned forward and my friend began to squeal in victory. A bit more and I told Garet, "Drink tea," and he straightened up. My friend collapsed in laughter. "At last, I understand ki—and from a little *gaijin* kid, a foreigner!"

Sit up Straight

In the mid-seventies my two runt teenage sons with a dozen hyper classmates, and myself with a band of my kooky friends —writers, a Tibetan Living Buddha, artists, orientalists, etc.— were studying aikido intensively. For three hours every morning I was with the kids, three hours more each afternoon with my adult group. We were under American teachers sent down to our town from Tokyo by Tohei. First came Paul Cascarot, a tall, gentle cowboy who looked like a Gandhara Buddha sculpture and was the best teacher-in-English of any martial art I have known. He taught pure Tohei style—start with meditation, then two hours of ki-generating drills and eventually some *waza,* forms. He was succeeded (but never replaced) by less graceful, more aggressive Steve Seagal, not quite as good a teacher though possibly a better street fighter. Steve stayed on in the area, married a black belt aiki-ka whose mother owned the most beautiful dojo in Japan becoming its dojo-master and thus an ex-officio 5-dan. Years later Steve learned proper English, re-accented his name and improved his choreography to greatly spread the name (if not exactly the pacific spirit) of aikido.

It was marvelous watching barely-out-of-his-teens cowboy Paul instructing a senior lama in meditation posture. Tibetans are essentially hippies, all, regardless of rank. They always hang loose, slouch even at prayer and meditation, scratch their navels. But Paul insisted that rinpoche sit martial art style spine straight. He was far senior to everyone else, but as

268

a true leader recognized the situational authority of the class leader, Paul. After a week, rinpoche publicly acclaimed the superiority of a straight back position to a Tibetan slouch.

After our early afternoon adult class of three hours held in the tatami-matted grand reception room of writer David Kidd's luxurious feudal lord's mansion, we would retire to his Japanese garden—formal bamboo glade and moss around a patch of grass on which orientalist Dave had set up a more comfortable occidental table-and-chairs arrangement. There we'd sit and chat over cool drinks, reviewing the lesson while waiting for the mosquitoes to drive us back inside. The fifth day, which had been a particularly satisfying lesson, nothing happened. No bites, no buzz. Then I noticed a black buzzer quietly strolling down my bare arm without sampling me. I looked around at ten sets of bare arms. There were plenty of skeeters, but no one was being bitten.

Then Reverend Shinji swept in, his priest's robes billowing. This noted Shinto cleric with a large popular following and media support, for all his brilliance came off as a pompous know-it-all—he never just conversed, he preached. He had recently returned from a quick tourist trek to Cairo so we listened to all there was to know about the pyramids and UFOs. He finally talked himself out and leaned back, self-satisfied. "Any questions?"

No one stirred. No skeeters buzzed, yet there were many on the bare forearms. Shinji's fat white flesh showed off the most black spots, but none of them squatted down to imbibe. No one swatted. No one else even noticed the skeeters. I sat farthest from Shinji, by choice, and after a long pause asked, "When was the last time a mosquito bit you?"

Previously unaware of my presence, he looked at me quizzically, then at the black blots on his bare arm. His eyes flashed sudden awareness. He looked at me again and smiled, "Come to think of it, not since my satori—my great enlightenment."

It seems that all of us after experiencing the mild enlightenment of getting our ki flowing, were impervious to mosquitoes. And according to Shinji's experience, all bug bites including bedbugs and fleas. Since that summer of intensive ki study I have not been bothered by bugs, even desert vermin in Iran.

I had long been puzzled by the fact that great masters did not have great successors, did not run in dynasties. Kano was an amazing martial artist in the cinematic tradition of the little guy of fabulous mysterious power. Ueshiba, originator of aikido, was a wizard in human form. Seeing him bare-handedly catch arrows fired point blank, contend with half a dozen burly US air police (see earlier), then make it a dozen (easier, he said) adding six Kodokan judo-ka, or special *randori* free-for-all for Rube Goldberg when he took on his entire dojo, or Tohei, with his raised pinkie, pushing back four burly MPs—all make it plausible to accept the tall tales of medieval wizardry by past masters, true-life supermen.

But neither Kano nor Ueshiba nor medieval wizards developed able successors. Ueshiba Morihei's son and heir, Kisshomaru, has beautiful form (*waza*), but is not even a shadow of his father, except perhaps in choreography. And Tohei, though Morihei's ace student, is quite different, even if every bit as important in his own way, in making it comprehensible. A superman, perhaps, but no wizard.

Like the comic strip Popeye, O-Sensei, Tohei, Kisshomaru, Ugajin all have ordinary biceps, but immense, soft, forearms.

"Western books on martial arts disparage the esoteric side of the art," says Crowley in *Moving with the Wind*—but, in all fairness, so do most Eastern practitioners. O-Sensei's noted spirituality is ignored, rejected. The threefold, spirit-mind-body participation at the heart of all martial arts, the meaning of *to-itsu* in the name for Tohei's school Toitsu Aikido, parallels the neurological discovery of interaction of left and right brain, of the holographic quality of the brain-mind. To move with ki is to move in the hologram: is to move the hologram.

Dojo politics in all of the martial arts are as downright bitchy as any college sorority, to the great detriment of the arts. Oyama's incessant snide remarks about Ueshiba were sophomoric. The 'low ki' verbal duel between the schools of aikido is a travesty—and the branch-offs from Morihei's system legally cannot call themselves 'aikido' (without a modifier) as it is a registered brand name like Kleenex, and equally generic.

It also doesn't help that aces develop fantastic egos. And the phoney machismo of Hollywood samurai. There is little if any of the humility of the sumo rikishi as exemplified by Chiyonofuji when he logged his all-time record thousandth victory and was asked, "What is your next great goal?"

His laconic response: "1,001!" —One day at a time.

270

Kyogen Dance of Wild Words

Most Japanese traditional arts are more than mere performance of some skill. Like calligraphy, ink-painting, noh theater, classical dance (even the avant-garde buto dance as well)—each is a Way of Life, a '-do' with discipline as strict as any martial art. Watching noh is like undergoing yoga heart pulse control. I went to my first noh show in Kyoto—just before the dramatic climax, fell asleep. I was embarrassed, but my host had snoozed, too, complimented me that it is an old saw that true noh aficionados dose. At subsequent performances I noted my pulse, how some dances would drop the rate from my normal low 70s to a stupor-inducing 50. At my wife's being given medical anesthesia, I was amazed how her voice simultaneously deepened as her speech slowed like a tape-player with its battery running down—she then sounded just like a noh actor. I learned that noh actors are descended of shamans and put themselves into trance in the Green Room before going on, so that may account for the similarity.

An assistant editor joined us in Japan from California. Third day we took her to a performance of the noh ghost play *Sumidagawa*. I had her take her pulse before the play—77. Twenty minutes in she took it again—63. I almost had to wake her up to take the next when the ghost was about to appear—45. At the climax, where stage action returns to normal speed, she was jolted upright as her pulse hit 80.

The following year I was in Iran at the Shiraz Arts Festival, watching Japanese noh by torchlight in an old Persian garden. Sengoro, heir of the great Shigeyama family of performers of *kyogen*—'wild words' or comic noh—mesmerized the audience. No one who has heard the voice of Sengoro can ever forget it, it is as much an exercise of martial art as theater art. On the Persian stage he went through the hilarious antics of one of a pair of alcoholic servants, trussed up by the master in his absence, one tied at the wrists behind him, the other crucified to a broomstick across his shoulders, cooperating to loot the boss's wine supply. His drunken laughter intoxicated the audience. His voice compares to others like an American bullfrog to a mouse. His physique matches his voice—he is a barrel chest and gut with feet. A theater critic who had sat next to me for information, asked, "I know the Japanese are geniuses at electronic miniaturization and can hide tiny amplifiers in the billowy kimono, but what about the woofer-speakers? Where are they hidden?"

Next day at Sengoro's press conference I translated and added commentary. Persians were aware 'special power' had been projected on stage. We decided to demonstrate its reality. Sengoro is shorter than I, but hefty. He centered himself, inhaled, and glided across the stage in the characteristic noh shuffle.. As he passed me I threw my arms around his neck and dug in—only to skid along with him, his pace unbroken. Then he walked forward against three journalists as easily as would Tohei. I told him the story of my pulse rate reduction. He laughed, "Yes, and I can *raise* your pulse so high so fast as to kill you." There was, thankfully, no call for demonstration.

Born of Simplicity

The basic budo teaching dictum of blindly following the sensei's action like a lemming is misunderstood to both extremes on both sides of the Pacific. But I think it more a generational difference than cultural. Both shores are equally at fault. To discuss it I defer to my first archery sensei, Onuma Hideharu:

> Some...argue that any attempt to control the human spirit stifles creativity. They find themselves unable to adhere to the strict guidelines and ceremonial procedures so typical of the traditional Japanese arts, and prefer a more casual approach. Such an attitude is usually a cover for insufficient skill, however, so real technique is replaced with ostentatious display and unorthodox methods—all in the name of creativity. But true creativity is sister to the spirit, and both are born of simplicity. Neither can be learned, like some school subject, nor can they be feigned. They are not a product of the intellect, but flower only when the analytical mind is quieted and the intuitive thought process takes over.

> Most people believe that the teaching is kept simple and the ceremony strictly controlled to ensure that the techniques are transmitted correctly from generation to generation. That is partly true, but a deeper reason exists: Limiting the student to a certain pattern of movement forces him or her to discard all extraneous action and thought and move into a state of consciousness known as *mushin* (no mind).

> For most of us, the concept of *mushin* seems foreign because we associate 'no mind' with no thought—the equivalent of un-

272

consciousness or even death. But *mushin* is not the elimination of thought, it is the elimination of the remnants of thought: that which remains when thought is divorced from action. In *mushin*, thought and action occur simultaneously. Nothing comes between the thought and the action, and nothing is left over.

When explained in simple, straightforward terms, *mushin* does not seem particularly difficult to understand. Still, people who have actually experienced *mushin*—through practice of Zen or martial arts—caution against intellectual acceptance of *mushin* without firsthand experience. They compare it to a man describing what it's like to give birth. He may be able to sympathize with the pain and appreciate the wonder of it all, but because he lacks experience of giving birth, he can never truly understand it in the same sense that a woman does.

That is why a master ... keeps explanations to a minimum and encourages his students to find the answers for themselves. He knows that over-teaching only further stimulates the intellect and inhibits intuition, thus denying the student the chance to experience the hidden, inner workings of the art.[4]

The error of "over-teaching" that Onuma warns against is a common ill, but I feel explanations by teachers are too minimal, often nonexistent—Tohei excepted. Japanese are not good explainers. For many years instruction booklets for fine equipment were jokes, even in original Japanese. Then Canon camera had an American write one—and translated it into Nihon-go.

Most teachers—including Japanese—do not comprehend ki, are unaware of its reality. Explanations must not be limited to verbal, must involve the student physically. Tohei's teaching technique is probably best. This is proven by its adaptation to other activities—not the least, baseball and sumo. But I admit to having learned as much from Onuma's and Nakamura's traditional methods.

The *Yellow Emperor's Classic of Medicine,* by China's counterpart to Hippocrates, developed over the first millennium B.C. An inscription on a Chinese ritual bronze of 11th–8th centuries B.C refers to qi, to its 'extension' and its two types, 'heavenly' or constitutional, which we are born with and must conserve, and 'earthly' or acquired, which we draw on when needed. Elsewhere it is stated that our physical structure is but vibrations, or energy, manifested—as in quantum physics.

[4] *Kyudo, The Essence and Practice of Japanese Archery,* by Onuma Hideharu with Dan & Jackie DeProspero; Kodansha International.

My dancer-kid sister Ruby watched me start an aikido warm-up on her living room floor, sat down and acted as my shadow doing the exact same actions, confirming my ideas of 'choreoptic quintessentials' (p.108). "I don't know what you call what you're doing, but we call it the Martha Graham Warm-up. You know, Martha Graham, founder of American modern dance, studied Japanese dance early in her career." A few stretches later she added, "... insisted we not just stretch, we must extend ... mentally and physically ... we must reach out to infinity, mentally project our action out to the universe."

That is the best instruction of how to turn on ki I know. "Ki=Modern Dance extension or projection." The best, easiest way to 'turn on' ki is by mental projection, visualization. Just as Oyama had early on admonished, "dancers make the best karate-kas.... I have only one prerequisite to studying here; you must like music. If you haven't got rhythm, you can't learn karate."

All forms of 'do' use basic ki-generating exercises. We are all aware of the slow graceful circular arm waving and dance steps of tai-chi and kung fu. Karate has the *kata* (forms) of pinans, which are best done with careful projection, at slow steady pace, in circular movements. Kendo has its basic drills, done correctly (thus rarely) with projection, but alas lacking proper circular motion—naginata drills are more effective because of choreoptic footwork and sweeping, circular, even spherical, pole reverses. Kyudo has its slow circular arm extensions, expanding full breath while expanding-stretching bow and bowstring and projecting self as arrow—plus educational bonus that if you don't extend correctly and get your ki turned on you suffer the teaching of "the sound of no-hand," the slap on the cheek of the incorrectly released bowstring. You will do anything to avoid repeating this form of instant enlightenment—even to the extreme of doing things correctly.

In *The Japanese Art of War*, Thomas Cleary cautions: "The West cannot afford to be mystified by the mystery of Japan [or the Orient],...those who glamorize Japan...[or those] who vilify Japan.... Both extremes are casualties of *the art of war*, who in turn victimize others."

Takuan insisted on strict adherence to standard form and rite, just as modern Onuma. Both induce the student to get the feel intuitively. The ultimate goal is freedom and sponta-

274

neity, which are ends to a stage in education, in turn to become means in the next stage. Knowledge of ki is passed on IF the practitioner correctly learns ki-generating warm-ups.

Dowsing Aura and Chakras

Chakra power points on your body can be located by a dowser, or 'water witch' using a divining rod—forked branch, L-rod or pendulum. Anyone can do this with instruction and a few minutes of practice.

The aura is a layer of energy said to envelop the body, which people alleged to have psychic powers are able to see, as ethereal cloudlike substance or layers of colors. The location of this also can be dowsed. Good budo-ka sense it and make use of their opponent's.

To locate, we here learn to dowse. A pendulum is easiest. To start, take a string or thread 4 to 8 inches (10-20 cm) long and knot it to 5- or 50-yen coin or pierced bead, fishing weight, etc. so that suspended it swings free. Sit squarely, feet flat, knees two fists apart. Center yourself. Hold the string by your right forefinger and thumb, hanging an inch over the right kneecap, left hand at left side; stay still. Now play patient fisherman and wait. Think a message to the string, "Show me 'Yes.'" In time—seconds, minutes, hours—there will be some motion. Then it will move in a clear way, in circles or to-and-fro. Most likely a clockwise circle. Now, move pendulum so the right hand holds it over the left knee. Movement will come opposite to previous test, that is counterclockwise if first was clockwise and if to-and-fro then 90 degrees off. This is "No." Repeat from beginning, thinking message, "Show me a stronger response." Thank you. You are now a dowser.[5]

To drill a well, think of water—good, potable water or you may find a sewer pipe. Lost something?—think of it, ask for its direction from you, move over, repeat and triangulate. Taking a yes-no exam?—ask the pendulum ('it' doesn't know the answer, your subconscious does). Always say "Thank you."

What is this 'human energy field,' the aura? UCLA professor of kinesiology Valerie Hunt does not believe, despite its electric aspects, that it is electromagnetic. She writes, "... it is much

[5] To learn more, write American Society of Dowsers, PO Box 524, Danville, VT 05828 for booklist and list of local chapters. Best single book, *The Divining Hand* by Chris Bird—history, scientific analysis, how-to, fascinating.

more complex and without doubt composed of an as yet undiscovered energy."

To find someone's aura, have subject stand still. Starting at ten feet away, dangle your pendulum held out at shoulder height. 'Ask' to be shown target aura; move slow and steady towards subject. Pendulum should react in some way, different from when simply suspended, definitely at about arm's distance out. There are several auras, one about arm's length, one halfway at elbow, one inches out. Artists, actors, budo-ka will give an indication farther out. If indication is too close it warns your subject's ki is weak, so probably is his/her immune system and may be open to illness or become accident-prone.

MRT, Muscular Reaction Test of kinesiology can be used to locate the aura. Extend either arm out to the side at shoulder height. Tester tries to push hand down while subject resists. Hold a cigarette in other hand, now press down on extended arm. Oops! Weak = no good for you.

Tester should now slash through subject's aura with karate hand sword and instantly MRT extended arm—which should drop. This sudden loss of strength repairs itself in a few seconds—but illustrates the real combat value of the feint.

Hold a cigarette in the subject's aura and MRT arm. Move cigarette closer or away and MRT arm to locate aura.

Ki is undoubtedly a basic aspect of this energy field. Many budo masters can project ki like spook-movie sorcerers. (Dig out your old Boy Scout compass, set it on table, center yourself, point forefinger at it and imagine you can move the needle … oops.) Ki's effect seems not to diminish with distance as do other energies, and so will be best explored seriously through an understanding of quantum physics.

But for playful science, experiment with this MRT yourself. Test foods, supplements to see which agree with you. Visualize a person (friend or foe?) and test visualizer's arm. Have fun.

Understanding bioenergy, alias ki:
'Next step upward in what we are in relation to the universe'
—Dr. Robert O. Becker, M.D.
author of *The Body Electric*, in the video *BIOenergy*

If this talk of 'Way' is difficult to comprehend,
the *Tao Te Ching* reminds us:
"A Way that can be articulated is not a permanent Way."

WHAT SHOULD I STUDY?

WHAT SHOULD I STUDY—aikido, karate, judo, etc.? Go for the good teacher, the true sensei—there aren't many around.

As I prophesied a generation ago, aikido is spreading more in the West than in Japan. It fits our love of personal freedom. Karate is also thriving, especially the true round movement, though linear head-on direct contact style has a proper place—it depends on what you want out of your martial art.

And no age limits. My grandson Richard, pugnacious nine-year-old, went with fellow martial arts movie-fan brats to karate class to become instant ninjas. Sensei, an otherwise capable karate-ka, could not cope–a kid is tougher to handle than a stevedore. He got more pugnacious but, realizing with the native wisdom of innocence that he was not learning value, dropped out. His father as a child in Japan had studied aikido. He was sad. On a visit to the US I found an aikido dojo near their home and enrolled him. It worked wonders.

Praise comes, too, from those who don't like sweaty exercise —though sweat is part of serious advancement.

After the original edition of *Zen Combat* an in-law in Berkeley wanted to do a martial art with her low-teen kids. There was no aikido or karate, but a Kodokan dojo young American sensei taught 'judo with ki'—reinventing true Kano judo, what Kano meant judo to be.

If you can't find an MA teacher who knows ki, study any martial art—those in this book, or taekwando, kung-fu, tai-chi chuan—and get a Japanese longbow set and book[6] and learn ki- control by "Way of the Sound of No-hand."

Remember "*Zen-ken-shu*—Zen is Sword is Brush." Study other ki-control arts—calligraphy, ink painting, oriental dance, chado, noh-chant for diaphragm control. In Japan, do Ohmoto (Shinto sect) summer seminar in traditional Japanese arts,[7] boot camp month of 8 hours daily aiki ken-jutsu, noh dance, brushwork, chado, meditation.

Ki is the key to life.

[6] Dan DeProspero, 501 Sleepy Valley Rd, Apex NC 27502, fax 919-303-5726 or Zen Mountain Monastery, PO Box 197AT, Mt Tremper NY 12457.

[7] International Office Ohmoto Foundation, Kameoka-shi, Kyoto 621, Japan

KEMARI PLAYERS

年中行事

nen-ju gyoji

APPENDIX A – DATEBOOK

*O*ther ancient sports are seen at festivals and listed in our 'Personally Oriented' guidebook *Japan Inside Out* in area DATEBOOKs. These include: *yabusame*, archery from horseback; *kemari*, soccerlike 'pepper' game played in ancient court costume; *toh-gyu* (bull)-sumo, bloodless fight between bulls; bloodless dog-fighting is dying sport. Boat races and water polo are also features of shrine fetes in summer, as also tugs-of-war and ceremonial free-for-all, often near-naked in midwinter. Windy seasons see aerial dog-fighting of giant kites.

FIREWALKING RITES

Page ref (p.1043) to guide *Japan Inside Out*

January 17 Firewalking 1pm Yama-dera temple Yamagata; onlookers welcome to walk after priests pass; (p.1043).

February 3 *Goma Firewalk*, led by *Yamabushi* walk slat-bridge over, not on, embers, 1-2pm, Gango-ji Gokuraku-bo 2 blocks SE Nara Hotel, near my private Orient museum (p.385, 390-1).

February 15 *Firewalk*: Near Yamaguchi, W. Honshu, Hanayaji, Hiraocho Yanai city; rites 11am, walk noon (p.677).

March, 1st Sunday *Firewalk*: suburbs of Tokyo, Nagatoro Saitama Pref, Fudo-ji Temple, 1-4pm; info town office *cho yakuba* tel.0494-66-3111 (p.1266).

March, 2nd Sunday *Firewalking*, 11am. Crowded so go early; starts with yamabushi, then 2pm any who want to try—like you. Kotsu Anzen Kitosho, Yakuo-in, tel.0426-26-3111; nr. Takao-guchi stn, on Keio line from Shinjuku, Tokyo.

April 14, pm, *Hiwatari* Firewalking at Mineji temple, Mitoya-town, Hi-no-misaki, Izumo area, with lovely ancient shrine, early lighthouse, British built 1903, (¥80), fine beach with glass-bottom boats. Bus 30min S of Izumo-city on Rte 54, 35min bus from Taisha Izumo Shrine tel.(0854)45-2111 (p824)

April 15 Sacred isle of Miyajima, near Hiroshima, under bank of pink floral mist, noon exorcise ills of winter— *firewalk* Daisho-in temple (see p.118), near exit of shrine (was atop Mt. Misen more dramatic locale, may shift back); eve 6pm richly costumed *bugaku* ancient imperial court dances in main shrine on stage over water (p668-9).

April 15 *Firewalking*, Saitama Pref Taka-yama Fudo-san, noon. Seibu Chichibu line to Agano bus; info 0429-78-0027.

April 18 *Firewalk*, Shoryaku-ji, tel.(0742-62-9569; rites, bugaku ancient court dance 10am, pyre lit 1pm, walk 2pm; JR Sakurai line Tenri, bus to Kubonosho, temple bus awaits.

April 28-29 Kyoto, Iwaya-yama Hiwatari, Fudo's feast day; rite led by *yamabushi*, huge bonfire burns down to coals men, women, kids walk embers: Iwaya-yama Shimyo-in [L-1], 1pm past Yase (p509)

April 29 *Firewalk* Yamato-machi Niigata, Mt Hakkai, 10am, info tel.(0257)-77-3111 (p.950).

July 1 *Firewalking* Hakkai-san shrine, 10am, at Muika-machi trailhead, Niigata; tel.(0257)-73-6672 (p.950).

July 27 *Firewalking* Tanuki-dani Fudo-in Ichijoji Sagarimatsu tel.781-5664; 5pm chant bonfire, 7pm faithful walk

August 8 *Firewalk* at Makihata Satomiya shrine, Shiozawa; tel.(0257)-82-0250, town office (p.950).

October 20 *Firewalk*, Osaki-guchi trailhead to Mt Hakkai, Yamato-machi, Niigata special bus from Shinkansen Urasa stn; tel.(0257)-77-3lll (p.950).

November 7 *Firewalk*, Akiba Shrine, Matsugaya Taito-ku, 15min walk from Inari-cho stn subway (p.1271).

November 15 noon *firewalk* atop flamered-mapled Mt Misen reach by ropeway 15min on main path; *see* Apr 15.

December 6 Odawara City 400-year-old secret fire rite *yamabushi* at Ryokaku-in. Massive torches, prayers ward off illness, 6pm firewalk; bus for Hakone-Yumoto from Odawara stn, 5min to Itabashi stop, 10min walk on (p.257).

December 15-16 *Firewalking*, Shimizu City, Akiba shrine, priests undergo cold water rites, 9pm.

December 16 *Firewalk*, Akiwa Shrine in Entsu-ji complex, Atsuta-ku downtown Nagoya: subway Tenma stn; pyre lit 10am, exotic exorcism rites all day, walk 7pm—dramatic in dark (p.310).

YABUSAME

Kamakura City Yabusamé-baba (mounted archery lane) spanning 300m between W&E toriis. Along it Yoritomo's warriors honed martial skills galloping full speed controlling horse with knees while rapid-shooting arrows at running dogs—now humanely small stationary wood targets.

Yabusamé begun by Yoritomo 1187 here, became integral part of ceremonies. Serious display skills, winners rewarded; honor to participate. Colorful event twice yearly: April part of Kamakura Matsuri, September 16 Yabusame Matsuri. Master archers Ogasawara archery school in Kamakura period hunting dress vie for top honors. Must see if in town, but crowded! If you miss it here Yabusame takes place elsewhere at different times.

April 1st Sat under sakura blooms by Sumida River, Senso-ji temple.

2nd nearest Sun. Tsuwano, feudal-style town in mountainous far west of Honshu Washihara, Hachiman Shrine fete, 10am, 2pm (*Japan Inside Out* p.818).

4th Sun Mizu Inari Jinja, Shinjuku.

Mid May: Kashima end of JR Kashima Line, 25min from Sawara), shrine of same name was patronized by famed samurai, enshrined deity is Takemikazu-chi-no-mikoto, warriors' guardian. Most structures here date ca 1620 when 2nd Tokugawa shogun Hidetada restored it. 10min walk stn. Beyond huge vermillion Ro-mon Gate, on R is Main hall, giant 2,000-year-old sacred tree soars behind. On left past shrine office is Homutsu-kan Treasure House (9:00-16:00, ¥300), martial offerings left by dignitaries as Minamoto Yoritomo. Among them, 2.7m/8.5-ft long sword 7th century. Path here where archery once done. Mid-May yabusame, feudal-costumed archers gallop between next gate and Oku-no-In pavilion, shooting at small targets. Far back is 'bottomless' Mitarashi pond.

September 14-16 Tsurugaoka Hachiman Autumn Fete, Kamakura; hilite 15th shrine-procession, 16th Yabusame.

October 3 Tokyo, between Waseda and next tram stop Omokage-bashi is Sweet Spring Garden, Kansen-en. Once daimyo feudal manse named for spring in nearby Mizu Inari Shrine bubbles cool water favored by tea masters. In October fete, mounted archers race down shrine's pathway firing arrows at wooden targets.

November 3 Culture Week Emperor Meiji's birthday Grand Autumn Festival, Nov 1-3: Nov 1 10:30 am bugaku music-dance, 12:30 ancient polo; Nov 2 10:30 noh, 12:30 dance; Nov 3 archery 9am, 11 aikido, 12:30 martial art, 1pm yabusame; Nov 5 ceremonial tea by head of one Senke schools. Culture Week, Seinen-Kan (youth hall) Meiji Park is locale for 2 days of best rural folk theater from all Japan. Nov 23 Harvest thanksgiving. Dec 23 Emperor Akihito's Birthday. Dec 31 exorcism ends year.

* * *

January 15 Sanjusangendo Temple, Kyoto (see *Japan Inside Out* p.491, map # I-10) *Kyudo* archery contest of long-shooting over distance of block and a half-long veranda with height of lob-shots limited by roof overhang; hundreds of archers in formal dress, both sexes.

SUMO

TOURNAMENTS: Tokyo mid-January, May (which emperor visits, sitting in his special box), September, with three others in Osaka March, Nagoya July, Fukuoka November. Each, runs 15 days, begins Sunday nearest 10th of month, ends Sunday; at Kokugikan, 10,000-seat Sumo 'National Sport Pavilion' in olde-Edo Tokyo Ryogoku area (see *Japan Inside Out*–TOKYO: ASAKUSA). Check hotel desk for ticket availability. NHK TV covers them live daily 15:30-18:00 with intelligent English commentary on bilingual sattelite channel. Regular NHK replays hilites 23:00. Kokugikan also hosts college championships November, amateur playoffs in December.

Tickets up to 3 months ahead: or at your hotel desk, arena (TOKYO (03)-3623-5111, OSAKA (06)-647-6301) or PlayGuide; some early same day at arena. Box 4, ¥36,-75,000 w/bento-lunch most fun, sgle from ¥7,500 in pairs, cramped on tatami. Discomfort salved by camaraderie, food and drink hawked, passed around. Arena entry thru food-stall-lined alley, *chaya*, run by ex-rikishi —who run boxes, so if speak Japanese, check with one of men in medieval costume if any open. If no box, settle for bleachers, eat-drink into mood of crowd. Fans skip early matches so you can quietly, politely squeeze into empty box, alert to withdraw with bows or nods of thanks or apologies when owner appears — sometimes never in early days, as most reserved for season by company for possible out-of-town business guests. Tickets different system Tokyo, Osaka. Tokyo boxes for 2 & 4 box, charge per person ¥7,500-9,500 (no bento); rsved seats ¥2,300, ¥5,-7,000; ¥1,500. Osaka box 4, ¥70,-82,000 w/bento, souvenir; rsved ¥15,-16,000 bento, souvenir; SRO ¥500.

Get in and see inside Kokugikan other than during tournament. Part of building Sumo Hakubutsu-kan Museum thousands of sumo items. *Free*, 9:30-16:30, X-weekends, holidays; and during tournament fortnights only sumo bout admission tickets may enter museum.

USHI-ZUMO BULL SUMO

UWAJIMA, one of Shikoku island's larger towns, but pulling into station, you feel you're at road's end. It draws many spectators for bloodless tohgyu or ushi-zumo (bull sumo). Records date it to 1801, according to local legend it started in Kamakura Era, 12th century, by farmers. Found over much of SE Asia— especially places inhabited by Malays— South India thru Sri Lanka and Burma, Thailand and isles of Indonesia and north to Philippines, Okinawa and on Japan Seacoast's Oki Isles. Champion earns master higher stud fees, value of sport lay in improving breed. Bulls used are farm work animals relieved of chores about one month before tournament and put into fighting shape by practicing technique (there are certain neck-holds used) and by rest and diet— includes two dozen raw eggs (interesting reversal of steak'n eggs), meat of poisonous mamushi snake and lightly fermented garlic. He is dressed in ceremonial costume much as human sumo wrestler (and work bulls in Hiroshima rice-planting festivals), some of which are works of art worth thousands of dollars. Fight not completely bloodless, tho' very little and that infrequently. Unlike human sumo match may last hour until one animal gives way, is forced out of ring or down on its knees or moos. Bulls average 800 kilos, 1,760 lbs.

Matches now at city Tohgyu Center on Maruyama Hill near stn. Regular bouts are: New Year match Jan 2nd; Spring tournament 3rd sun May. Summer Jul 24, Aug 14; Autumn 3rd sun Nov. Each starts 12:00 for at least 2 hours; ¥2,500 per person. Also arrange offseason matches, City Tourist Office tel.(0895)-22-3934, or Tohgyu Center tel.25-3511 at ¥45,000 per match depending rank of fighters you wish to see, ¥85,000 two bouts, negotiable.

July 23-24 Warei Shrine Grand Festival; giant dinosaur demon cows paraded with fireworks, hundreds flag-bedecked fishing boats jam scenic harbor. Tohgyu 24th offering for good catch at sea; 24th nite main event Hashiri-komi, several mikoshi hauled from boats in harbor carried by young men race up waist-deep Suka River to Warei Shrine.

Uwatsu-hiko Shrine Fall Fete Yatsu-shika (8-deer) dance. Wear deer heads, 7 antlered-males, 1 female dance to giant drum. Started 1615, Daté Hidemune made lord Uwajima, brought dance from home in Sendai where similar dance still seen.

Demon-cows appear this day. Other autumn festivals feature mikoshi parade, big taiko-drums competition, lion dances: October 14 Mishima Shrine; 16 Hachiman Shrine, 19 Tenman Shrine. October bout may be rescheduled to Hachiman Fest.

OKINAWA CITY: West Grand Ave, past sports ground,...Kanko Togyu-jo, where Okinawan bullfights. Similar to Uwajima Shikoku, introduced by Satsuma clan since Okinawan farmers first pit bull against bull for entertainment mid-17th century. Benefits farmer for stronger bull is more valuable as breeding stock. Now, bulls bred only for fighting (no menial labor for them, unless losers), undergo training and special diets one month before main tournaments. Rankings like human sumo, Okinawa City annually hosts two national championships and four inter-isle championships. As name implies, Kanko Togyu-jo Tourism Arena has biweekly fights (tues, fri 7pm, ¥300). Scheds for main tournaments in newspapers; or Okinawa City Tourist Bureau, tel.(09893)-2-8735, on SW corner of Grand and Nakanomachi Avenues.

JAPAN SEA, Oki Isle noted for bull-sumo started 750 years ago by emperor Go-Toba to amuse court exiles—others rank healthy bulls. Spring Bout May 5 (sometimes April 29), Summer August 15, champs September 1, October 13.

All held on Dogo: September at Chayama Ushitsuki-jo, October Take-yama Ushitsuki-jo or Nijiyama Togyu-jo by Kokubun-ji temple. Finals free, others ¥2,500 4hr tour. Daily for summer tourists at Kanko Ushitsuki-jo nr Mizuwaka Shrine. July 1 to August 31, ¥500 for 1 or 2 matches, tour buses visit.

Bullfighting also part of rural Echigo's festivities since early 17c. Here too, began as mix of sport and way to select bulls. Matches May–Nov around Yama-koshi village near Ojiya and Hirokami villages on Tadami Line. Matches alternate rings, check: Yamakoshi Togyu-kai tel.(025859)-2375, Hirokami Togyu-kai tel.(025799)-2867 Yamakoshi rings all 7-15km from Ojiya stn, cab or bus (special buses from Nagaoka city on match days): Koguriyama Togyu-jo, 18 min bus Ojiya to Jotaki, 15min walk; Mushikame Togyu-jo, 50min bus from Nagaoka or cab from Ojiya; Yamakoshi Togyu-jo, 35min bus Ojiya to Katsuraya and 10min walk. Hirokami village ring Imogawa Togyu-jo is 15min drive from JR Tadami Line's Hirokami stn. Regular seat¥1,000, box seat ¥2,000; not much difference.

KEMARI

Soccerlike except no heading due to tall horsehair hats 'pepper' game similar to Siamese takraw except that it's played in ancient Heian court costume, usually in Kyoto imperial palace.

January 4 Kemari-hajime 'First-of-year': Shimogamo-jinja Kyoto, 2pm.

July 7 Shiramine Shrine [G-6] Kemari 3pm, also Tanabata Star Fest 2:30pm Kitano Tenman Shrine [E-6] 1pm.

Traditional sports of Japan are still very much alive, best seen in Tokyo. Most high schools and colleges also clubs for kendo-fencing, karate, judo, kyudo, perhaps aikido and sumo, and if you visit school request to see their dojo.

APPENDIX B – FURTHER READING

"As learning is a gate, when you read books don't think this is the Way. This misconception has made many people remain ignorant of the Way no matter how much they study or how many words they know." —Yagyu

KARATE: A plethora of good books: Start anything by Oyama or Nishuyama–or whoever your dojo master. Originator Funakoshi *Karatedo Nyumon*. As pure mechanics without ki or 'soul' Donn Draeger is OK.

NINJA: Much bunk, most Ninja 'art' is hokey. Cat burglar with black belt is real ninja. Reflecting this reality is Shoto Tanemura in *Ninpo;* Gruzanski *Ninja Weapons* & Draeger *Ninjutsu: Art of Inviasibility* amusing,

ZEN: of truckloads published, must is *Zen Teaching of Huang Po* (Grove) translated Blofeld. If you don't dig this, get a new spoon and poke at anything at random, it won't matter. Still tops as he does not presume, any Daisetzu Suzuki texts (himself not Zen, but Jodo Shinshu 'Pureland' Buddhist). Tibet books of Alexandra David-Neel. AmeriZen movement started with promise at Asia Institute, New York, 1951 (Suzuki's first lectures N.Y. and where Chao Li Chi introduced Tai-chi/taiqiquan to non-Orientals), blooms only in some minor artists, scribes and too many self-proclaimed honky roshi.

FIREWALK: Loring Danforth, *Firewalking and Religious Healing*, Princeton.

KENDO: US's top kendo-ka, fabulous pegleg Gordon Warner, *This is Kendo* and *Kendo, Japanese Swordsmanship*, tho' as historian he's fine swordsman; Nicklaus Suino *Art of Japanese Swordsmanship & Practice Drills for Japanese Swordsmanship.* Japanese sword as weapon-art: *Nippon To* by master smith Inami Hakusui; *The Samurai Sword*, John Yumoto; *Primer of Japanese Sword Blades* B.W. Robinson; *Sword and Samé* trans Joly & Inada; *Manufacture of Armour and Helmets in 16th Century Japan* trans Wakameda; *Armour Book in Honcho-Gunki-Ko,* Arai Hakuseki; *Iaie Art of Drawing the Sword,* C. Darrell. (Tut)

Several new authors with aikido background are for real–kendo best studied in parallel with aiki or kyudo to learn reality of ki.

KYUDO: *Kyudo, Essence and Practice of Japanese Archery* by Onuma Hideharu with disciples Dan & Jackie DeProspero; should come as basic accessory to every Japanese longbow, profusely illustrated, mustread for all budo-ka; DeProspero, *Illuminated Spirit–Conversations with Onuma Sensei*, both Kodansha.

SUMO: Bible is Andy Adams' mag *Sumo World* published each bimonthly tournament–background, profiles, scores etc. Don't go to bout without. Best books: Adams, Hatano *Sumo History and Yokozuna Profiles*; Sumo Association *Sumo*, Patricia Cuyler's *Sumo from Rite to Sport*; John Wheeler's wonderful as-told-to *Takamiyama*. Good survey J.A. Sargeant, *Sumo: Sport and Tradition*. Gem by superscientist Lyall Watson,

Sumo (Channel 4 Book, London), who brought full-fledged 5-day tourney to UK '91 Japan Festival, also hosted sumo program TV 4. US picking up; Hawaii satellite NHK intelligently commentated English.

AIKIDO: fortunately best live (second best ever) master handles English. Unfortunately Tohei in *Aikido* thinks his English in esoteric Japanese so book of little use to those not trained in aiki, yoga or perhaps modern dance. Final draft *Zen Combat* 'Aiki-do' & 'Ki' chapters were modified in sincere hope to serve as introduction to Tohei books—must be for anyone in budo. *This is Aikido*, also his *Aikido in Daily Life* and variant *Ki in Daily Life*, get either, or any by him, classics. 'Aikido' is copyright brand name. *Aikido and the Dynamic Sphere*, Westbrook & Ratti (Tut); *Zen & Aikido* Kamata & Shimizu; *Secrets of Aikido* John Stevens, or anything by him; *Aiki News Encyclopedia of Aikido; Aikido Masters: Prewar Students of Ueshiba Morihei*, fine series on aiki masters all by Stanley Pranin ed *Aikido Jnl*; also *Aikido: Heart & Sword* by André Nocquet; all Aiki News {*see* below}. VIDEOTAPES on Ueshiba O-Sensei, 1/2 hr: #1-1935, #2 1952-58, #3-1958, #4-1958-62, #5-1962-69; Yoshinkan Tomiki, Shin'ei Taido, Daito-ryu Aikijujutsu; & Koichi Tohei late '96, Aiki News Inc. 1-800-473-6040

KI: *The Body Electric*, Robert Becker MD & Gary Selden. *Moving with the Wind: Magick & Healing in Martial Arts*, Brian & Esther Cowley (Llewellyn Pub). *QiGung for H;ealth & Longeviity*, Simon Wang MD. *The Holographic Universe*, Michael Talbot gives ki a scientific pedigree. *Silva Mind Control*, Phillip Meile complement to ki Watannabe & Avakian *Secets of Judo* which 'Secret" is Ki.

GENERAL: *Secret Path* by Paul Brunton (Dutton) basic to make any 'jutsu' a true 'do.' *Book of Five Rings* of Miyamoto Musashi himself, very readable translation yuppy businessman cult text 1970-80s. *Japanese Art of War*, Thomas Cleary (Shambala), fine compendium writings of Musashi & Yagyu Munenori, another ancient philosopher-swordsman. *Secrets of the Samurai*, Ratti & Westbrook (Tut). *Japanese Cult of Tranquility* Karlfried Durckheim (Weiser), cultishly German, yet helpful.

PERIODICALS RECOMMENDED
Black Belt, macho grampa MA mag: PO Box 918, 24715 Ave Rockefeller, Santa Clarita, CA 91380-9018

Dojo, 821 W 24th St., Erie, PA 16502
Journal of Asian Martial Arts, more academic *vs* dojo angle, same house

Furyu, Tengu Press, PO Box 61637 Honolulu, HI 96839

Qi, Insight Graphics, PO Box 18476, Anaheim Hills, CA 92817

Aikido Journal, quarterly, Aiki News Inc., Tokyo, address below.

Aikido Today (6x yr), address below.

BEST SOURCES for books and tapes, write/fax for mail order catalogs:
Aikido Today Book & Video Service, 1420 N. Claremont Blvd., #204C-D, Claremont, CA 91711; Fax 909-398 -1840; publish *Aikido Today* mag; mail orde by credit card.

MA Books, Aiki News Inc Tamagawa Gakuen, 1-25-21 B-305, Machida City, Tokyo-to 194; Fax + 81-427-28-4380; USA 1-800-473-6040.

Ohara Publications, publisher MA books POBox 918, Santa Clarita, CA 91380-9018; Fax 1-805-257-3028.

Peterson Book Co, Northbank Berryhill Industrial Estate, Droitwich Worcs, WR9 9BL England.

INDEX